Class Representation in
Modern Fiction and Film

List of Previous Publications

Keith Gandal

2002
Cleveland Anonymous: A Novel. Berkeley, CA: North Atlantic Books.

1997
The Virtues of the Vicious: Jacob Riis, Stephen Crane, and the Spectacle of the Slum. New York: Oxford University Press.

Class Representation in Modern Fiction and Film

Keith Gandal

First published in 2007 by
PALGRAVE MACMILLAN™
175 Fifth Avenue, New York, N.Y. 10010 and
Houndmills, Basingstoke, Hampshire, England RG21 6XS.
Companies and representatives throughout the world.

PALGRAVE MACMILLAN is the global academic imprint of the Palgrave
Macmillan division of St. Martin's Press, LLC and of Palgrave Macmillan
Ltd. Macmillan® is a registered trademark in the United States, United
Kingdom and other countries. Palgrave is a registered trademark in the
European Union and other countries.

ISBN-13: 978-1-4039-7792-2
ISBN-10: 1-4039-7792-5

Library of Congress Cataloging-in-Publication Data

Gandal, Keith.
    Class representation in modern fiction and film / by Keith Gandal.
        p. cm.
    Includes bibliographical references and index.
    ISBN 1-4039-7792-5 (alk. paper)
    1. American literature—20th century—History and criticism. 2. Social
classes in literature. 3. American literature—19th century—History and
criticism. 4. Motion pictures and literature—United States. 5. Poor in
literature. 6. Difference (Psychology) in literature. 7. Hurston, Zora
Neale—Criticism and interpretation. 8. Crane, Stephen, 1871–1900—
Criticism and interpretation. 9. Miller, Henry, 1891–1980—Criticism and
interpretation. I. Title.
    PS228.S63G36   2006
    810.9'355—dc22
                                        2006051054

A catalogue record of the book is available from the British Library.

Design by Scribe Inc.

First edition: May 2007

10 9 8 7 6 5 4 3 2 1

Printed in the United States of America.

for J.L.V.

Contents

List of Abbreviations

AK followed by page numbers
Michel Foucault, *The Archeology of Knowledge,* trans. A. M. Sheridan Smith (New York: Pantheon, 1972).

Cap followed by page numbers
Henry Miller, *Tropic of Capricorn* (New York: Grove, 1961).

CM followed by page numbers
Henry Miller, *The Colossus of Maroussi* (New York: New Directions, 1958).

DT followed by page numbers
Zora Neale Hurston, *Dust Tracks on a Road* (New York: Harper, 1991).

HM followed by page numbers
Robert Ferguson, *Henry Miller: A Life* (New York: Norton, 1991).

HS followed by page numbers
Michel Foucault, *The History of Sexuality: Volume I: An Introduction,* trans. Robert Hurley (New York: Vintage, 1980).

JGV followed by page numbers
Zora Neale Hurston, *Jonah's Gourd Vine* (New York: Harper, 1991).

LMF followed by page numbers
David Macey, *The Lives of Michel Foucault: A Biography* (New York: Pantheon, 1993).

M followed by page numbers
Stephen Crane, *Maggie: A Girl of the Streets* (New York: Norton, 1979).

MC followed by page numbers
Michel Foucault, *Madness and Civilization*, trans. Richard Howard (New York: Random House, 1965).

MF followed by page numbers
  Didier Eribon, *Michel Foucault*, trans. Betsy Wing (Cambridge, MA: Harvard University Press, 1991).

PMF followed by page numbers
  James Miller, *The Passion of Michel Foucault* (New York: Simon and Schuster, 1993).

SC followed by page numbers
  John Berryman, *Stephen Crane* (Cleveland: Meridian, 1950).

SCAB followed by page numbers
  Robert Wooster Stallman, *Stephen Crane: A Biography* (New York: George Braziller, 1968).

SO followed by page numbers
  Claudia Roth Pierpont, "A Society of One: Zora Neale Hurston, American Contrarian," *The New Yorker*, February 17, 1997.

SS followed by page numbers
  Zora Neale Hurston, *Seraph on the Suwanee* (New York: Harper, 1991).

TC followed by page numbers
  Henry Miller, *Tropic of Cancer* (New York: Grove, 1961).

TE followed by page numbers
  Zora Neale Hurston, *Their Eyes Were Watching God* (New York: Harper, 1990).

TE followed by roman numerals
  Mary Helen Washington's foreword in *Their Eyes Were Watching God* (New York: Harper, 1990).

TM followed by page numbers
  Stephen Crane, *The Monster*, in *The Red Badge of Courage and Other Writings* (Boston: Houghton Mifflin, 1960).

TMH *followed by page numbers*
  Zora Neale *Hurston, Tell My Horse* (New York: Harper, 1990).

ZNH followed by page numbers
  Robert E. Hemenway, *Zora Neale Hurston* (Urbana: University of Illinois Press, 1980).

ZNH followed by roman numerals
  Alice Walker's foreword in Robert E. Hemenway, *Zora Neale Hurston* (Urbana: University of Illinois Press, 1980).

Acknowledgments

This book has been a dozen years in the making. My students at Northern Illinois University have made contributions, as have colleagues at Northern and elsewhere: Dan Andries, William Baker, Robert Ducharme, James Giles, Don Hardy, William Heath, Melody Lawrence, Amy Levin, Ross Peddicord, Robert Self, Roger Shattuck, and Palgrave-MacMillan's reader. Financial support over several summers was supplied by Northern Illinois, Mount Saint Mary's College, and the National Endowment for the Humanities; Northern also supported the book's completion with a sabbatical. Thanks to Didier Eribon for agreeing to be interviewed for this project. Thomas Wortham and James Miller supplied encouragement, and Liz Maguire supplied perfect advice about publishers. This book was made possible by the ongoing support of Walter Michaels and John Wilkins and the generosity of Michel Foucault. Once again, my greatest debt is to Eric Sundquist.

Introduction

An Apology for Studying Class, Not Culture

There was a strange and telling moment in a 1998 PBS *Frontline* special on the class division between "the two nations of black America," the tragic class split ironically created in the wake of civil rights gains. Henry Louis Gates talked to a number of poor African Americans, but his only discussion with a member of the underclass ended in a quick, uncomprehending dismissal.

The man, who Gates felt represented the sort of violent gang members that make the news, talked openly about being involved in crime, asserting that he would get his share of available American wealth, at any cost. He also said, "I'm not stupid. But I've got a problem, though, a problem I can't solve because," he added, pointing in turn, apparently to those filming and conducting the interview, "because you don't help; he don't help; he don't help." He also said, "We're already dead—the black people—but we're walking." The moment's intensity was augmented by the eerie finger pointing: the young black male was not only violating the television convention that allows the film crew to remain as if nonexistent, he was clearly accusing each and every person present in the interview room, presumably for a failure to do anything about the poverty and social isolation of the black underclass.

Gates's response to this singular interview in the PBS special was to cut it short and, most strikingly, to reject immediately and essentially the gang member's comments as irreducibly foreign: Gates said the man sounded to him like "a Martian." Gates could not remember such a violent attitude of entitlement when he was growing up—though, by the way, the renowned musician Quincy Jones, a contemporary of Gates who appeared in conversation with him, could indeed recall from his youth criminals with just that sort of disposition. Jones seemed to be correcting Gates's almost nostalgic rendition of pre–civil rights era poverty and segregation.

Gates's dismissal of this unrepentant criminal was typical of current middle-class reporting on the poor, and hardly remarkable—except in the context of the show's theme of a tragic split between classes. Gates's de rigueur and well-motivated eagerness to distance himself from this specimen of underclass culture was odd here because the man was speaking to exactly the sort of problem that the show was at other moments elucidating:[1] namely, the fact that the black poor have been—quite literally—left behind by blacks who have managed to enter the middle class and move out of the inner city in the last forty years. The man's pointed claim of abandonment was allowed to pass without comment. Apparently, the man's shameless endorsement of crime and violence—and Gates's need to repudiate him for it—meant that everything he said had to be dismissed. If this program was about black middle-class responsibility for solving the problem of the inner city, the man's comments and finger pointing could hardly have been more poignant. But the thug's utter Otherness—a staple of current, standard middle-class reportage—overruled the unusual relevance of his words.[2]

Gates's choice to refuse to engage the thug's self-justification for criminality and reject his words as sounding "Martian"—though casual, slightly comic, and perhaps charming—is telling. To be a Martian is to be completely foreign and incomprehensible, to hail from another planet where everything is different because life itself is different. This dismissal of the thug as essentially and incomprehensibly different marks a break with Progressive Era attitudes, which gained steam in the late nineteenth century and held sway until the failure of the 1960s "War on Poverty." The Progressive line was that the thug started out just like you and me, but had become hostile and arrogant in response to a threatening and demeaning social environment. Progressives talked to thugs because their account of themselves was important to understanding the way they could be reformed and because talking with the thug was itself part of the method of reforming him (as in psychological social work). You had to change the thug's mind, and you could.[3]

Gates's refusal to engage in dialogue with the thug and his cute application of the label "Martian" asserts an irreducible difference in identity between the middle class and the underclass: it is as if the middle class were dealing with people from another planet. And though Gates's particular term of dismissal is idiosyncratic, it is indicative of a change in our own thinking about class. Gates's application of the

"Martian" label is itself comprehensible because if, in this post-Progressive era, we are not used to thinking of the underclass as inhabiting a separate planet, we are used to thinking of them as inhabiting a separate culture, a "culture of poverty." We do not really believe that the thug is biologically different from us (as a Martian would be), but we have in the last few decades come to believe that he is culturally different from us, and cultural differences, we have learned during the same period, are, like biological differences, not something you can argue with. So we get Gates's gist. Cultural differences are thought of as identity differences, not ideological differences; they are not a matter of what you think, but who you are. Another culture is something you can try to understand, respect, and tolerate or, alternatively, find incomprehensible, gawk at, and dismiss. Somewhere in between, you can also find another culture frightening and titillating: witness the multibillion-dollar industry of marketing "ghetto style" to middle-class youth in the form of rap music and clothes—a gigantic "class-ploitation" industry. The under*class* has become a *cultural* Other.

We live in an era of increased sensitivity to issues of race, ethnicity, and gender. Classic exploitation films can no longer be unconsciously made and circulated, and absent from the screen are the "mammy" and the "happy darkie" minstrel figures who enjoy their subordination, as well as the "weak-willed" woman who lives only for her man and likes to be taken by force. Meanwhile, though, the movie industry is still allowed to churn out happy-go-lucky poor folk who prefer the expansive freedom of poverty to the burdens of economic viability and upper-class responsibility.

Since the 1970s, the rule in Hollywood seems to be that sexploitation and blaxploitation are fine if the women or minorities being exploited are powerful or defiant. Thus, in our era, we have become acquainted with sexploitation movies in which the sexy women themselves employ force and violence. And 1990s "gangsploitation" films, arguably the next generation of blaxploitation cinema, can produce denizens of a black urban underclass trapped in a culture of hypersex, hyperviolence, and supermasculinity, which is both thrilling and utterly Other to the upper classes.

No such self-consciousness is exercised with regard to the lower classes. In fact, the happy-go-lucky poor are often the stuff of blockbusters and Academy Awards: witness James Cameron's *Titanic*, Best Picture of 1997 and the highest grossing movie of all time. Why are cheerfully subordinate minorities and women off limits but the happy poor still fair game?

As recent commentators such as Walter Michaels have pointed out, multiculturalism has functioned not only to edge out issues of economics but also to obscure them.[4] The focus on cultural identity has changed the way we think about class. This sea change, and the triumph of "cultural" thinking, is neatly summed up in the now familiar concept of the "culture of poverty," a term that is still highly suspect to progressive thinkers. For William Julius Wilson, for example, the focus on "the alleged grip of the so-called culture of poverty" diverts attention from "joblessness and economic exclusion." To see the poor as having a culture that reproduces itself from one generation to the next, rather than seeing the poor as the effect of an economic or class structure, is a radical idea that would be incomprehensible to writers and scholars of the 1930s and 1940s.[5] Equally radical is the idea that the rich need to appreciate the "culture of poverty," the way the underclass live, or on the flip side, the idea (Gates's idea) that the way the underclass live is incomprehensible and essentially Other. For leftists of previous generations, the issue was to ameliorate their conditions.

Of course, classploitation narratives are nothing new and cannot be blamed on multiculturalism. They clearly play a psychological role in a society in which wealth has always been distributed very unequally; class ascension (à la "the self-made man") has long been the American Dream, and class demotion is often a very real possibility.[6] But the striking popularity of classploitation movies and books, in our own time, depends on multiculturalism, not only for ruling out other classic exploitation narratives (such as classic sexploitation and blaxploitation), but also for subordinating class concerns to cultural ones.

The rise to the top of the canon of Zora Neale Hurston (one of the literary figures focused on in this book) is a literary marker of the dramatic subordination of class issues to cultural ones. It is easy to see how multiculturalism has championed African American and female Hurston as an early Black Nationalist and feminist. What is perhaps forgotten is that Hurston's *Their Eyes Were Watching God* (1937), written during the Great Depression, was once virulently rejected by the leading black writer of her day, class-minded Richard Wright, for romanticizing and thus exploiting black poverty and entertaining whites with it, rather than accusing them of perpetuating it through racism. Like cinematic "screwball comedies" of the same decade, Hurston's novel, for Wright, made (black) poverty fun and took the edge off of the guilt of the rich (whites). Hurston's ascension beginning in the late 1960s was made possible by her double-victim status (as black *and* female), but was also unthinkable before the issue of cultural identity began in that decade to replace that of class identity. That the book's heroine's trip from an all-black middle-class town to a poor black migrant-worker community run by whites can be described by a leading Hurston critic as taking the reader "deeper into blackness,"[7] is a testament to our acceptance of the primacy of this mystical, race-based category of "culture." To underline the arbitrary nature of this claim, imagine a critic observing that Stephen Crane or Henry Miller, the two other literary figures treated at length here, go "deeper into whiteness" by turning their attention from white middle-class communities to white slums.

And if multicultural themes today often circumscribe class issues, multicultural studies also are regularly considered somehow superior to or more important than studies of class. Sometimes multicultural studies assert a virtual monopoly on certain terms and issues that could be fruitful in the discussion of class. I had the strange—but, I imagine, by no means unusual—experience of being advised by a leading journal not to use the word "trauma" to describe a genre of class-ploitation film I discuss here. The reader's report explained: "in Holocaust Studies, the term 'trauma' has been used to describe a systematic investigation of cultural expressions dealing with such significant cultural and political events. While, of course, 'trauma' studies doesn't own the term, I encourage the author to change the title of the grouping to avoid belittling those studies by linking them with this set of films." Certain multicultural studies have an almost holy status in our academic culture. Class studies today have nothing like that status.

Fictions of Poverty Old and New

It has been nearly one hundred and twenty years since the publication of Jacob Riis's seminal *How the Other Half Lives* (1890), the first photojournalistic and "modern" book about the American urban "slum problem." I would suggest that perhaps we don't know or care much more than they did a century ago about solving this problem, and part of our inability to make much progress in this domain is due to our continued imaginative investments in the poor or our middle-class myths of poverty.[8] Bluntly put, the upper classes have an active and tortured fantasy life about poverty that seems to play a role in their psychic equilibrium. Perhaps this is not so bizarre in a nation in which identity is profoundly tied to one's status in economies of scale well beyond that of the home and the local community, in what might be called a "fame/shame culture." (And shame is a very live issue in the United States despite certain clichéd anthropological fallacies about the guilt culture of the West versus the shame culture of the East). Here, in contemporary America, I would suggest, shame is obviously tied much more to material wealth, class, and career status than to traditional moral concerns, but shame has been so personalized and mystified in popular discourse that one begins to wonder, naively, if this mystification—like the mystification of "culture"—does not function principally to obscure class and status issues.

This book attempts to investigate the middle-class's fantastical and schizophrenic representation of the poor and lowlifes—focusing on fictional narratives that center on contact between poor individuals and those of higher classes in the American literary tradition primarily and, secondarily, in contemporary American film. Its subject is, thus, our current class-crossing or cross-class "classploitation" narratives and their geneses, and by classploitation narratives I mean stories about the poor that are exploitative in the sense that they seem to come out of middle-class fantasies and serve those fantasies more than any other social aim. They are fantastical outsider accounts meant ultimately to titillate, mollify, or terrify. Expanding on Richard Wright's and also Alain Locke's attacks of Hurston's *Their Eyes* back in the 1930s, one can generate a working notion of exploitation: in the treatment of its subject class, an exploitation narrative drums up envy, laughter, or horror in its audience.[9] Exploitation movies have traditionally contained a "digestible" element of social outrage—even *Titanic* has its exposé of the upper-class's abuse of the class in steerage—but the social critique component is swamped by a sensationalist rendition of the subject. Most of our current stories about the poor, our classploitation ones, fall into one of three very different genres, in which the poor and socially marginal have three very different profiles:

1. *The poor and lowlifes have it better* because they are free of status and money concerns and live for enjoyment, love, and art and music in a primitive social harmony. They have much to teach the upper classes, and thus the plots in this genre involve happy downward mobility and liberating liaisons across classes. This particular sentimental theme—what might be called "*slumming drama*"—is a major motif among blockbusters, and the largest grossing film of all time, *Titanic*, is a prime example of such a movie. *Shakespeare in Love* (John Madden, 1998) and *American Beauty* (Sam Mendes, 1999) are other recent Academy Award winners for Best Picture that depend upon this motif. Toward the end of the nineteenth century, when this

genre first appeared, "slumming parties" were actual outings taken by upper-class tourists to the slums, sometimes in the company of policemen. By "slumming" here, I am refining today's much expanded colloquial use of the term, but I mean any voluntary class-crossing foray into a lower-class domain.

2. *The poor and lowlifes have it worse* because they repulsively prey on and humiliate each other in a foreign, immoral world, in which transcendence is impossible and nobody is immune to irreversible psychological damage. This motif can be realized without a class-crossing theme; the action can play out entirely among lowlifes. But those who enter their world from outside are especially vulnerable to damage. This *"class trauma"* motif is the province of 1990s independent films; the shock movies *Kids* (Larry Clark, 1995) and *Boys Don't Cry* (Kimberly Peirce, 1999), for example, partake of it.[10]

3. *The poor and lowlifes have it both better and worse.* They live in a difficult and dangerous environment but, as a result, the survivors are tougher, (street) wiser, and, thus, cooler and more effective. This particular class motif underlies 1990s "black action films" or "gangsploitation movies" about street gangs and gangsta lifestyle, such as *New Jack City* (Mario Van Peebles, 1991) and *Boyz N the Hood* (John Singleton, 1991), which have been seen as a second generation of blaxploitation movies.[11] (And these movies, along with the more generalized marketing of "ghetto style" to middle-class youth, involve not only race but also class exploitation.) But this motif also animates class-crossing tales, which I will describe as *"slumming trauma,"* such as *Fight Club* (David Fincher, 1999).[12] This third genre is a chemical compound of the first two. In these tales, the characters are defiled, but they embrace their defilement as a means of liberation and transcendence.

These genres are all products of our modern age; the familiar fictions of the poor of the nineteenth century were quite different. One of the most popular cross-class classploitation genres of the eighteenth and nineteenth centuries was the seduction novel—in its sentimental (for women) or sensational (for men) varieties—in which a poor girl is seduced and ruined, usually by a man of a higher class. She experiences a moral fall and generally ends up dead, though occasionally the higher-class man rescues her by marrying her, making for a Cinderella finish. George Lippard's *The Quaker City; Or, the Monks of Monk Hall* (1845), the best-selling American novel before *Uncle Tom's Cabin* (1852), involves such a sensational seduction subplot.[13] Another very popular classploitation story was the Horatio Alger Jr. "rags to riches" or "rags to respectability" tale, in which a poor and low-life boy meets a rich person (boy, woman, or man) who teaches the boy how to transcend poverty through virtuous hard work and self-restraint.

In our own time, by contrast, the rich tend to be attracted to the ragged—but hardly for the Christian virtue and restraint of the poor—and so shed their class affiliation at least temporarily. There is downward mobility in slumming dramas. The slumming romance is perhaps the most familiar version: Rich girl meets poor or low-life boy who liberates her from middle- or upper-class social constraints and pettiness and then is cast off (by death or some other means). Meanwhile, in the class trauma "love story," a weak, vulnerable, innocent, naive, or somewhat socially exalted girl meets a poor or low-life boy who trashes her (and sometimes then is trashed in turn by another girl, or the initial girl trashes someone else). Here the key interior experience of the girl is not a moral fall—as in the nineteenth-century sentimental seduction genre—but a traumatic humiliation, and the class of the girl varies, but she is not as socially degraded as the male who traumatizes her. In effect, the older "seduction genre" has, for the most part, been inverted and split into two separate newer variants, of the slumming drama and the class trauma varieties.[14] The ascension narrative (rags to riches) has also been *partially* inverted, with a *temporary* riches-to-rags trajectory.[15]

Where do these three current stories come from—these newer stories that turn "the Cinderella myth" inside out and upside down? Though these different classploitation tales are today doing a brisk business in Hollywood and on the Indie scene respectively, they are not inventions of the 1990s, or even, I want to suggest, of our contemporary era. They have, as I will examine, older roots in the turn of the last century and the first few decades of the twentieth century.

Genres have long life spans. So do cultural myths. The fictions that we are today producing about the poor have their roots in the late-nineteenth and early-twentieth centuries. A significant break in American writing about the poor came in that period, and we have not since surpassed the genres that were then invented. For the first four-fifths of the nineteenth century, most stories about the poor were either sentimental and moralistic tales of uplift or sentimental and moralistic tales of fall. These were tales of moral transformation. Poor shop girls were seduced and destroyed by men of a higher class or else managed to resist sexual temptation; bootblacks stopped gambling, saved their money with the help of an upper-class benefactor, and became generally virtuous. There were also tales of the American Renaissance sensationalists, romantics, and transcendentalists, in which the poor—the common people—might be blessed with innate goodness.

In the 1880s and 1890s, new genres concerning the poor and lowlifes were invented. We usually account for the new writing of this period under the rubrics of realism and naturalism. But realism tends to be used loosely, and naturalism likewise is a bit of a catchall. We can be more precise. What we call realism about the poor and naturalism (by definition about the lower orders) resolve themselves into the three genres suggested above: the slumming drama, the class-based trauma, and the slumming trauma. Briefly, we can distinguish these genres in terms of their imaginations of the poor and of the inner lives of their protagonists.

Sentimental and sensational moral tales of the nineteenth century were based on Protestant mental philosophy, in which moral conscience or character is supposed to control the passions. The inner conflict is against the temptation to sin. Again, the seduction novel (in which a poor girl is seduced and ruined by a man of a higher class) and the sentimental tale of class ascension popularized by Alger (in which a poor boy meets a denizen of the upper classes and learns middle-class habits of self-control) are the most familiar tales in this genre. The fictional poor in the mid-nineteenth century tended to experience dramatic moral transformations (rises and falls), but there were exceptions. American romantic and sensationalist writers sometimes imagined the poor and socially marginal as ennobled from the start. There is the natural or savage nobility of James Fenimore Cooper's Mohicans and Herman Melville's South Sea Islander, Queequeg. George Lippard's *Quaker City* contains urban poor people who are thoroughly virtuous and others who, though degraded, are still capable of good (and the book demythologizes the upper classes, exposing their corruption and cruelty). Nathaniel Hawthorne's *Blithedale Romance* (1852) plays with the typical seduction formula by turning it on its head. The poor woman seduces and saves the morally broken man of a higher class, instead of being ruined by him.

Meanwhile, sentimental slumming heroes of the late nineteenth and the twentieth centuries reject conscience or moral character, which is seen as an inhibiting social construct, and discover the inner resource of a deeper, truer self. As with the American romantics, the poor are once again idealized: in the slumming genre, they may be morally outrageous by middle-class standards, but they are in touch with a deeper, truer life. Their depth and nobility derives from an unconcern with money and status.

This *slumming* genre was given its realist-era incarnation by Mark Twain with *Huckleberry Finn* (1885) and its modern "female" signature in the 1930s with Zora Neale Hurston's *Their Eyes*. *Huckleberry Finn* staked out the two most popular male variants in this genre: the solitary vagabond trickster tale and the buddy story, the latter of which joins together a white male with a male companion of another class and/or race.

Hurston was apparently one of the first to put together all the elements of and elaborate the now phenomenally popular female variant in which a higher-class woman meets a lower-class (and often "swarthy") man who liberates her, and then is removed from her life, usually by a dramatic deus ex machina.[16] The taboo love story of the rich, light woman who ventures across classes and coloring was of course an older story (which haunted the white Southern imagination and notoriously led to many lynchings); one can find versions of it in previous African American literature as well, such as James Weldon Johnson's *Autobiography of an Ex-Colored Man* (1912). Hurston reworked it as a romantic slumming tale of personal liberation and development from the woman's point of view. Hurston's conscious grafting of the taboo class/color-crossing motif onto the tale of female liberation and development is made clear in the genesis of her novel: Hurston based her heroine Janie's relationship with the character Tea Cake in *Their Eyes* on her own relationship with a man of West Indian parentage who was not, like Tea Cake, a lower-class migrant worker, gambler, and vagabond, but a college student studying to be a minister.[17]

The reversal of the seduction tale formula is complete: the woman, now of the higher class, is not ruined but "saved" by the relationship; the lower-class man is the one who is cast out or dies. This slumming romance is today so common and overplayed that an alternative New York literary press can warn writers that "We are not interested in...the following: Whimsical tales of love and laughter as petit bourgeois women travel the world and find true love after facing the hard realities of having sex with a swarthy ethnic type."[18]

In the *class trauma* genre, traditionally a genre authored by males, the poor do not have inner resources; they are driven by shame and the need to avoid shame. This need results in humiliating others and in violence. In the 1890s, Stephen Crane developed the tale in which a vulnerable female is used and then tossed aside by a lower-class man. (And then the man is tossed aside in turn.)

Crane's *Maggie: A Girl of the Streets* (1893) is about a slum girl who is unrelentingly demeaned, rejected, and ostracized—unto death.

Her mother and the older generation in the tenements find her unchaste street behavior damnable; meanwhile, the hippest street types reject her as boring and nice. Finally, when she turns to prostitution, she gets rejected there too once she is no longer a new item for sale on the streets. Apparently, the degrading treatment she has received from early child abuse on has left her too humiliated and self-doubting to develop the flair and grit necessary for the life of a streetwalker.

Though Crane's protagonist Maggie Johnson is of the same class as Pete, the man who uses and rejects her, she is importantly somewhat of an anomaly in the tenements, not possessed of the callousness and brutality that characterizes everyone around her, including the local women: she "blossomed in a mud puddle,"[19] as Crane puts it. Crane's conscious and purposeful fashioning of Maggie as a girl of the streets who is not streetwise can be deduced from the fact that in Crane's initial short story sketch of the Johnson siblings, the Maggie figure is a gum-chewing, tough-talking, street savvy girl indistinguishable from the other women in the tenement world of the finished novel.[20] In inventing Maggie, Crane borrowed an element from the sentimental seduction story, in which the lower-class heroine was somehow spiritually removed from her slum element so that the middle-class reader could care about her. He changed the seduction tale in almost every other way: making the treacherous lover a lower-class, not an upper-class man, and creating characters motivated by pride and shame, not conscience and remorse. But he needed the figure of a female victim to retain the skeletal plot of the seduction tale while reworking its characterizations, and, to be a victim of a lower-class man, Maggie needed to be almost magically ignorant of the world right around her, just as the old lower-class heroine of the seduction novel would naturally be ignorant of the upper classes and their perfidy. Which is to say that Maggie, who has a promiscuous thug for a brother but is nonetheless blindsided by another promiscuous thug, is in effect a stranger to her own class.[21]

The *slumming trauma*, also usually a male genre, is a cross between the slumming drama and the psycho-sociologically minded trauma. The slumming trauma protagonist discovers the resources of a deeper self, but does so through self-defilement, degraded sex, and violence. It is the defilement and degradation that separates this genre from that of slumming drama. McTeague in Frank Norris's novel by that name is an 1890s example of such a protagonist: he becomes a bum and abuses his wife on his way to the discovery of his mystical masculine powers. And Norris seems equally interested in the subject of universal instincts released at the social bottom and that of Gilded Era social exclusion. Henry Miller helps transform the genre into its contemporary heroic and "Beat" form (and paves the way for the likes of Jack Kerouac, William S. Burroughs, Norman Mailer, Hunter S. Thompson, and Kathy Acker), by explicitly identifying the writer with the slumming and self-defiling protagonist—who in turn becomes a more obvious hero.[22]

To sum up, following are two contrasting lists:

Popular nineteenth-century cross-class classploitation tales:

1. Sentimental rags-to-riches: Poor boy *aided* by rich person.
2. Sentimental/sensational seduction: Poor girl *ruined* by rich boy.
1+2. Cinderella seduction/redemption: Poor girl *ruined* then *rescued* by rich boy.

New popular cross-class classploitation tales:

1. Slumming drama: Rich girl or boy *liberated* by poor boy or girl or by downward mobility.
2. Class trauma: Vulnerable girl *degraded* by lower-class boy.
1+2. Slumming trauma: Rich boy or girl *degraded* and *liberated* by poverty.

As becomes clear in the plot kernels and in the various examples of the genres, race is often relevant in these class tales (for example, the low-life liberator in the slumming drama is often "swarthy"), and gender is almost always crucial—gender roles, in these plots, are almost always fixed (only slumming tales of liberation seem to be flexible here in terms of gendered roles, and, even there, the male as savior, female as saved, is still more common). Which is to say, these stories are often "race-ploitation" and almost always sexploitation tales on top of being classploitation. While race and gender will often come into my discussion, my subject is, for practical reasons, limited to stories about the poor, and, as a result, I will not venture to make conclusions about race-ploitation or sexploitation narratives in general. More than this, I am asserting here that there are remarkable continuities and discontinuities in the fictional representation of the poor that cut across racial or ethnic lines. Racial or ethnic representations—in all their complexity and variation—would have to be addressed in a complete study of the subject of fictions of the poor; they are simply beyond the scope of this book. But my point in taking up this subject is that classploitation narratives are lasting American phenomena and not just epiphenomena of blaxploitation and sexploitation stories.

New Mental Philosophies: Depth Psychology and Shame or Self-Esteem Theory

It is a common perception that our great advance in the understanding of the human person comes with Freud at the beginning of the twentieth century. Prior psychological theory tends to be imagined as primitive, shallow, and based on an absolute distinction between sanity and insanity. Moreover, we tend to attribute our current "shame theory" and the "self-esteem movement" entirely to Freudian theory, to see these as direct derivations of Freudian ego and self psychologies (which get developed in the mid- and late-twentieth century). But current shame theory and self-esteem psychology have older historical roots as well: in American literary realism and naturalism of the 1890s that described the poor—especially in the "trauma" literature I am identifying. By "shame theory" and "self-esteem theory," I mean simply the sum of psychological, sociological, and pop psychological thinking that attributes central importance in human behavior and mental well-being to one's self-esteem or propensity for feelings of shame—as opposed to those older schools of thought (first formalized in textbooks in the mid-nineteenth century[23]) that stressed and still stress moral character as the determining factor in behavior or the relatively newer (early twentieth century), classic Freudian views that stress any number of unconscious conflicts that come out of desire and its repression. (I am distinguishing between these classic Freudian approaches and the even newer post–World War II Freudian ideas about unconscious conflicts that come out of narcissism or personality disorders.) Post–World War II Freudian ego and self psychology and theories of narcissism and our current pop self-esteem psychology mark the linking up of two initially separate strands of psychological thinking—namely, classic Freudian psychology and the self-esteem and shame theory of realism and naturalism—and the application of self-esteem and shame theory to the middle class.

Though it is often regarded as a contemporary phenomenon, the self-esteem movement in fact started up in the 1890s in relation to the urban and immigrant poor. After decades of hand wringing about urban immorality, American journalism and literature experienced a breakthrough in the 1890s. A few nonprofessional "psychologists of shame" emerged to provide a new view of slum thuggery, debauchery, divorce, drinking, and rudeness.

Jacob Riis, the first photojournalist of the American slums—whose camera was an essential ingredient in the reconception of the poor in America—explained that boys became "toughs" (or thugs) out of a perverted expression of their self-esteem, an expression that was twisted or stunted by a lack of opportunity. Riis shocked his police friends and many middle-class readers by claiming that the urban tough, who—though the worst of the worst morally since he often maimed and killed and always swaggered—really represented a hopeful sign in the slums, a sign of a preserved self-esteem in an environment that often killed pride and, as a result, left human wrecks. Riis wanted to make sure that boys' asylums didn't manage to do to the tough what even slum misery couldn't, namely, crush out his pride; Riis wanted social programs and the penal system to nurture self-esteem.

In Crane's little novel *Maggie*, which no publisher would touch (until he was famous), he understood that the slum dweller was engaged in a constant battle to fend off insult: the insults of exploitative bosses and landlords, haughty church missionaries, intimidating policemen, and often abusive (because desperate) parents. And simply the insult of well-dressed middle-class people in the streets. Crane understood that any remark, or even a look, from such a well-dressed person might very well be met with violence. The gaze or glance of a middle-class person is felt as condescension and humiliation. This battle to fend off insult—and preserve a sense of self—was constant and all consuming. Middle-class calls for morality, insofar as they reached the slums, were so many further insults that had to be deflected. Crane explicitly described the slum dweller's experience of the middle-class calls for morality: while waiting for their soup, his slum dwellers act uncivilly in a mission church as the preacher tells them they are damned. Their rowdy behavior in church may strike the preacher as uncivil and immoral, but Crane understands it as a necessity for psychic health. The slum dwellers need to reject the preacher's message—even at the risk of not getting their soup. Crane understood the general belligerence, rebelliousness, profanity, intoxication, violence, and rudeness of the slums along the same lines. Crime and violence may be self-destructive, but in the context of slum life they are relatively healthy responses, the alternatives being depression and paralyzing self-hatred—like the traumatic incapacitation Maggie experiences.

Crane's "healthy" slum characters are likewise incapable of remorse, or self-criticism, because any self-accusation would open up the floodgates of toxic shame. Even to show respect for anybody else is to risk a keen reminder of one's own lowliness or a further lowering of oneself; indeed, indifference or disrespect must be shown. As Crane makes painfully clear, the alternative to constantly fending off the *shame* of poverty, of social inferiority—through swaggering incivility—is a self-loathing that is bound to become suicidal. In Crane's observed Bowery, the cool or disrespectful, always-uncivil swagger is the main device for masking shame.[24]

Meanwhile, if in America self-esteem theory initially developed in relation to the poor, classic Freudianism was first addressed to the upper classes. As several recent historical commentators have persuasively claimed, Freudian psychology originally became popular in America (in the early decades of the twentieth century) because white middle- and upper-class urbanites seized on it for their own personal redefinition in a moment of cultural identity crisis, in which the older notion of Horatio Alger–style, self-made, entrepreneurial individualism—and the moralistic Alger tale of self-transformation and class-ascension—was becoming untenable. As Joel Pfister puts it:

> America was entering a phase of advanced corporate or monopoly capitalism during the 1920s, and...confidence in the nineteenth-century ideology of self-making had eroded with the advent of corporate hierarchies. Discourses of "depth"—packaged in various forms by [Eugene] O'Neill's plays, Sherwood Anderson's fiction, pop psychologists, therapists, and others—provided a class of white-collar professionals and managers with a compensatory belief in and often sexy fascination with its own "psychological" significance and individualism, a "depth" that corporate authority seemingly could not standardize, control, or own.[25]

Indeed, the rise of corporations and the resulting middle- and upper-class masculine identity crisis that made way for the American embrace of Freudianism had their beginnings in the 1880s and 1890s, as various historians (from Ann Douglas to Jackson Lears[26]) have shown. There was a rising masculine "anticivilization" feeling and cult of experience and strenuous adventure in the 1890s, which was popularized by the likes of Teddy Roosevelt and Western-writer and artist Frederic Remington (as well as war and Western writers like Crane who also found new masculine adventure in the slums), a few decades before Freud essentially gave that feeling theoretical legitimacy in

Civilization and Its Discontents (1930). Likewise, 1890s masculine literary naturalism à la Frank Norris and Jack London—with their marvelous blond brutes and heroic canines—already had a central fascination with base, sexual and violent animal instincts, and with a primitive, deep, buried self, before the more elegant, less racist concept of the unconscious Freudian "id" came on the scene.

What might be added to these accounts is that Freudianism also was acceptable to urban professionals and managers because it did not really involve a tremendous intellectual leap from traditional middle- and upper-class thinking about the human mind, the nineteenth-century Protestant mental philosophy of character. Like Freudian theory, nineteenth-century mental philosophy divided the mind into component parts, which it also hierarchized; moreover, moral "character" played much the same role as Freud's "superego," while the passions that traditionally needed to be controlled by character in Protestant mental philosophy were similar to the id. Freudian theory involved some twists and revaluations that made it appealing to the masculine crusade of the turn of the century—it set out expressly to lower the demands of the superego and give more credence to the needs of the id for a healthier psychological balance; it also provided some mystification of what had been considered base or mundane passions. But it hardly marked a fundamental break in long-standing ruling-class notions of the human mental equipment. In this sense, Freudian psychology was not only an upper- or managing-class philosophy because the upper classes seized on it and applied it (for many decades) only to themselves and not to the working classes but also because it was largely in the tradition of upper-class Victorian thought.

A more dramatic break in American writing and thought came with some realism and naturalism—specifically, with *class* and *slumming traumas*. True enough, the fantasies of escape and the recovery of youth, native to American romanticism, were still there in these new genres, but a fundamental difference entered between the slumming drama and the trauma writer, namely, defilement. The association with the poor, with the slum, with the thug, was no longer an association with the common man or with natural impulses, but instead with something degraded. Walt Whitman complained or lost interest in the Bowery Theater when it became vulgar—as opposed to common.[27] Here Stephen Crane's interest really began. In fact, he detailed the vulgar acts of the Bowery Theater at some length in *Maggie*. Whitman was a democrat, universal in his embrace, embracing the lowly along with the rest, but he balked at vulgarity, at degraded spectacle. Crane shunned the upper- and middle-classes with a contempt that perhaps only exaggerated the romantics', but he also embraced the defiled. In *Maggie*, he wrote not only about an innocent girl who was driven to prostitution but also depicted the mentalities of a ruthless female hustler (who knows how to edge out the competition) and a sophisticated john (who develops a disturbing connoisseurship of street girls). Perhaps shocking to our sense of the possible in the Gilded Age, Crane even planned a novel (that he apparently never wrote) about a male prostitute.[28] Between Whitman and Crane is the big change in the bohemian's sensibility and also in the conception of the human mental equipment, of the interior life of the human person.

The more dramatic break in the imagination of the human mental equipment is not between the Christian (especially Protestant) notion of character and Freud's model; again, these are in fact very similar. Both propose a controlling part of the self and a subordinate part— character and passions, superego and id—both are concerned with the issue of guilt, even if Freud noted that guilt could be an unconscious process. Crane and some of the other realists and naturalists who adopted trauma or "humiliation" themes were not writing principally about guilt, but about shame, not about something their characters have done, but about the way they are seen by others. They were writing not primarily about an internal conflict between separate parts of the self, but about a feeling of stigma and the fierce reaction to it. (Likewise, there are contemporary forms of shame theory that are non-Freudian: for example, *affect* shame theory, à la Silvan Tomkins, starting in the 1960s, does not deal on the one hand in deep or unconscious Freudian drives and conflicts or on the other in personal Protestant conscience, but in affects triggered in reaction to external stimuli, especially interaction with others.[29]) Hawthorne, for all his subtlety about personality, was still centrally concerned (in *The Scarlet Letter* [1850] and elsewhere) with guilt and the internal conflict between passions and conscience. Crane was not. With Crane, the moralistic seduction novel, which had dominated the novel of the poor for a century, came to a screeching halt. More largely, the novel of "conscience" or "moral character"—seduction as well as Alger's rags-to-riches—was finished with Crane. His "fallen woman" is not guilty, and that means she is not ashamed of having fallen; she feels the stigma of social rejection, whether that rejection comes in the name of traditional chastity or alternative street smarts.

Another difference between these new psychological approaches was in their initial application. While the middle and upper classes would seize on Freudianism for self-redefinition, this early shame- or self-esteem-based psychological thinking—the brainchildren of street-wise 1890s "trauma" realists such as Crane and Jacob Riis—was applied mostly to the lower classes.

But, for all these differences, depth psychology and shame theory (and, likewise, slumming drama and class trauma stories) have more in common than might be immediately apparent. Though shame the-ory arguably comes out of social humiliation and was initially applied to the lower classes, it does not follow that depth or "individuality" psychology (which the upper-classes applied to themselves) comes simply out of social affirmation or superiority. As historians have sug-gested, the popularity of depth psychology comes out of a middle- and upper-class identity crisis in the transition to corporate capitalism—one might say it comes out of *historical* humiliation (rather than class humiliation). In that case, one might suspect that depth psychology and shame psychology have intimate connections; one might even say that they represent two intellectual responses to the multiple identity crises of industrialization, and two responses that are veritable inver-sions of each other. Much the same might be said about the two seem-ingly very different tales of slumming drama and class trauma, which these seemingly very different psychological theories underpin.

Indeed, it might be said that in the earliest stage in the development of these psychological theories in America, the two models were not greatly differentiated. Another way of saying this is that in the 1890s "individuality" had not yet taken on the mystical valence that it has in contemporary culture; it had not yet been invested with inner depth, as it would be in the course of the twentieth century. For example, for Riis in the last decade of the nineteenth century, the terms "self-esteem" and "individuality" were used interchangeably. The reason Riis preferred the violent thug was precisely that, though morally warped, he pos-sessed an "individuality" or "self-esteem" that the beggar had lost.

Nor is it the case, then, that the tale of liberating slumming (and related depth theory) was developed by writers from the upper classes while the story of humiliating trauma (and related shame theory) came from the social bottom. The developers or early practitioners of these different genres do not break down neatly along class lines. Rather, what can be argued is that slumming sentimentalists and trauma writers alike—those writers who broke with Protestant men-tal philosophy in favor either of depth psychology or self-esteem psy-chology—came out of some sort of marginalization, exclusion, or humiliation, whether class-based, racial, familial, or personal.

And—to bring this brief sketch of the history of psychology again up to the present—the class distinction in the application of these tales and psychological theories would eventually erode. After World War II, self-esteem theory in psychology and the trauma genre in literature and film would no longer be applied solely to the poor. In literature and film, there would be trauma narratives set among the upper class: stories of the privileged, humiliated and humiliating in the rat race. Meanwhile, many practicing psychiatrists of the 1950s and 1960s reported a crop of adult middle-class patients with problems little seen before World War II—problems that inspired a major transformation in clinical practice and theory, away from classic Freudian approaches and categories. These problems, distinct from the familiar symptom neuroses (such as compulsive "hand washing"), came to be called "character or personality disorders,"[30] and they were responded to with self-esteem and shame theory or, more specifically, their new Freudian-psychology forms: ego psychology, self psychology, and the theory of narcissism. In effect, when middle-class adults clinically applied self-esteem theory to themselves, it was often done in Freudian, depth psychology form. And the two separate models of subjectivity were combined; the concepts of individuality and self-esteem were reunited.

Humiliation and Writers of the New Classploitation

Though we might expect to, we do not find sustained shame theory or "trauma literature" written by the socially and economically oppressed in mid-nineteenth-century America; either the nineteenth-century poor and oppressed simply had no voice, or, like the former slaves who wrote abolitionist narratives, they generally had to pitch their voices moralistically to reach upper-class Northern Protestants. We must look for the earliest examples of trauma literature, not only among the oppressed, but also among those who might appear economically, socially, or racially privileged, but who nonetheless underwent some experience of humiliation.[31]

Friedrich Nietzsche suggested that Christianity was a slave morality—that it issued from the socially oppressed. In a similar way, I want to consider that both depth psychology and shame theory got their start as psychological theories of the humiliated. Writers of slumming dramas (such as Twain and Hurston), slumming traumas (including Norris and Miller), and class "docu-traumas" (including Riis and Crane) were, for different reasons, poised to reformulate the social problem of the poor in their different ways: some were immigrants or from ethnic minorities, some were black or from the lower class, and many had experienced social stigmatization or humiliating poverty firsthand before emerging as middle-class writers. But others grew up in middle-class families and experienced shames of other varieties, voluntarily associating with the poor and lowlifes out of their personal compulsions.

Traditionally (that is, before the poststructuralist turn in literary studies that has resulted in New Historicism and cultural studies), writers who associated with low-life, so-called bohemian writers—no matter how they wrote and which of these genres they fall into—were seen as exemplars of individualism. That is to say, they were integrated into the mythology of slumming drama: they tended to be celebrated as bohemian individualists, and, thus, treated with a depth psychology approach. Poststructuralism essentially neutralized—or at least put a chill effect—on the discussion of authors' personal motivations, discovering suspect social or political agendas behind the construction of the author as heroic individualist.[32]

The developers or early practitioners of our current classploitation tales of rejection—the class trauma tale as well as the story of slumming love and loss—were shaped by varieties of shame (not just class shame) and are therefore themselves apt candidates for a shame theory analysis. In the exploration of that contention, this book will zero in on the literary pioneers Hurston, Crane, and Miller specifically, submitting them to such analysis, a shame theory analysis that certainly draws on depth psychology ideas—and even admits the usefulness at times of the notion of sublimation—without sinking into pop psychology platitudes and sentimentality: an analysis that looks to particular ongoing experiences (not universal primal scenes) in childhood and youth to understand an adult identity particularly attuned to shame. However, it attempts to avoid, as Eve Kosofsky Sedgwick puts it, "the engulfing, near eschatological pathos surrounding shame in the popular discourse...of the self-help and recovery movements and the self psychology that theoretically underpins them."[33] All three of these writers have been championed as daring individualists who flouted middle-class convention in their voluntary association with the poor. But it is also possible to reconstruct their biographies and psychological habits or reflexes along the lines of shame theory, to trace the various racial, sexual, class-based, and familial humiliations that can be seen to give them the perspectives they needed to generate their classploitation writing.[34]

Hurston, born black, female, and working-class just a generation after the Civil War, and Miller, born to an urban working-class immigrant family during an era of intense industrialization and poverty, seem more obviously situated for such an approach. Their familiarity with humiliation is easy enough to imagine. But less than obvious is how Hurston's experiences of gender and race stigmatization and Miller's of class humiliation translate into their development of the seemingly self-affirming genres of the slumming romance and the slumming trauma, respectively. Also less immediately clear is socially privileged Crane's experience of shame and his resulting affinity for the class trauma genre. Crane, white, male, and from a middle-class family, seems at first glance immune to humiliation, but shame—or feeling "queered," to use a phrase that pops up in his *Maggie*[35]—comes in many forms.[36]

"A Tiger's Leap into the Past"

The body of the book will proceed by genre, turning in each part first and fairly briefly to current film[37] and then, in much greater depth, to the writers I consider literary pioneers of these genres: Hurston, Crane, and Miller. These latter chapters in each part will attempt to link these authors' very different experiences of shame to the particular classploitation tales I want to give them credit for helping develop: to explain socially privileged Crane's production of sociological trauma and socially stigmatized Hurston's and Miller's development of slumming drama and slumming trauma.

There are different sorts of genealogies one could attempt to give of these newer film genres—and any genealogy is of course going to be a partial one. It would be possible, for example, in accounting for the appearance of 1990s trauma films, to focus on developments in film and popular culture post–World War II.[38]

This book attempts a different sort of genealogy of these classploitation stories that are so popular today. It will leave out the more recent developments and influences and try to get at the older historical roots, focusing especially on literary sources. The reason for this choice of focus is twofold: First, I want to show that these seemingly very contemporary classploitation stories have been around in American culture longer than we tend to think. The New Historicism in literary studies has tended to have a prejudice in favor of historical and cultural discontinuities and differences rather than continuities and similarities; I want to point up the continuities in our fictions of the poor and lowlifes. And I want to investigate reasons why these tales or genres might have come into being in the first place with a close look at three writers who were decisive in the development of these genres, Zora Neale Hurston, Stephen Crane, and Henry Miller, and the "reasons"—at once personal and cultural—for their ground-breaking literary productions.

Here again I will depart from standard New Historicist and cultural studies practice, which has "uncritically" embraced Michel Foucault's conception of discourse—as an impersonal, or metapersonal, reality—and, thus, describes cultural forces that subsume authors rather than discussing authors' personal experiences of and adaptations to cultural forces (such as shame and reactions to shame in response to the social constructions of race, gender, class, appearance, and so on). In short, theory has been used to disqualify biography, but biography can in fact be employed to think about theory. It is, for example, possible to discover behind Foucault's influential notion of "the death of the author" personal motivations, or a personal adaptation to cultural forces: it is possible, in fact, to submit Foucault's creation and practice of that desubjectivizing notion to a shame theory analysis, as I do in an appendix.

Walter Benjamin advocated "a tiger's leap into the past," which would allow historical thinkers to illuminate aspects of the past that were invisible then as well as to learn about the present by exposing surprising continuities with and developments from the past.

The counterintuitive and unbalanced procedure of the book—to jump in each section antichronologically from a brief look at current film to a much more substantial inquiry into the pre-postmodern writers, including their biographies, reflects the fact that this book attempts just such a "leap in the open air of history."[39] (I include biographical information for the writers and not the filmmakers here because the writers' and filmmakers' relationships to these genres are quite different. I see the writers as innovators of the genres that are just being developed, and their biographies help explain where these innovations come from; I see, by contrast, the filmmakers as consciously partaking in established genres and tales. Their biographies would at most explain their interest in these genres, and so are not relevant in the same way.)

The book is not meant to be a full and comprehensive account of certain trends in contemporary film but a merely suggestive description of genres, basically limited to issues of plot and character (and excluding *mise en scene* and editing).[40] Rather, this book is ultimately an attempt to rethink certain realist, naturalist, and modernist literature, in the light of some relatively obvious developments in current film. It is to a lesser extent an attempt to inflect these rather obvious cinematic developments by drawing links from them to the literary tradition. I want to reflect on these older literary forms, to which Crane, Hurston, and Miller are usually assigned, through the prism of our current cultural productions.

I

Slumming Drama

Award-Winning Hollywood Blockbusters

"Call me a tumbleweed blowing in the wind."

—*Jack in* Titanic

Several of the Academy Award winners for Best Picture in recent years are based on a by now very familiar slumming romance of lower-class life, one that is already fully articulated in Hurston's *Their Eyes*. *Titanic*, *Shakespeare in Love*, and *American Beauty*, for example, all depend on the charms of downward mobility into lower-class existence—at least in the short run. As strange as it sounds at first, it seems hardly an overstatement to claim that the middle-class conceptions of itself today at the turn of the century—both its romantic fantasy and its acerbic realism—are heavily mediated by its imagination of the poor.

In *Titanic*, this romance of lower-class life is most fully and painstakingly realized. In several objective ways, Jack Dawson is a lot like the character Telly in the class trauma film *Kids*: he has obvious connections to lower-class life, he lives for the moment and has no plans for the future, he is a sensualist, he is rootless and likes to drift, he seduces a girl from the upper-middle class and introduces her to the joys of premarital sex. Both of them also seem, in particular, to like to spit. But their treatments in the two films could hardly be more different. Indeed, in *Titanic* Rose's genteel mother sees Jack much as the upper-middle-class viewer of today might see Telly: he is "a dangerous insect which must be squashed quickly." But while the film *Kids* could be said to demonize Telly, the movie *Titanic* romanticizes Jack (first of all by casting teen heartthrob Leonardo DiCaprio in the role).

Jack in the film is, of course, the instrument of Rose's liberation and salvation from the straightjacket of upper-class life, just as lower-class, free-spirited Tea Cake is explicitly seen as delivering Janie in *Their Eyes*. Jack not only helps rescue Rose from the sinking of the Titanic; he more profoundly saves her "in every way that a woman can be saved." Quite similarly, Tea Cake not only saves Janie from drowning in a flood; he saves her from "bein' dead from the standing still and tryin' to laugh";[1] as she puts it to him, "God snatched me out de fire through you" (172).

At the beginning of the film, Rose has been affianced to Cal, a despicably arrogant and class-conscious man of wealth and no taste. (To make his tastelessness perfectly clear, the audience sees him scold Rose for buying Picassos and hears him declare that Picasso "won't amount to a thing, trust me.") Rose rushes across the deck of the boat to leap off and commit suicide at the beginning of the story, as she looks forward to an "endless round of parties and cotillions and polo...the same narrow people, the same mindless chatter. I felt like I was standing at a precipice, no one to pull me back...no one who cared." Janie in *Their Eyes*, along similar lines, has had to contend with a previous husband, Joe Starks, who is focused on wealth and status and has expected her to play the confining role of the mayor's wife. Jack, who was on deck appreciating nature, of course pulls Rose back from the precipice of the ship's railing and goes on to liberate her from those people and that chatter and the narrow social role staked out for upper-class wives. Though Tea Cake doesn't free Janie from Joe Starks (who has died), he does liberate her from the suffocating emptiness of the middle-class existence Joe has set up for her.

Jack introduces Rose to the liberated mores of the lower classes. He not only teaches her how to spit like a man; he introduces her to the rowdy dancing, cavorting and drinking of the crowd in "steerage." He promises to teach her how to ride a horse Western style, and he of course engages in passionate, literally steamy lovemaking with her, in an automobile in cargo. Tea Cake likewise includes Janie in male activities; he teaches her to play chess and use a gun, and he introduces her to juke joints.

Jack's character is singular insofar as he is a composite of two different stock figures of slumming liberation dramas: the noble, independent,

Western outdoor proletarian and the urban bohemian artist. For on top of being born poor in Wisconsin, losing his family young, and providing for himself through a variety of jobs while drifting, he has been to Paris, is an excellent artist, and has sketched a prostitute in the nude. This is a prostitute, not incidentally, whom he hasn't slept with—because that might make him seem decadent, and he is too healthy in a Midwestern American way for that. On the other hand, he is too red-blooded and grounded in his body ("just go with it, don't think," he instructs Rose when teaching her to dance in his style) to refrain from sleeping with a prostitute because of a moral caveat, so we learn that the prostitute had only one leg. Meanwhile, it might seem callous or arrogant to reject a woman sexually because she is deformed, so Jack must comment that she had a good sense of humor. The movie falls all over itself in this scene trying to carve out for Jack the right combination of adventurous worldliness and good-hearted innocence.

Jack is also in possession of a homely bohemian philosophy, that is corny partly because we have heard it—and heard it said better—a hundred times before (by the likes of Hurston, Henry Miller, and Jack Kerouac), and partly because, again, he is a country boy from Wisconsin. When Rose's mother asks if he finds his "sort of rootless existence appealing," he replies, "yes, ma'am, I do,...the air in my lungs, a few blank sheets of paper....I love waking up in the morning, not knowing what's going to happen....I figure life's a gift, and I don't intend on wasting it....Make each day count." We can aptly, if a little awkwardly, agree with Jack to "call [him] a tumbleweed blowing in the wind"—which is to say, part honest Westerner, part Dylanesque bohemian spirit. (He even says, borrowing from Bob Dylan, "when you got nothing, you got nothing to lose.")

Jack survives the humiliating "snake pit" of the upper-class dinner table and the general arrogant sniping at his lower-class status ("tell us of the accommodations in steerage," Rose's mother nastily asks) because he has a host of talents and experiences that money can't buy. He is impervious to such shame because he simply doesn't desire money and status. He understands it is a trap.

In this now familiar romance of poverty, lower-class status has quite simply allowed Jack—like Hurston's Tea Cake—to develop a freedom and a joy in living that is inaccessible to the rich. And not only does this romance of downward mobility indulge in the genre's familiar notion that the lower classes have better sex, dancing, music, and appreciation of the beauties of the natural world, it turns out that in this romance of the poor, the lower classes are better in a disaster.

While the rich are ready to shoot the poor—and often to climb over each other—to get seats in the lifeboats, Jack and his gang spend most of their time helping and rescuing each other, and little children. (Rose's fiancé Cal meanwhile ignores a crying girl until he sees a way to use her to get on a lifeboat with the women and children.) Moreover, Jack in particular has an almost instinctive knowledge of how to ride an ocean liner down when it is sinking and breaking apart (while others are flying and dying all around him).

The working—and vagabond—class in *Titanic* (like the spirited community of migrant workers on the "muck" in *Their Eyes*) is assuredly not a community of the demeaned. It is quite the opposite, in fact. Members of the lower class regularly show respect and good will to each other, sometimes to the point of absurdity. When Jack and Rose are running from Cal's manservant and cross through the ship's boiler room, Jack somewhat ridiculously excuses the intrusion with kind words of encouragement to his fellow workers: as he dashes by, he calls, "don't mind us, you're doing a great job, keep up the good work." Members of the working class accept each other regardless of trade or national origin; Jack's bunk room is a veritable *multicultural* micro-cosm—and this is of course another marker of its virtue—with a couple of Swedish men and an Italian, in addition to the American Jack. (The upper class provides here again a foil to lower class brotherhood and equality: those from established families snub "new money.")

And fair play rules among the poor. When Jack wins tickets on the Titanic from a couple of Swedish workingmen in a card game, it seems there might be trouble and double-dealing. One of the Swedes grabs Jack by the lapel, and Jack cringes in anticipation of a punch. But the Swede slugs his friend instead, who has foolishly wagered the tickets. Jack's own honesty becomes a major theme in the film, when a huge diamond belonging to Cal and Rose is planted on him. Jack insists loudly on his innocence, even though the coat he is wearing is also not his own. But Jack maintains he has "borrowed" the coat and intended to return it (he has merely taken it so he can move among the upper class without creating suspicion), and the audience and later Rose believe him. (Tea Cake's honesty in *Their Eyes* is also thematized; though he sneaks off to gamble with Janie's money, he doesn't steal it and isn't a thief; he was simply secretive because he was worried Janie would look down on him on account of his vice.)

If Jack and, say, Telly of *Kids* are both vagabond, basically parent-less kids but depicted in utterly opposite ways, the lower-class communities in these two movies are also complete inversions of each other.

The community in "steerage" on the Titanic is not only not demeaned and degraded by its lower class status and here its literal confinement to the lower spaces on the ship. It is rather a utopian multicultural community of civility, justice, and fellowship, apparently—judging by Jack's response to Rose—with feminist notions about the equality of women as well. Furthermore, the disturbing physical plights of poverty, such as filth and disease, are swept from the recreated steerage. The only time rats appear in the film is in a moment when they are not only nonthreatening, but rather charmingly helpful: the rats lead the way to dry ground when the ship starts sinking. As a buddy of Jack's puts it, "if that's the way they're heading, it's good enough for me."

Titanic may be the grandest imaginable rendering of this now signature American romantic theme that Hurston helped develop (in all its current dimensions) in *Their Eyes*—rich girl meets poor or low life boy who liberates her, then is removed. It is certainly the most expensive and lucrative movie of all times. But *Shakespeare in Love* cleverly manages nothing less than to "overwrite" the most famous romance in the Western literary tradition with this same American class-busting formula. The "star-crossed" lovers of *Romeo and Juliet* become the "class-crossed" lovers of *Shakespeare in Love*.

Shakespeare, here dubiously reconfigured as a poor bohemian artist ("a poor player"), becomes the model for Romeo, and Juliet is inspired by the aristocratic Viola de Lesseps whom he helps (for a time) break out of the chains that bound women in Renaissance court life. She not only discovers passionate love and sex prior to marriage and the ribald joys of the street tavern but also gets to act on the all-male Elizabethan stage. The character Shakespeare (in the film) presumably had to smooth out the class theme in his adaptation of his more dramatic real life, making Romeo and Juliet both of noble birth, in order not to offend the aristocratic element in his pre-American audience.

Shakespeare in this movie is, like Jack in *Titanic*, blessed with artistic ability and a lust for life that make him indifferent to money and social status; he only cares about his reputation as an artist, and this makes him irresistible to the soulful aristocratic woman. (It should be made clear that almost all literary historians would take issue with this portrayal of Shakespeare as a poor bohemian indifferent to social status; historians generally see him, rather, as a social climber. We know very little about him for certain, but one thing we do know is that he worked very hard to procure for his family a coat of arms and the attendant social class and privilege.) And like Rose in *Titanic*, Viola de Lesseps has an upper-crust, arrogant fiancé who is ready to make her his domestic chattel and strangle the hidden but deeper life out of her. Again as in *Titanic*, the cuckolded, upper-class fiancé is angry, but powerless to take revenge on his rival, largely because the bohemian artist type is too busy living and creating to worry about upsetting the powers that be.

American Beauty is not an example of this special American inter-class romance, but it shares the theme of liberating downward mobil-ity. When corporate downsizing hits Lester Burnham, he decides to go down in flames, savaging his boss and ridiculing his job. His joy in his socioeconomic downgrade surprisingly continues when he dumps the middle-class rat race and returns to a job of his youth, flipping burg-ers at a fast-food joint. He also returns to the illicit drugs and now illicit sexual fantasies of his adolescence, buying dope from a neighbor kid and lusting after a teenage friend of his daughter.

American Beauty also suggests a second quest to escape from sta-tus. Just as Lester has left his job, his daughter, Jane, and the kid next door, Ricky, will drop out and run away, leaving the provincial popu-larity-driven world of suburban high school—in which they are both unappreciated—for the adventurous and cosmopolitan city.

What links these blockbuster films is that their male heroes are impervious to the issue of class status that dominates everyone else in the film; they instead enjoy a liberated, slumming appreciation of lower-class life. (This enjoyment of the lower class is made possible, ironically, by luck with money or offbeat financial ability. Jack wins his Titanic trip in a card game; Shakespeare seems to be able to string along his producers and get necessary advances; Lester manages to arrange a good severance deal by threatening to damage the reputa-tion of the boss who fires him with wild claims of sexual harassment, and Ricky participates in the underground drug economy.)

Depth Psychology

These films also, not surprisingly, share an investment in the familiar Freudian or deep-self psychology (which trauma films reject). Rose, in fact, approvingly mentions Freud near the beginning of *Titanic*, in mocking one of the Titanic officials who is consumed with its unprece-dented size. She implies that he might be suffering from a deficiency in penis size and manliness, and her offhand remark seems to be borne out later in the film, when, in the midst of the disaster, he takes the coward's way out and sneaks on the lifeboats along with the women and children. Shakespeare visits a kind of Freudian apothecary at the beginning of *Shakespeare in Love*, who analyzes his phallic-packed dreams and makes it clear to the audience that his writer's block is tied to sexual frustration; Shakespeare has perhaps been "humiliated in the act of love." In any case, he hasn't "scored" in a while.

These direct, comic references to Freudian psychology aside, the blockbusters at issue here provide their characters with deep, repressed selves that will be liberated and developed in the course of the films. These adventurous and erotic selves are importantly beyond the narrow roles that the higher-class codes confer on people. We watch Rose, Viola de Lesseps, and Lester Burnham blossom into charming, passionate, brave, and thoughtful people. In a similar way, Ricky and Jane in *American Beauty* have been cast by their high school peers as "freaks," but they have inner capacities and sensitivities to beauty that the narrow world of high school social life cannot fathom.

Importantly, Lester doesn't consummate his lust for his daughter's cheerleader pal Angela when he has the chance. Instead, when she throws herself at him, needing an ego fix, and he discovers she's a virgin, he comes to his (other) senses, recognizes her need for reassurance, and affirms her worth without using her. He talks to her and makes her a sandwich instead of having sex with her. She has been put down by the quirky, drug-dealing kid Ricky next door, when her popular-kid gambit of humiliating him has as a freak and "mental case" in front of her friend Jane fails, and he in turn mocks her as boring and ordinary. We couldn't be further here from the humiliate-or-be-humiliated world of the trauma film, in which a girl in Angela's wounded and needy condition, fresh from a failure as a victimizer, would be ruthlessly exploited and left further demeaned. Lester breaks the cycle of humiliation, with humane restraint and compassion. He is here gifted with exactly the interior mental space—of sensitivity and capacity for conscience and compassion—that trauma film characters conspicuously lack. And we get the feeling that his escape from the corporate shark-tank of status competition has much to do with his enhanced capacity for care.

While these films depend on depth psychology and ascribe to their class-crossing heroes romanticized individualities that can only be discovered outside of upper-class society, they also rely on familiar notions of self-esteem in describing those upper-class societies driven by status and ego. The writers of *Titanic* and *Shakespeare in Love*, like Hurston in her *Their Eyes*, depend upon two very different types of characters, which seem to be ontologically distinct: the petty and the heroic, the first set motivated by ego or status, the second set magically free of this concern and instead motivated by freedom, vitality, and self-discovery (and even a mystical relation to God in Hurston's case). So on the one hand you have the fiancés and upper-class society generally in *Titanic* and *Shakespeare in Love* and the middle-class porch sitters and Janie's first two husbands in *Their Eyes*, then on the other hand you have the heroic couples and the romanticized lower class generally.

Deus Ex Machina

What finally links these bohemian romance narratives is that, interestingly, none of them allow the class-crossing to last. In the tales of romantic love, the class-crossing relationships are temporary; Jack dies, and Viola must still marry Lord Wessex and move to Virginia (Janie in *Their Eyes* has to kill Tea Cake and returns to the middle-class town where she lived with her oppressive mayor husband). Lester's non-upper-middle class behavior is brought to an end by a bullet from a troubled neighbor who tragically misinterprets Lester's unconventional client-drug dealer relationship with his son as homosexuality.[2]

In these blockbuster escape fantasies of downward mobility, the fantasy can only last so long. It seems this is the case because these movies get their punch from breaking the rules—from the thrill of liberation from the restrictions of upper-class life—not from a vision of an enduring bohemian lifestyle outside of status concerns.

Rose literally has to pry herself loose from Jack's dead, frozen hand to get saved by the rescue boat from death. Though he has saved her from dying in the disaster, his corpse has become a burden to her, and it is not hard to imagine that if they had landed together in New York he would have become a burden to her in life. (Very similarly, in Hurston's tale, Tea Cake becomes a threat to Janie before he dies: he goes mad with rabies after saving her from the hurricane and flood. Rose has to discard Jack's corpse lest she drown; Janie has to shoot Tea Cake lest he kill her.) Jack has told her as they float in the freezing water that she will live to have children, and it is hard to imagine how Jack, with his pennilessness, vagabond habits, and lower-class status, will be much help in that enterprise beyond the act of conception. The combination of these traits of Jack is enough to cut her off from socioeconomic success—which the elder Rose has clearly enjoyed. In any case, it is precisely at the moment that Rose announces to Jack "when this ship docks, I'm getting off with you," that the iceberg is sighted. This laughable timing is no coincidence. The film cannot imagine the relationship beyond this point; nor must it allow the audience to think about the terms of a lasting liaison. The iceberg is, in this sense, a kind of deus ex machina that saves the relationship from an internal unraveling by an external catastrophe that eliminates Jack— and leaves Rose poised to be a "saved" woman in every sense, including a social-class sense. Jack has served his purpose in Rose's life, which is to liberate her from a narrow definition of womanhood and to open her up to a wider female possibility as represented in the snapshots on the elder Rose's bedside table (Rose riding a horse Western style, standing next to an airplane wearing pilot's goggles, and striking a sexy, glamorous pose).

Titanic has in fact insured that we never need worry about Rose's socioeconomic status—we don't like the idea that she might end up as a seamstress, as her mother worries she herself will if Rose doesn't marry Cal. By happenstance, the rescued Rose carries in the pocket of her coat the fantastic diamond Cal gave her as a present. She never in fact cashes in the diamond—the elder Rose drops it into the Atlantic when she returns to the scene of the catastrophe years later. This is the movie's way of letting us know that Rose was never corrupted by a desire for wealth and high status, but, again, the diamond also served the purpose of assuring the audience she would never drop too far down on the socioeconomic scale.

In a similar way, *Shakespeare in Love* doesn't want the audience to imagine what would happen to Viola de Lesseps if she left her moneyed status and royally approved marriage for an actually illegal life in the Elizabethan theater. Virginia Woolf in her famous extended essay *A Room of One's Own* has imagined at some length what might have happened if Shakespeare had had a sister who was likewise inclined to the theater and ran away to London to try her chances. The result is not pretty: she ends up killing herself at a crossroads, unable to break into the theater and pregnant with a child she doesn't want but won't be able to abandon.

American Beauty also doesn't want to take us very far down the road with Lester's class downgrade. Lester has to die, much as Jack must be eliminated from Rose's life, and Viola de Lesseps must be taken far away from the temptations of Shakespeare and theater. We couldn't easily stomach the sight of Lester flipping burgers at age fifty-five or sixty.

In each case, an external force intervenes to end the slumming romance—this way the characters themselves never have to pop the bubble of the fantasy and question the long-term prospects of downward mobility. If the deus ex machina is the catastrophic sinking of the ocean liner in *Titanic* (and the hurricane and flood in *Their Eyes*) it is the awesome—and likable—Queen Elizabeth herself who plays the god-like role in *Shakespeare in Love*, instructing Viola not to break the divinely sanctioned vows of a marriage the queen herself has also blessed. The external force that does the dirty work in *American Beauty* is less magnificent, but more thematically tight: it is Lester's hard-ass marine neighbor with repressed homosexual desires and a serious Freudian conflict who shoots him after Lester rebuffs his sexual advances. Lester is killed because of his neighbor's Freudian guilt and shame.

Incidentally, *American Beauty* does not here metamorphose suddenly from a black slumming comedy into a trauma film. Lester's neighbor is indeed traumatized and ashamed, but his shame is not rooted in his social rejection (the type of humiliation native to trauma films). Lester does not in fact reject his neighbor as undesirable or as a pervert; rather, he explains that he himself simply does not have homosexual desires. The neighbor's trauma is rooted in his moral guilt over his own forbidden impulses, which now have been revealed to Lester. The neighbor is a typical Freudian case of illicit, unresolved, repressed desires and the resulting tension and conflict. In fact, his traditional and restrictive military code of behavior makes him something of an anachronism in the anything-goes, consumer, suburban society the other characters in the film inhabit. Lester is not gunned down by one of the socially demeaned or humiliated; rather, Lester's own free-spiritedness has managed to begin to liberate a deeply repressed man who cannot cope morally with the sudden revelation of his desires—and ends up apparently shocked by the murder he has committed. The neighbor is not a conscienceless monster, like the victimizers in trauma films (who of course are not themselves traumatized by their acts of destruction), but rather a kind of opposite: a monster of conscience.

The Historical Slumming Drama

The historical romances *Titanic* and *Shakespeare in Love* of course let audiences heave a sigh of relief—on the way out of the theater—that we today live in a society where women will not perish miserably if they try to follow their dreams of art and accomplishment. Why do we take pleasure in revisiting these eras when upper-class women were virtual chattel? There is not just national self-congratulation at stake.

Of course these blockbusters are "escape" movies, but what do they allow us to escape from?

If these movies are two of the most celebrated in the United States in recent years, it is largely because, as they take us into an idealized downward mobility, they allow us to escape momentarily from our unending American preoccupation with status—precisely what trauma films throw in our faces. And we need these unenlightened past eras because they tied higher-class status to highly restrictive social codes— something our society no longer does. In these historical slumming romances, then, the downward escape from social class status is not principally an escape from status worries, but an escape from restrictive codes. The escape means freedom, the opportunity for pleasure, and personal development. There is quite an ingenious sleight of hand at work in *Titanic* and *Shakespeare and Love*. The audience can escape from oppressive status concerns (perhaps even from feelings of being demeaned, as trauma films suggest) without ever consciously confronting the nature of this escapist respite because the escape in these movies is instead from the social constraints once associated with class. These movies show female characters being liberated from restrictions we no longer endorse or experience. No one in the audience is going to be offended by the code busting of Rose's learning to spit or Viola's acting on the stage—while they might be disturbed by "status crashes," such as Rose becoming a vagabond like Jack or Viola becoming a prostitute like some of the other women Shakespeare has truck with. Thus, these films are completely noncontroversial and are upbeat because they give us escape from status concerns we all care about in the form of escape from quaint social taboos that mean nothing to us.

This device of the historical slumming romance goes back to the beginning of the development of the slumming drama genre in the late nineteenth century: *Huckleberry Finn* gains much of its power through this device. Though Twain hated the historical romances of Walter Scott that dominated his era, he did not discard the genre, but rather transformed it. For of course, *Huckleberry Finn* is a historical romance set in the early nineteenth century during slavery—and published in 1885. Huck's *radical* "abolitionist" behavior in helping free the slave Jim is somewhat acceptable to a Northern audience in the 1880s, who have since Huck's time fought a war that freed the slaves—much as Rose's and Viola de Lesseps's "unwomanly" behaviors are completely acceptable in the 1990s. While Rose and Viola heroically break taboos that no longer exist, Huck heroically breaks a taboo that no longer has the same prohibitive force.

Since social status in today's American world does not involve obedience to restrictive codes of behavior, a movie such as *American Beauty* is trickier and comes off as a "black comedy" and a "satire" (to quote the TV guide review[3]). Lester's status dive from a white-collar managerial position to a burger-flipping entry-level job obviously directly confronts the issue of rejecting the pursuit of status. This confrontation is diluted to some degree by the fact that his downward mobility also involves the regaining of certain freedoms that we associate with youth and that are often put aside in the pursuit of status or a stable upper-middle class life and livelihood, such as indiscriminate lust and recreational drug use. The fact is that one can of course pursue illicit sex and drugs while working as a white-collar manager or professional. Thus, in presenting Lester's wholesale life change as a unitary, coherent package, the film finesses or softens the controversial and potentially uncomfortable notion of trading in a managerial career for low-level service work. In effect, it allows the audience to digest the explicit, potentially bitter theme of lost status with some sugary spoonfuls of liberation.

Nonetheless, *American Beauty* does not entirely mystify the nature of the escape that these slumming romances deliver up to audiences. Because *American Beauty* is set in the present, it depicts not only a romanticized escape from social constraints, but also explicitly shows the escape from a hideous middle-class competition for status. It is the latter theme that makes this movie satirical and dark, while *Shakespeare in Love* or *Titanic* could never be labeled as such. These historical dramas may in fact satirize the upper classes of the past, but no one in the audience of course has belonging in them. Audience members do, however, work in offices like Lester, sell real estate like his wife, Carolyn, and attend high school like his daughter Janie.

One of the most uncomfortable scenes in *American Beauty* involves the rejection of Lester's wife Carolyn, who in her total—and inevitably miserable—commitment to the world of status competition serves as a foil to her husband and daughter. Buddy Kane, "the real estate king," abruptly ends his affair with Carolyn when she becomes a status risk to him. After Lester confronts them at the burger joint where he now works and where they have come for "a little junk food, after the workout" they've had in bed, Buddy feels the need to cut her loose. He hardly has to explain; as she fights to hold back tears, she says she understands and painfully repeats the formula for success that he introduced her to in their first exchange: "In order to be successful, one must project an image of success at all times." She understands that she has become a handicap to his image of success. As he drives away, she is left crying in the car, and as in an earlier scene of career frustration when she has had trouble selling a house, she tells herself to stop crying. Only this time, she can't, and the scene ends with her screaming in a way that is not entirely funny. Next we see her, she is listening to an empowerment self-help tape in her car, repeating the "mantra," "I refuse to be a victim," and fingering a gun that she intends to use on her husband. Not unlike a trauma film victim, Carolyn has been repeatedly humiliated and rejected (she has also been stingingly rebuked at various times by her husband and daughter) and reduced to the desperation of consuming pathetic self-help products and contemplating lunatic violence.

American Beauty is finally a romantic fantasy about fleeing two different, menacing communities of the demeaned: Lester sidesteps the corporate feeding tank (depicted also in a trauma movie such as *In the Company of Men*) and his daughter and the neighbor kid Ricky escape from the mutual humiliation society of teenage life (represented also in a trauma movie such as *Welcome to the Dollhouse*). In effect, *American Beauty* might be thought of as a romantic, slumming antidote to the trauma film. Carolyn, meanwhile, might be thought of as trapped in a trauma film comedy for which no antidote is provided; this too accounts for some of the darkness of the film. *American Beauty* makes explicit the cultural function of the sentimental and escapist slumming genre—a temporary escape from the status-driven communities we inhabit, communities of the demeaned that are inescapable in trauma films.

Slumming Drama Returns to Rags to Riches: *Forrest Gump*

"An imbecile, a moron who makes a fool of himself on TV in front of the whole goddamn country gets the Congressional Medal of Honor!"

—*Lt. Dan to Forrest in* Forrest Gump

The indie class trauma film and the Hollywood blockbuster slumming drama movie are at first glance mirror opposites: in class trauma tales, the struggle for status and against demotion is continuous, brutal, and inescapable in communities of the socially degraded; in slumming escapist movies, the upper classes are socially poisonous, but there are lower social zones where one can escape status and its horrors. But, as is the case in recent winners of the Academy Award for Best Picture, most of those escapes are only provisional, temporary ones; they cannot be sustained in a long-term vision of a status-free, bohemian life.

If the seemingly insoluble question of the slumming romance is how to escape the concern with class and status—and the narrowing of self and distasteful arrogance that goes with it—without either sinking into humiliating, impoverished circumstances in the long run or avoiding the long run by dying suddenly, the answer is to be somehow handicapped in your ability to comprehend class and status, but meanwhile lucky enough to make a fortune and become an out-and-out celebrity. For, if one follows the trauma film *Being John Malkovich* (and many current films do in this regard), nothing short of wealth and fame will provide adequate status in today's culture. And indeed one film seems to have come up with just such a solution, albeit radical, to this conundrum that otherwise plagues the status-escapist slumming film: perhaps not surprisingly, another winner of the Academy Award for Best Picture, *Forrest Gump* (Robert Zemeckis, 1994).

Forrest Gump manages nothing less than to fold the slumming drama back into the rags-to-riches tale—but without introducing a concern for status. The classic Alger American Dream is achieved, not out of a desire to become respectable, but by accident. Respectability is eschewed, as in all slumming dramas, because the upper class is a hotbed of bigotry (in *Forrest Gump*, of racial prejudice); the pure heart untouched by class aspirations is preserved. Forrest Gump is an "incorruptible" Ragged Dick, with a mental disability that insures he'll always remain an innocent child when it comes to invidious issues of status.

Mental disability provides the solution, and this will seem less strange and arbitrary once we examine the exceptional role it consistently plays in the trauma film. Mental disability is a kind of magical charm in trauma films because it removes the afflicted from sensing humiliation and thus from the zero-sum game of status and ego; it also has the power to inspire rare tenderness because the afflicted do not perpetrate humiliation. Mental disability can function similarly in the escapist romance: because of his disability, Forrest Gump can remain not only not traumatized by the extreme childhood teasing he gets for being "stupid" and also, initially, physically disabled (he wears leg braces for a bad back), but also blithely indifferent first to poverty and later to status, even as he enjoys the fruits of fantastic economic and social success. This might be why the "stupid," rich Forrest Gump is a hero of our status-obsessed time.

Forrest Gump the movie is by no means unaware of what it is doing; Forrest has a number of foils in the course of the story who are not blessed with his "stupidity" and so have normal, arrogant, American desires for status that are self-destructive. Forrest's lifelong love, Jenny, is the prime example; she tells him she wants to be "famous" while he, in response to her question about what he dreams of being, says, "aren't I going to be me?" He has a similar exchange with his platoon lieutenant, Dan Taylor, who has lost his legs in Vietnam. "I should have died out there, but now I'm a goddamn cripple, a legless freak," says Lieutenant Dan. "This wasn't supposed to happen, not to me; I had a destiny; I was Lieutenant Dan Taylor." Forrest replies, "You're still Lieutenant Dan." Both Jenny and Dan suffer greatly over their identification with status and their inability to value themselves for their intrinsic qualities. Since the movie is a romantic tearjerker and not a social satire, they are both allowed to come to "peace" with themselves, much influenced by Forrest's incorruptible loyalty and integrity. After years of running from Forrest and (we understand) herself, willing to be exploited, for example, as a stripper in her search for fame, the hippie Jenny eventually returns to him with AIDS, and with their son. And after years of boozing and sleeping with prostitutes, the humiliated Vietnam vet Lieutenant Dan makes a fortune working with Forrest and then investing, and eventually purchases artificial titanium legs and finds a bride of Asian descent.

Along with these other Academy Award winning slumming blockbusters, *Forrest Gump* partakes in the conception of an essential self that is outside of social status, even of physical capability. Forrest is the perfect spokesperson for this notion because, in essence, he isn't able to perceive status. He is of course completely unchanged when he gains celebrity and wealth (several times over); he is nonplussed by his appearances on television and the like (at one point he compares himself to Captain Kangaroo); his various visits to the White House to receive one honor or another get tiresome. His inner life centers around his "momma," his friends, and of course Jenny; he can never be made sad by economic or social ill fortune, only personal losses.

The movie's escapist, paradoxical conceit is that Forrest's incredible wealth and celebrity follows precisely from his indifference to these things. This conceit is actually a familiar romantic notion about the essential self. Authentic, unaffected individuality is supposed to bring its own economic and social rewards because, as the romantic notion has it, it is the people who are truly themselves, who are indifferent to public opinion and acclaim, that we admire and learn from. Thus,

Forrest in fact becomes a kind of guru at one point in the movie when he starts running across the country, and continues for more than three years, "for no particular reason." Forrest's authenticity or unaffectedness is again of course guaranteed by his severe intellectual limitation.

Forrest is not only a natural celebrity; he is also blessed by a mystical "dumb luck" with money that is an extreme version of the financial good fortune that attends the heroes of the other slumming movies at issue here. He happens to be out on his boat when a storm hits that destroys every other shrimping vessel in the area, thus giving him a temporary monopoly. His money gets invested for him in "some kind of fruit company," namely, the fledgling Apple Computer corporation.

Forrest Gump can be seen as a slumming movie because Forrest not only embodies romantic notions of individuality and is magically removed from the status concerns of the other characters but also lives in a markedly bohemian way. Like Jack in *Titanic*, he has no plans for the future and enjoys traveling around with no particular destination—whether it is walking around Vietnam (as a soldier), sailing on a boat (as a shrimp-boat captain), or running across the nation. He has a vagabond spirit, a knack for taking things as they come, and an appreciation for natural beauty, much as Jack has and as Ricky in *American Beauty* has. And despite his mental disability, he does manage to articulate the fundamentals of a bohemian philosophy. Actually, he is only slightly less articulate than Jack, and again, as with Jack, his homey inarticulateness is part of his charm. (While Jack is a humble Western man of few words, Forrest is a Southern bumpkin of even fewer.) He has inherited his mother's corny notion that "life is like a box of chocolates; you never know what you're gonna get." And he also says to Jenny in her grave, "I don't know if we each have a destiny, or we are floating around accidental like on a breeze; I think maybe it's both." In fact, Forrest's reference to floating around on the breeze—and the mystically floating feather that the camera follows at the beginning and end of the movie—is reminiscent of Jack's self-description as a "tumbleweed blowing in the wind."

The deus ex machina of the slumming drama is here too—though transposed. Since Forrest, through a combination of dumb luck and an inability to understand status can achieve financial security without losing his bohemian humility, he need not die young. But the same mental incapacity means that an adult love relationship is impossible for him: so while he can provide sanctuary for Jenny, she has to die quickly upon their ultimate reunion. Just as Lester's or Jack's long-term socioeconomic prospects are grim, and sudden death comes as a deliverance from the issue, Forrest's long-term prospects in an adult relationship are dim, and so Jenny has to die. That way he keeps her (she doesn't leave him once again), and he can carry on a believable, childlike relationship with her grave. The specter of Jenny and Forrest negotiating an adult sexual relationship would be grotesque—and the movie doesn't want that.

Forrest Gump is in fact a sort of updated version of Twain's realist-era slumming historical romance, *Huckleberry Finn*. Huck and Forrest are both innocent vagabond tricksters, sometimes accidentally inter-rupting the machinations of the powerful and corrupt: Huck unknow-ingly brings the feud between the aristocratic families to a boil, and Forrest unwittingly drops a dime on the Watergate burglars. They also each become iconoclastically committed to a black buddy in a preju-diced Southern setting—Huck because of his youth, Forrest because of his mental limitations. Their stories are both set in the recent past—and now their attitudes about blacks, once completely scandalous, are closer to the norm for their audiences. They are both homely in speech and become unwitting vehicles of social satire. They are both rich almost by accident, but have no interest in money.

Forrest Gump may be the ultimate slumming romance of our time, not only because it solves the problem that afflicts the other escapist slumming Best Pictures, but also because it provides a direct rebuttal to the trauma film. This movie might indeed be thought of as staging a contest between the slumming drama and trauma genres, in which the slumming romance triumphs. As a mentally *and* physically disabled child from a poor home, Forrest is of course a likely candidate for stigmatization and unending abuse in a trauma story. Indeed, he faces a world of tormentors, humiliators, and rejecters in adulthood as well as childhood, in the army as well as in school. Even his best friends at times reject or mock him for his mental disability; Jenny is constantly leaving him for other men, at one point claiming he doesn't know what love is, and Lieutenant Dan mocks his plans to become a shrimp-boat captain.

But Forrest never does become a demeaned victim. He is protected, again, by his mental disability—which neutralizes or takes the edge off feelings of humiliation and also allows him to be winningly loyal to the friends who sometimes reject him. He is also equipped (by his mother) with a comeback line that quiets most people who are merely unwitting humiliators: to the people who reflexively ask if he is "stu-pid," he invariably replies, "stupid is as stupid does."

Forrest is finally protected by his ability to run. This ability to run—from his willful tormentors, whether school kids on bikes or high school boys in pickup trucks—importantly seems to issue out of the fact of his physical disability. As a child he wears leg braces for his a curvature of the spine; and, as with Olympian Wilma Rudolph who also grew up in leg braces, his legs become marvelously strong as a result. His ability to run across the entire country—which depends not only on his physical prowess but also his mental vacancy—likewise saves him from one of the few personal rejections he cannot escape feeling, when Jenny abandons him the morning after they first make love.

In the end, Forrest defeats a world of the demeaned (who are sometimes humiliators as well), managing to bring those who get the closest to him into the fold of the escapist romance. Jenny and Lieutenant Dan are two deeply demeaned characters—Jenny by a childhood sexual abuse by her father that metamorphoses into adulthood abuse of her by men and her abuse of drugs, and Dan by the loss of his legs in Vietnam, especially in the context of a warped family tradition that considers death on the battlefield the only honorable outcome of serving one's country. But again, by the end of the movie, Forrest's undying gentleness, love, and respect for them has helped them stop the processes of degrading themselves. Symbolically, Forrest has in fact healed the two groups alienated and degraded by the American traumas of the 1960s (the hippie runaways and the traumatized Vietnam vets) as well as healed the breach between them (thus the importance of Jenny and Lieutenant Dan meeting and embracing on the occasion of Forrest's wedding). On an allegorical level, Forrest has done nothing less than heal the national shame over Vietnam and the accompanying civil unrest.[4] Forrest then is a superhero of his sentimental slumming genre.

And his benighted success suggests that the slumming drama does not merely overturn the rags-to-riches tale but partakes of its magic as well. The luck with money in all of these slumming tales—Jack and Rose's, Shakespeare's, Lester's, Ricky's, and most obviously Forrest's— is not just a necessary plot device but also an ideological fantasy, borrowed from Alger's rags-to-riches story.[5] The slumming drama and the rags-to-riches tale share a very American logic or ideology that reaches back perhaps all the way to the American Dream of Ben Franklin: The hero of both of these types of tales, because he is honest and pure at heart (whether hard-working or drifting), gets rewarded with financial good luck. *Forrest Gump* makes the financial reward large enough to last a lifetime and can do so because Forrest's mental disability makes him immune to the corruption of money and status.

2

A Shameful Look at Zora Neale Hurston

A shame theorist would question the critically popular "multicultural" account of Hurston as an avant-garde Black Nationalist and feminist, a portrait constructed by ignoring, explaining away, or dismissing as "out of character" aspects of her fictions and her life, certain of her works, and her later political positions. Instead of a racial and gender hero, who somehow transcends or escapes the racism and sexism of American culture, Hurston shows up as a multiply shamed identity, but one who might be characterized, in contrast to Stephen Crane, as exhibitionist rather than paranoid. Her love of the public eye, patterns of short intense relationships with men, expeditions as a folklorist to cultures of poverty in the South and the Caribbean, participation in voodoo and animal sacrifice, and reactionary political positions: these can all be understood in terms of an abjection that issues out of her beloved mother's early death, her father's abandonment of her, her encounters with sexism, and her experiences of racism and color consciousness as a dark-skinned black child.

Meanwhile, *Their Eyes* is predicated on a variety of disturbing aspects that critics have mostly explained away in their celebration of the main love story as feminist and black nationalist, aspects that the shame theorist would find telling. Namely, and of particular relevance here, is the classploitation of the story in the form of sentimental slumming liberation: the heroine Janie's temporary bohemian flirtation with poverty and the emphasis on her light skin (in contrast to the dark skin of her young lover, Tea Cake) as she moves toward self-discovery. There is also Janie's adult indulgence in girlhood and her violence against men, which mirrors the misogyny in the works of Crane and Henry Miller.

The main contemporary narrative in leftist multicultural studies is of race, gender, and sexual oppression and marginalization and the heroic fight against it—by blacks, native peoples, women, gays. Those writers that can be enlisted in the story are rising to the top of the canon; others are being exposed and demoted for their willful or unwitting complicity in the oppression. This grand critical narrative has now largely replaced and displaced the leftist intellectual social realism of previous decades, which focused on class inequities. Hurston's meteoric rise in the canon is particularly revealing of this displacement, as her work, including *Their Eyes*, was once considered reactionary by leftist progressives. This is not to deny Hurston's important contributions to African American and feminist literature, but it is to retrieve her from a critically reductive deification as Black Nationalist and feminist that misses her important, creative role in an American mythology that is much more popular than the multicultural critical one because it is mainstream: the slumming drama.

What are Hurston's contributions to African American and feminist literature, and multiculturalism, considered to be? For one thing, she has been embraced by popular contemporary black women writers—not just critics—as a kind of literary godmother. Alice Walker, in particular, has honored her, making the pilgrimage down south to the cemetery where Hurston was buried in an unmarked grave and providing her with a headstone. Walker has declared that "condemned to a deserted island for life, with an allotment of ten books to see me through, I would choose unhesitatingly, two of Zora's: *Mules and Men*, because I would need to be able to pass on to younger generations the life of American blacks as legend and myth, and *Their Eyes Were Watching God*, because I would want to enjoy myself while identifying with the black heroine, Janie Crawford, as she acted out many roles in a variety of settings, and functioned (with spectacular results!) in romantic and sensual love. *There is no book more important to me than this one*" (ZNH, xiii).[1]

As for Hurston's contribution to American letters, most critics would agree that she enjoys the major distinction either of having invented modern black vernacular fiction or of being the first master of it. Important critics also credit her with an African American classic in *Mules and Men* (1935), as a vernacular account of African American folklore, voodoo, and conjure—which is an insider, and not a "colonialist," anthropology. In addition, she receives deserved credit for having set the stage for figurations of the conjure woman in contemporary black women's fiction.[2] Finally, more generally, and as

Walker's homage implies, she is widely recognized as having paved the way for today's black female authorship with her affirmation of black cultural traditions. As Houston A. Baker Jr. puts it:

> When we witness the forceful expressive succession of Zora's conjure woman found in works like those of Walker and [Toni] Morrison, we know that the creator of *Mules and Men* did, indeed, accomplish the foremost task of the authentic Afro-American cultural worker. To seek a habitation beyond alienation and ancient disharmonies in a land where Africans have been scarred and battered, shackled in long rows on toilsome levees, is the motion of such cultural work.[3]

Their Eyes is the work of Hurston's that is most celebrated and from which her reputation as *both* a black cultural revolutionary and a feminist issues, and the love relationship at the center of the book between Janie and Tea Cake, which has been seen by critics as ideal (or just short of ideal), has everything to do with that reputation.[4] The novel, indeed, has become "perhaps the most widely known and the most privileged text in the African American literary canon." And Janie has been given the status of "earliest...heroic black woman in the Afro-American tradition" (SO, 86).[5] As Mary Helen Washington writes in the foreword to the popular Perennial edition (1990):

> What I loved immediately about this novel besides its high poetry and its female hero was its investment in black folk traditions. Here, finally, was a woman on a quest for her own identity and, unlike so many other questing figures in black literature, her journey would take her, not away from, but deeper and deeper into blackness, the descent into the Everglades with its rich black soil, wild cane, and communal life representing immersion into black traditions. (*TE*, viii–ix)[6]

According to Washington, the novel makes a "unique contribution to black literature: it affirms black cultural traditions while revising them to empower black women." Janie's progression through a series of three marriages is seen to be "on the track of autonomy, self-realization, and independence" (*TE*, x). The first two marriages, with Logan Killicks and upwardly-mobile and white-emulating Joe Starks, are perceived by critics as quickly or ultimately stultifying and the last, with lower-class and dark-skinned Tea Cake, is celebrated for the possibilities of self-fulfillment and self-expression that it offers.

If Washington—and others—now find problems with the novel in terms of its feminist message, these qualms concern "its uncritical depiction of violence towards women" (*TE*, xii) (there is violence in Janie's relationship with Tea Cake) and its placing "Janie in the position of romantic heroine of Tea Cake's quest, at times so subordinate to the magnificent presence of Tea Cake that even her interior life reveals more about him than about her." But, for Washington at least, these antifeminist aspects of the book can be chalked up to the "difficulties in 1937 of giving a woman character such power and such daring" (*TE*, xiv).

Critics have not only seized on Hurston's books as feminist and culturally revolutionary texts but they have also seized on her life, on the person of Hurston herself as a modern black feminist folk hero. (This is an even trickier deification, given Hurston's reactionary politics in the 1950s.) In this rendition of Hurston's autobiography, she chooses work and independence over men without sacrificing the pleasures of sex and, in essence like Janie, she discovers herself by exploring the roots of African American culture in the rural South and the Caribbean. So Alice Walker can write about "the way [Hurston] tended to marry or not marry men, but enjoyed them anyway, while never missing a beat in her work" (SO, 84). Walker can also say:

> Zora's pride in black people was so pronounced in the ersatz black twenties it made other blacks suspicious and perhaps uncomfortable; after all, *they* were still infatuated with things European—*everything* European. Zora was interested in Africa, Haiti, Jamaica—and for a little racial diversity (Indians), Honduras. She also had a confidence in herself as an individual that few people (anyone?) understood. This was because Zora grew up in a community of black people who had enormous respect for themselves and for their ability to *govern* themselves. Her own father had written the Eatonville town laws....In her easy self-acceptance, Zora was more like an uncolonized African than she was like her contemporary American blacks... (*ZNH*, xiii)

What about Hurston's well-known politically incorrect actions and works, such as her opposing the Supreme Court's historic decision on behalf of school integration in *Brown v. Board of Education* and her joining in the anticommunist fever of the McCarthy era? Walker simply implies that these are "out of character" for Hurston. The device Walker and some others use is to cordon off from the heroic Hurston a later Hurston, who had been beaten down by the need for money and would eventually die in a county home. As Walker writes, in Hurston's later years, she and "her work, too, became reactionary, static, shockingly misguided and timid. This is especially true of her last novel, *Seraph on the Suwanee*, which is not even about black people, which is no crime, but *is* about white people who are bores, which is." Walker would also like to excise from the category of the "real" Hurston her not-so-late autobiography, *Dust Tracks on a Road* (1942), for Walker "the most unfortunate thing Zora ever wrote. After the first several chapters, it rings false." Walker finds in this work an "unctuousness" that is "out of character for Zora" (*ZNH*, xvi, xvii). Maya Angelou too has commented that in *Dust Tracks*, "it is difficult, if not impossible, to find and touch the real Zora Neale Hurston."[7] Hurston is seen in her later work as not only compromising her racial loyalties in an attempt to please editors and readers but also watering down her feminism for similar reasons: Deborah E. McDowell finds that her "feminist bite seems toothless" in *Seraph* (1948), and *Tell My Horse* (1938), her book about voodoo in Jamaica and Haiti, has been criticized along similar lines.[8]

Hurston's literary contributions to modern African American vernacular and women's fiction and to African American folklore or anthropology seem secure. But the rationalizations or excuses given about aspects of her work and her life make her reputation as a Black Nationalist and feminist suspicious. These rationalizations suggest ideological desires. Walker contends that the "telling of [Zora's] life [is] a 'cautionary tale,'" but it seems that the major lesson Walker wants to draw is too blunt and unspecific to Hurston and her unusual, very distinctive life, namely that "without money of one's own in a capitalist society, there is no such thing as independence....And so we have Zora sincerely offering gratitude and kinds words to people one knows she could not have respected" (*ZNH*, xvi–xvii). Of course, one can make aesthetic and political selections among Hurston's works and deeds, but to divide up Hurston's achievements between the "true" and the "out of character"—by implication setting aside the latter—is to disregard fundamental and troubling continuities across this artificial divide, to design an idealized Hurston, and ultimately to fail to come to grips with her work as well as her life story.[9]

Does the idealized account of the younger Hurston, which depicts her as an all-confident black feminist hero, really explain her behavior in her love life, her choices as a fiction writer, and her adventures as a researcher? In fact, this account ignores essential, intriguing, and disturbing aspects of her personality. She did not simply enjoy men (marriage or no marriage) and always place her work first; rather, her relationships were torturous, haunted by fear, anger, shame, and doubt—searing emotions that are registered in her fiction and even in her mostly stoical autobiography. Likewise, Tea Cake's "magnificent presence" is not accidental, a function of the prefeminist 1930s, but is instead therapeutic for Hurston. The violence of *Their Eyes*, violence against and by women, is not at all peripheral to her imagination of relationships (after all, Janie kills Tea Cake in a gun battle at close range), but central to it, and also therapeutic for her. Moreover, her trips south were not simply a matter of pride and interest in black traditions but indeed served psychic compulsions. Hurston's attraction to voodoo and animal sacrifice and her fascination with zombies are not fully explained by anthropological interest, Black Nationalism, or even inspiration about creativity; that is, her trips down south were not simply about rediscovering and celebrating black culture. Rather, they were about using black cultures of poverty for self-empowerment, for an immediate status boost, and for stabs at fame. Her repeated participation in voodoo violence against animals and her fascination with zombies only become fully intelligible if one considers her private demons.

In coming to grips with Hurston, one has to understand why *Their Eyes*—this book that is now given credit for changing everything in black women's fiction—is the book it is. Again, is it really what most critics have said it is—a pure affirmation of blackness and a feminist love story—except perhaps at a superficial level, at a level of political and moral rationalization, at a level of alibi? The book's reputation as Black Nationalist and feminist love story does not, for example, explain Tea Cake's youthfulness: Tea Cake "must be around twenty-five and here *she* [Janie] was around forty" (*TE*, 96). We know that the character of Tea Cake was based on a real person, with whom Hurston was involved, who was in fact some twenty years younger than she. But this does not dissolve the question: Tea Cake's youthfulness is not an accidental fact in the novel; it is a major theme. The question becomes: why was the youth of the male lover so important to Hurston, both in her novel and in her life?

And is the book actually a pure affirmation of blackness, or is it an exploitation of blackness? For oddly, when Janie becomes involved with dark-skinned Tea Cake, she herself seems to become lighter, or, more accurately, her lightness suddenly becomes a motif of the novel. The reader finds out fairly late in the book that Janie is relatively light skinned, with a "coffee-and-cream complexion" (*TE*, 134) and "Caucasian characteristics" (139). Indeed, by the time she reaches the Everglades, Janie starts to resemble the beautiful mulatto of romantic literature, as some critics have noted but barely explained (SO, 86).[10] Also, this fetishizing of light skin seems hardly minor or peripheral to the book. Indeed, the editors or publishers of the contemporary Harper Perennial edition seem to understand that Janie's light-skinned appearance is part of the romantic appeal of the novel (even as they declaim on the back cover that "Janie is one black woman who doesn't have to live lost in...romantic dreams"). In the summary of the book on the back, the third sentence begins with a description of Janie as "fair-skinned, long-haired, dreamy as a child..."[11]

Similarly, is the book an affirmation of lower-class black life—or classploitation? Critics often downplay the fact that Janie returns at the end of the novel to the middle-class town she supposedly hated, leaving behind the poor but vibrant life on "the muck" that the novel celebrates. But this finish allows her return to middle-class status and comforts while also distinguishing herself from her middle-class peers with her slumming adventures.

In order to understand what this book is about and how and why Hurston produced it, one has to explore the circumstances of her writing it, and they are dramatic. She wrote the book in Haiti, in flight from an intense and short-lived love relationship with a much younger man in New York, while involved in excursions into voodoo. And singular as these circumstances may seem, they in fact take us to repeating patterns in her life.

Hurston was married three times, in each case for a matter of months; most of her relationships were with significantly younger men.[12] Meanwhile, she consistently lied about her age, pretending she was a good deal younger than she was. She made a number of trips south, most of them ostensibly with anthropological aims, but they also coincided with troubles at home. And, in the cases of two trips at least, which produced her two books of folklore and voodoo and her novel *Their Eyes*, she was running from love relationships. Twice in her life, that is, she fled an uncomfortable intimacy with a man to seek refuge in temporary exile among the black rural poor, in initiation into voodoo, and in fiction writing. She traveled to Florida, to New Orleans, to Jamaica, to Haiti, to Honduras, all for purposes related to research; she also retired to a riverboat in Florida. Meanwhile, her novels tended to be produced or at least imagined on these excursions.

There are a number of questions to answer. Why did Hurston pursue relationships with younger men? Why did they last so little time? Why did she consistently lie about her age?[13] Why were black rural cultures of poverty a refuge for her? What did her voodoo association with death—with the spirits of the dead, with seemingly "undead" zombies, and with animal sacrifice—offer her? And, also, what was her fiction more fully about, especially *Their Eyes*, with its light-skinned, middle-class heroine who kills her seemingly ideal, younger, poorer, blacker mate?

Youth and Chronic Adolescence

For a moment, let's think about Hurston, who is somewhat unknown to us, by juxtaposing her with a much more familiar and spectacular contemporary artist, Michael Jackson. Jackson, with his Neverland Ranch, replete with an amusement park, a pet monkey, and other animals, his many plastic surgeries, delicate speaking voice, and sleepovers with young boys, seems fixed somehow in childhood. We understand that he behaves the way he does because, in an important way, he still experiences himself as a young boy.

One could say something similar about Hurston and adolescent girlhood—though one cannot point in her case to unmistakable physical trappings as in the case of Jackson. To see this in Hurston, one has to examine her relationships and her fictions. But, having done so, it seems irresistible to conclude that part of her self-image was lodged in girlhood, and, as an adult, she sometimes experienced herself, and indulged herself, as an adolescent girl. Hurston, too, is fixed in and fixated upon youth, and, like it or not, this fixation has everything to do with the books she produced.

What are the trappings of extended childhood that we can point to in the case of Hurston? To begin with, it is worth repeating that she chronically fiddled with her age. She did not have access to plastic surgery, like Jackson, but she did consistently lie about her age: usually to the tune of ten years but sometimes up to as many as twenty. She was born January 7, 1891, but her "second marriage license lists her date of birth as 1910" (SO, 81). Even when she appeared as a defendant in court and thus took a risk by lying (she was arrested on charges of child molestation that were eventually dropped), she kept up the lie about her age, claiming to be forty-five when she was fifty-seven.[14] She fooled a lot of people, including some of those who have studied her carefully. As Arnold Rampersad writes, she "so willfully misrepresented herself that even her diligent biographer [Hemenway] believed that her year of birth was 1901."[15] And as Claudia Roth Pierpont likewise notes, "Alice Walker, who put up a tombstone in 1973 to mark

Hurston's Florida grave (inscribed "'A Genius of the South' 1901–1960...") got this basic fact wrong as [her] honored subject would have wished" (SO, 81).

In her writing, moreover, Hurston sometimes seems to render a horror of aging. Her description of her heroine Janie's impressions of her middle-aging husband Joe Starks, in *Their Eyes*, gives a sense of Hurston's visceral distaste for the aging body:

> Then too she noticed how baggy Joe was getting all over. Like bags hanging from an ironing board. A little sack hung from the corners of his eyes and rested on his cheek-bones; a loose-filled bag of feathers hung from his ears and rested on his neck beneath his chin. A sack of flabby something hung from his loins and rested on his thighs when he sat down. But even these things were running down like candle grease as time moved on. (*TE*, 77)

Then, there is the fact that Hurston repeatedly married and became involved with much younger men, as did her most famous protagonist, Janie, in her idealized love affair with Tea Cake in *Their Eyes*. Again, Tea Cake is a significantly younger man—as was the real-life man upon whom Tea Cake was based, a man whom Hurston referred to her as the love of her life (whom she misleadingly calls A.W.P. in her autobiography[16]) and whom she fled by going off to pursue her anthropological research and fiction writing in Haiti. Tea Cake "must be around twenty-five and here *she* [Janie] was around forty" (*TE*, 96); according to Hurston's newest biographer, A.W.P. (actually Percival McGuire Punter) was twenty-three to her forty-four.[17] The spread was sometimes wider in Hurston's life: Hurston's third husband (James Howell Pitts) was twenty-three to her forty-eight.[18]

Another compelling piece of evidence of Hurston's at least partial conception of herself as a girl comes again in *Their Eyes*. The recapturing of girlhood is actually a central aspect of the novel that has been mostly overlooked by critics, no doubt because ideologically motivated critics have wanted to see the relationship between Janie and Tea Cake, based loosely on the real relationship between Hurston and A.W.P., as an ideal love and Tea Cake as an ideal mate. At a 1969 conference in Los Angeles, the main speaker, novelist Toni Cade Bambara, asked the women in the audience, "Are the sisters here ready for Tea Cake?" (*TE*, ix).

For the critics, Tea Cake is an ideal mate because he represents, in his person and behavior, blackness and black rural vernacular traditions. But Tea Cake is not simply an embodiment of the black cultural heritage, or perhaps one could say that his particular embodiment is tied up with his youthfulness. Tea Cake being much younger than Janie is not at all incidental. Indeed, he "looked like the love thoughts of women" (*TE*, 101). Janie has a hard time at first believing that the younger Tea Cake would be interested in her romantically—and physically. She wonders if he is "getting ready to laugh at me for an old fool" (*TE*, 100). And she takes "a good look at her mouth, eyes and hair" after an early conversation with him (*TE*, 101). Tea Cake insists that age difference "'got uh whole lot tuh do wid convenience, but it ain't got nothin' tuh do wid love'" (*TE*, 101). This may be true for Tea Cake, but it seems that age difference does have something to do with love here for Janie and Hurston.

Tea Cake's interest in Janie—as with the real-life A.W.P.'s interest in Hurston—seems to be proof first of all of the older woman's attractiveness. As Janie says, after a rash of compliments about her looks from Tea Cake, "'You keep dat up, Tea Cake, Ah'll b'lieve yuh after a while'" (*TE*, 172). Why is this confirmation of Janie's desirability by a younger man important?—after all, older men in the town she lives in with Joe Starks have expressed interest in her all along. For one thing, it is known from Hurston's letters that she developed (as she put it) an "overwhelming complex" (*ZNH*, 310) about her looks in her teens, in the years following the breakup of her family.

Tea Cake is also given a paternal quality in regard to Janie, which is odd given his relative youth and Janie's financial self-sufficiency (Joe Starks's death has left her with a load of money in the bank). Tea Cake insists on providing materially for Janie, and Janie goes along with it. It is possible that Janie's allowing Tea Cake to support her and call the shots is not so much a failing of Hurston's feminism as it is an imperative of her psychic needs, which require exploring.

Yet another function of A.W.P.'s and Tea Cake's youth may be to give Hurston and Janie a certain sense of power or superiority in the dangerous realm of love relationships (that she and Janie would otherwise lack): a sort of psychological handicap in the perilous game of romance where one must make oneself vulnerable to rejection. What Janie did not manage to do in her relationship with the older Joe Starks was to speak up for herself—until a couple of decades had gone by and rage had accumulated in monumental proportions. Until Joe was beginning to show signs of aging—and a repugnant aging, as we have seen—Janie seemed to be in awe of him. With Tea Cake, Janie is able from the start to exchange words, and she will later be able to exchange blows as well. She behaves with a confidence that was lacking in her relationship with Joe. Her relationship with Tea Cake apparently lets her act out her childish impulses, which Joe regularly forbade her (as the mayor's wife). A similar dynamic seems to have existed between Hurston and A.W.P.: his youth would perhaps have allowed her a freedom with her actions and emotions that she might have felt embarrassed about with a man her own age.[19]

Most strikingly, though, Janie's relationship with Tea Cake is explicitly presented as an opportunity to live out the sort of girlhood romance that she was denied in her youth (Janie's grandmother marries her off to Killicks, an older man she doesn't love, soon after she first expresses sexual interest in an adolescent boy). As Tea Cake says to Janie in fairly explicit and extreme language at a heightened emotional moment, "'Don't say you'se ole. You'se *uh lil girl baby* all de time. God made it so you spent yo' ole age first wid somebody else, and saved up yo' *young girl days* to spend wid me.'" And Janie responds, "'Ah feel dat uh way too, Tea Cake'" (*TE*, 172, my emphasis). Of course, Janie's now famous fantasy of love as a seventeen-year-old girl, concerning a blossoming pear tree and the bees that pollinate it—which Tea Cake seems finally to answer—is the dream of a teenager. And from the beginning, the relationship with Tea Cake is given a flavor of childhood. At one point we learn that with Tea Cake, Janie "felt like a child breaking rules" (*TE*, 98). The name "Tea Cake" itself has a childish ring to it: it is the name of a sweet, and children are notorious for their sweet teeth. Paradoxically, then, Tea Cake plays the role of both father-protector and adolescent playmate.

It is worth mentioning in this context that Tea Cake and Janie never have children, talk about doing so, or contemplate the possibility of pregnancy—though they are sexually very active. Perhaps this makes sense as Janie is at this point in the novel around forty. But Janie's other marriages likewise produce no children or even any consideration of any. Hurston herself had no children; she once toyed with the notion of adopting a baby girl but soon abandoned the idea, realizing she didn't want to be tied down. Insofar as Janie is Hurston's alter ego, it makes sense that the subject of children never arises. But as for why Hurston and Janie don't seriously contemplate reproduction, it might be suggested that if Hurston still experiences herself in large part as a girl, then there is no psychic room to imagine having a child. It would mean ceding prerogatives that Hurston herself has no intention of giving up—or, perhaps, she does not have the ability to do so.

In Hurston's autobiography, *Dust Tracks*, she tells us that she wrote *Their Eyes* in Haiti on the run from A.W.P., her one true love, "the real thing" (*DT*, 190). "I pitched in to work on my research and to smother my feelings. But the thing would not down. The plot was far from the circumstances, but I tried to embalm all the tenderness of my passion for him in 'Their Eyes Were Watching God'" (*DT*, 188–89). It seems that what Hurston embalmed in her depiction of Janie's relationship with Tea Cake is her finding a relationship that let her feel again like a girl. Janie's marriage with Tea Cake is not really about a woman's independence and autonomy. It is about Hurston's adult indulgence of herself as a girl. The question is, why did Hurston need such an indulgence, both real and imagined?

The answer no doubt lies in Hurston's own tortuous girlhood. Her relation with A.W.P. seems to have been her best, and no doubt largely unconscious, attempt to heal herself of her girlhood trauma, an attempt to make herself whole by stepping back into a kind of healthy girlhood she had been deprived of. To say that Hurston, because of her family breakup and the radical self-doubts it inspired, was, like her character Janie, denied a carefree girlhood experience is to put her trauma mildly.

The tragedy of Hurston's own true-love story—when things heated up with A.W.P. she fled to Haiti for anthropological research, initiation in voodoo, and novel writing—is that the shame and anxiety of her childhood experience was also activated when she let herself indulge in her girlhood. This shame and anxiety eventually overcame the salutary and joyful side of her reversion to girlhood, and they poisoned the relationship with A.W.P. In the novel, the youthful lover and the escape to a culture of poverty and blackness are imaginatively—wishfully—combined in the figure Tea Cake. In Hurston's real life she fled her New York love relationship with a middle-class West Indian man and took refuge in the adventure, mysticism, flirtation with death, fiction writing, and special status among the black rural poor she indulged in during her Caribbean travels. And because, again, this slumming and anthropological escape to rural cultures of poverty was also a repeating pattern in Hurston's life, it can be suggested that her indulgence in girlhood was only one of a set of compulsions that shaped her unusual life.

Fame and Special Status in Exile

Perhaps Hurston's most obvious and well-documented compulsion was her thirst for fame. This intense longing for recognition sometimes

makes her appear to contemporaries and later critics, especially
African American ones, as pandering to whites.[20] Indeed, if she began
her fiction career dreaming of acclaim as a black novelist writing
about black culture, when this didn't seem to be bringing her enough
recognition, she tried to make a splash with a novel about white
Southerners, attributing to them the same vernacular that she had previously staked out as a part of black culture.

As Hazel V. Carby notices in her foreword to the Perennial edition,
"In *Seraph on the Suwanee* there are many phrases and sentences that
evoke the language of Hurston's black figures in her previous works.
Occasionally, the language is identical—whole phrases are lifted from
the mouth of a black character in an earlier novel and inserted into the
mouth of a member of the white Meserve family."[21] Moreover, in a letter to her editor, Hurston explained that "what is known as Negro
dialect in the South is no such thing....[Southern Whites] did *not* get
it from the Negroes. The Africans coming to America got it from
them."[22] As Pierpont rightly observes, in this repudiation, Hurston "at
once lay[s] waste to her professional past and her extraordinary personal achievement" (SO, 89).

Hurston's ambition for recognition was arguably the one continuity
in her career: for her fantasies of fame were by no means limited to literature or even anthropology. At another point in her career, she imagined that she would write the proper book on voodoo that "has never
been done, and it is crying for me to do it" (*ZNH*, 246). She would discover and report truths as yet unknown in the West; in particular, she
"determined to get at the secret of Zombies," rendering "a great service to Haiti...[and] to medicine in general" (*TMH*, 205). Toward the
end of her career, when her desire for success was getting absolutely
desperate, she traveled to Honduras, imagining not that she would
engage in racial diversity by learning about Indians (as Alice Walker
wants to imagine) but that she would become famous and rich by discovering a lost Mayan city and buried Spanish treasure (*ZNH*, 301–2).

Hurston's trips to the South also offered her a brand of immediate
celebrity or at least a rise in status. Hurston never really behaved as an
anthropologist. Her "field work" was not exactly an extension of her
organized course of studies with Franz Boas at Barnard; it was more like
an antidote. She purposefully did not behave like a scholar; she showed
her disdain for the profession by extensively plagiarizing during one of
her first excursions collecting folktales. (In 1927, as Hemenway reports,
Hurston "had made a special trip to Mobile to interview Cudjo Lewis,
the only survivor of the last-known ship to bring African slaves to

America in 1859." But her essay on Lewis is "25 percent original research and the rest shameless plagiarism from a book entitled *Historical Sketches of the Old South*....Despite her obvious use of it, Hurston nowhere acknowledges [it]...as her source, and her plagiarism...remained undetected for almost a half-century" [*ZNH*, 96–97].)

More might be said. In New York, she was just another talented graduate student. In Florida, she was a sensation: now a middle-class, educated woman returning to her small town or tramping through the backwoods and hanging out in juke joints. *Mules and Men* records the adventure of collecting folk-tales, but it also reveals the peculiar and singular status of the collector. If anything, the sensational quality of Hurston's status was only augmented in her next experience in collecting in Jamaica and Haiti. Here, she was not only different for being educated but was also different for being a "*femme Americaine*," as the Haitians called her. And these differences added up to make her absolutely special there: unlike most women in the islands, she was listened to, and she was also allowed to study under voodoo men. The latter is worth underlining because it is another indication that Hurston was something other than an anthropologist. In New Orleans and later in the Caribbean, Hurston was not just another anthropology student doing her fieldwork in voodoo practices but also an initiate in voodoo. And, again, her sense of her project was grandiose.

In short, her folktale collecting, her use of vernacular in her writing, and her participation in voodoo were not merely or even primarily political choices; they were psychological ones. Her excursions to the South were first of all trips to places that allowed her to forget her own desperate striving for recognition and to alleviate the anxiety that she felt in regard to herself, to her own status. It is significant that she found on one of the "remote" Haitian islands "a peace I have never known anywhere else on earth" (*TMH*, 135). With a sense of self as precarious as the one Hurston apparently had, she found it difficult to participate in organized, hierarchical institutions. She needed special status—precisely in order *not* to feel, and be tormented by, her drive for prestige. So the status had to seem to come, as it were, gratis: for being herself. Like Stephen Crane who ditched the striving of college for the bohemians and the lower class of the Bowery, Hurston was more comfortable—and more able to write—in the backwoods of Florida or the voodoo culture of Haiti than in graduate school in New York. The unspoken side of Hurston's love for lower-class cultures was the fantasy of fame, of being special, of difference from everyone else, which she was able to indulge in these places.

Her participation in voodoo in particular—unorthodox for an anthropologist—involved another psychological longing as well, a kind of antidote to the powerlessness she experienced in relationships with adults. Because in Haiti Hurston was involved in distancing herself from an intimate relationship (this was of course an important reason and perhaps the principal one [SO, 84] for her trip to the Caribbean), and because she construed her loneliness as essentially "cosmic," rather than familial and social, voodoo was particularly attractive to her. It gave her a method of connecting herself directly with cosmic forces—rather than with people. (One of the interesting aspects of voodoo in this regard is that it is generally supposed to do its work without the voodoo doctor ever confronting the person he is attempting to manipulate, help, or harm.) In terms of fulfilling a need for connectedness to the world, many people would probably find voodoo—with its sacrifice of animals and its tales of zombies—more daunting than personal intimacy, but this was apparently not the case for Hurston. And her experience with visions as a child had already suggested to her the possibility of this kind of direct communication with cosmic forces.

In fact, Hurston's fiction writing might be thought of as coextensive with voodoo, or vice versa—both involve conjuration[23] at a safe or empowering distance from the real-life subjects involved. Both the voodoo doctor and the author are in total control. Hurston's first novel, *Jonah's Gourd Vine* (1934),[24] can be thought of as an exercise by Hurston in setting things right in her family life: it climaxes with the philandering character—based on her father—being demolished by a train. Perhaps it is not incidental, in this discussion of the similar strategies of literature and voodoo, to note that in the dissolution of Hurston's third marriage, her husband accused her of threatening him with voodoo.

Slumming Vitalism: Love and Cultures of Poverty

Once one notices the consistency of the concern with status and pride in Hurston's life, apparent discontinuities across her career begin to dissolve. Her celebration of black folk life and her African American cultural nationalism is in fact consistent with her rejection of school desegregation (and her anticommunism), as Hemenway points out: both follow from her affirmation of black culture and her refusal as she put it, to join the "sobbing school of Negrohood" that sees black

life, under the pressure of racism, as in any way deprived or pathological (*ZNH*, 329–37). (To have been in favor of school desegregation
was to admit that there was indeed something wrong with all-black
schools as they existed in America in the 1950s, and to admit that
racism made it impossible for blacks alone to cure the problem.) And
this refusal to acknowledge and attack the effects of racism follows
from a personal, and not a social, agenda. Arnold Rampersad makes
a similar observation in regard to *Mules and Men*:

> In one sense, it is possible to say that Hurston had become more of an
> African-American cultural nationalist [with her folklore research and
> writing], seeing more of the world and herself in terms of race and her
> own blackness. This would be true only to a limited degree, as
> Hurston's later involvement with reactionary political forces and per-
> sonalities suggests. The power she gained from seeing her life in coher-
> ence with the storytelling imagination of country blacks and with the
> world of conjure and black magic represented by voodoo was placed
> largely in a different service—self-empowerment, to facilitate her emer-
> gence as a writer of fiction.[25]

Hurston's psychological needs determined her "political" positions.
Hurston's involvement with black folk culture was not primarily political but—like Janie's—essentially personal or bohemian. Richard
Wright's well-known critique of *Their Eyes* might be compared to
James Baldwin's critique of Jack Kerouac's *On the Road* (1957):[26]
according to these critics, both novels misunderstand and exploit poor
blacks. Hurston cannot be accused, like Kerouac, of racism (though
she might be accused of engaging in color consciousness), but she can
be described as romanticizing poverty. Both she and Kerouac create
heroes who take up migrant work, not out of economic need, but as a
temporary lifestyle choice.

These observations about Hurston's particular relationships to
poor black communities and to younger men challenge the critical
assumption that *Their Eyes* is culturally revolutionary in its depiction
of the Everglades and feminist in its representation of Janie's relationship with Tea Cake: namely, they challenge the idea that Janie's heading for the Everglades is primarily about going "deeper into
blackness" and the idea that her relationship to Tea Cake has anything
to do with autonomy and independence.

First, Janie's trip to the Everglades arguably takes her to a place
that is no more steeped in blackness than the place she is leaving:

namely an all-black town where the people speak in the black rural vernacular and spin wonderfully poetic and imaginative speeches and tales. This town, it is also worth noting, is modeled on her own all-black hometown of Eatonville, which was the site where she began her folklore collecting for the volume *Mules and Men*. So the question arises: if Janie's move south does not take her deeper into blackness, but is rather a lateral move, ethnologically speaking, what sort of a progression is it? An answer might begin by noticing that Janie is moving downward socioeconomically, something she supposedly cannot do in town because she has been "classed...off" (by her dead husband [TE, 107]). Likewise, she is leaving her money and property, which remains in the town, temporarily out of reach. What the muck offers is a difficult but enjoyable lifestyle devoid of materialism, social striving, and middle-class security—a lifestyle that strips her of various social protections, and thus eventually fulfills the promise of the book's title and takes her "to God," as she says at the end to her confidant Pheoby. In slumming fashion, then, she is temporarily joining a "culture of poverty" for its liberating spiritual possibilities.

Second, it seems it is only critical imprecision that allows us to see Janie's relationship with Tea Cake as being "on the track of autonomy, self-realization, and independence." Certainly, their relationship is about self-realization for Janie; however, it is not their relationship, but rather its disposal, that puts Janie back on the track of autonomy and independence. The relationship itself, which involves a jealousy as well as a violence that Hurston seems to find healthy, is not geared toward these values, but rather toward vitality, passion, risk, and rejuvenation: values that are, importantly, embodied in the lifestyle of Hurston's migrant workers on the muck. As Pierpont observes, "The recent incarnation of Hurston's lyric drama as a...feminist textbook is touched with many ironies." One of the paramount ironies is that "the author offers perhaps the most serious Lawrentian vision ever penned by a woman of sexual love as the fundamental spring and power of life itself" (SO, 85). Harold Bloom likewise compares Hurston to the "heroic vitalists" Theodore Dreiser and D.H. Lawrence. And he too concludes that *Their Eyes* bursts the categories in which critics have tried to contain it:

> Hurston herself was refreshingly free of all ideologies that currently obscure the reception of her best book. Her sense of power has nothing in common with politics of any persuasion, with contemporary modes of feminism, or even with those questers who search for a black

esthetic. As a vitalist, she was of the line of the Wife of Bath and Sir John Falstaff and Mynheer Peeperkorn.[27]

But something more might be said about Hurston's investment in the *vitality* of these cultures of poverty and of their vernaculars—which is the principle reason she celebrates them in her fiction. Bloom's claim here, if insightful, is somewhat unexplored, first of all because he seems to assume that vitalism is purely a good thing, a kind of straightforward manifestation of health.

If Hurston is indeed a vitalist writer, and she is so drawn to the linguistic and social vitality of cultures of poverty, one might speculate that it is again in part because of her own trauma as a child and her attempt at self-healing. It seems important that already by the age of seven Hurston remembers wanting "to be away from the drabness [of her home life] and to stretch my limbs in some mighty struggle" (*DT*, 41). The "emptiness" that Janie several times refers to in regard to her house in the all-black town is, perhaps, a reflection of Hurston's own feelings about Eatonville that come out of her childhood neglect. Joe Starks, Janie's husband, is pretty clearly a fictional version of Joe Clarke, whose store porch in Eatonville was in Hurston's renditions of her hometown a social center. And Janie's need to leave the all-black town in search of her identity may have more to do with Hurston's feelings about Eatonville than with any deeper "blackness" in the Everglades. John Berryman sensed in Stephen Crane a primitive animism;[28] Pierpont in a similar way finds "an archaic sense of power in Hurston's sexing of all things" (SO, 88). For reasons yet to be discussed, Hurston's childhood left her with a tendency to depression, and her vitalism was an attempt at an antidote.

And so, to some degree, is her conception of Tea Cake. Tea Cake clearly embodies the vitality and capacity for pleasure that Hurston associates with the black cultures of poverty she visits. As Henry Louis Gates and Sieglinde Lemke write, Hurston's story about the mythic figure High John de Conquer shows that "those who are deprived of material wealth discover that their principal asset is spiritual wealth, rhythm, and laughter. This reemerging theme in Hurston's fiction reaches its fullest form in the character of Tea Cake."[29]

In this context, one might notice a couple of other blind spots in Bloom's description of Hurston as vitalist. First, he places her in the company of a bunch of fictional characters: the Wife of Bath, Falstaff, and so on. Second, he seems to miss the class issue that is involved in this vitalism, at least in the cases of Falstaff and Hurston. We do not believe that Shakespeare was giving us anything like a full self-portrait in Falstaff, or alternatively that Falstaff was a sort of ideal for him, and we remember that Prince Hal repudiates Sir John in the course of his "maturity" and rise to power: isn't it fair to say that Shakespeare has mixed feelings about Falstaff, if also about Hal? If Hurston does not have the kind of critical distance on her heroine Janie that Shakespeare has on Hal, the book's ending—with Tea Cake's ugly death—definitely indicates that Hurston has some problems with vitalist and lower-class Tea Cake. Recall that Janie, not unlike Hal in *Henry IV*, will get rid of Tea Cake and take up again her "rightful" class position, just as Hal disposes of Falstaff.

Terrors of Love

Before attempting to answer the question of why Hurston felt so threatened in intimate relationships, more should be said about her characteristic flight from them. Hurston attributes the ultimate failure of her relationship with A.W.P. to his need for "master[y]": and so her conflict with A.W.P. is reminiscent of Janie's with her first two husbands. "He begged me to give up my career, marry him and live outside of New York City," Hurston writes in *Dust Tracks*. "I really wanted to do anything he wanted me to do, but that one thing I could not do. It was not just my contract with my publishers, it was that I had things clawing inside of me that must be said....One did not conflict with the other in my mind. But it was different with him. He felt that he did not matter to me enough" (*DT*, 186).

Another reason for the demise of the relationship according to Hurston was that she saw herself as standing in the way of his career progress. "Another phase troubles me. As soon as he took his second degree, he was in line for bigger and better jobs. I began to feel that our love was slowing down his efforts. He ought to go a long way. I grew terribly afraid that later on he would feel that I had thwarted him in a way and come to resent me" (*DT*, 188).

There is reason to be suspicious of Hurston's conclusions, though. First of all, she acknowledges a consuming anxiety about being rejected by A.W.P. In *Dust Tracks*, she says that she "would interpret his moods as indifference and die, and die, and die" (*DT*, 186). She herself admits that these doubts were not based in his behavior: "Really, I never had occasion to doubt his sincerity, but I used to drag my heart over hot coals by supposing. I did not know that I could suffer so" (*DT*, 187–88).

Secondly, Hurston plays down the role of her own grandiose career ambitions in this account in her autobiography. Her casual reference to the primacy of her career concerns in relation to those of her love affair with A.W.P. is telling. Hurston elsewhere reports: "no matter how soaked we were in ecstasy, the telephone or the doorbell would ring, and there would be my career again. A charge had been laid upon me and I must follow the call. He said once with pathos in his voice, that at times he could not feel my presence. My real self had escaped him" (*DT*, 188).

The first thing Hurston says about women in *Their Eyes* is that "women forget all those things they don't want to remember..." (*TE*, 1). And one central thing that Hurston seems to "forget" about herself—in her description of herself in *Dust Tracks*—is her drive for recognition and prestige, precisely the drive that makes Joe Starks of *Their Eyes* so flawed and unappealing. This drive in her is left out of her autobiographical account of her reasons for her inability to part with her career for her man (she cites only the passion to write and her contract obligations). Interestingly, this drive for success is ascribed solely to A.W.P.: "I began to feel that our love was slowing down his efforts. He ought to go a long way." *Their Eyes*, not incidentally, makes a sleight of hand similar to this one in her autobiography and generalizes about the maleness of such drive: from the first page of the novel, Hurston assigns ambition—the dream of sailing to the "horizon" (*TE*, 1)—to men alone and "forgets" the desire in women.

It is not hard to imagine that Hurston's dramatic ambition would color her perception of A.W.P. and his demands upon her, and, at the same time, cause him to act more jealously toward her. On the one hand, the intensity of Hurston's need for recognition and fame would leave her terrified of any incursion whatsoever upon her career and thus tend to make her see his demands and jealousies as severe threats. On the other, A.W.P.'s experience of that intensity of Hurston's might in fact have been alienating. After all, if Hurston would always interrupt their time together for her career—"no matter how soaked we were in ecstasy"—it is easy to suppose that A.W.P. might indeed have felt hurt and angry that she "had escaped him." It is possible that A.W.P. was a deeply insecure and possessive man—like the men Hurston later wrote of in a letter about the novel *Seraph*—though this is not exactly how Hurston presents him in general in her autobiography. Still, it is also probable that the "charges" and "calls" that Hurston felt from her career were dramatic, and that even a fairly sensitive man of the 1930s (but still suffering from the sexist prejudices of that age) would have felt threatened by Hurston's ambition.

It is telling that another of her important relationships—an earlier marriage to a man named Herbert Sheen—also came to an end in large part because of Hurston's career ambitions. Interestingly, Hurston's feelings of being impeded, her rationalizing of the separation in her autobiography as a result of the man's career, and her means of escaping the relationship by embarking on research travels were a pattern established with Sheen that she would live out again with A.W.P. She left the relationship by going on a folklore-collecting trip. She had told Langston Hughes, "Herbert holds me back," and wrote to a friend after the divorce, "He was one of the obstacles that worried me." But she explained her leaving in *Dust Tracks* as a way of forcing Sheen to pursue *his* medical career (*ZNH*, 94).

Hurston's Childhood

Hurston's cathexis on girlhood, her youthful complex about her looks, her discomfort and sense of powerlessness in intimate relationships are all compulsions that issued out of her devastating abandonment as a child. In broad terms, her mother died when she was thirteen and her philandering father remarried and more or less abandoned her. But her shameful sense of abandonment began long before her mother's death.

In her autobiography *Dust Tracks*, she describes the event of her mother's death as the "hour [that] began my wanderings" (*DT*, 65). The Hurston siblings were dispersed; she was promptly sent off to school in Jacksonville, and there was "just a jagged hole where my home used to be" (*DT*, 69). At the end of the school year, she

> was to stay there [at the school] and Papa would send for me.
>
> I kept looking out of the window so that I could see Papa when he came up the walk to the office. But nobody came for me. Weeks passed, and then a letter came. Papa said the school could adopt me. The Second in Command sent for me and told me about it. She said that she had no place for a girl so young, and besides she was too busy to bring up any children.
>
> It was crumbling news for me. (*DT*, 79)

After this signal rejection, Hurston was returned to her "father's house which was no longer home...." She writes:

> Papa's children were in his way, because they were too much trouble to his wife. Ragged, dirty clothes and hit-and-miss meals. The four older children were definitely gone for good. One by one we four younger ones were shifted to the homes of Mama's friends.
>
> Perhaps it could be no other way. Certainly no other way was open to a man who loved peace and ease the way my father did. (*DT*, 82)

As traumatic as this death of one parent and abandonment by the other must have been for a girl of thirteen, it seems Hurston's pain started a lot earlier. Hurston reports in *Dust Tracks* that she had several visions of "cosmic loneliness" (*DT*, 43) as a child that predicted future events in her life, including seeing "myself homeless and uncared for" (*DT*, 83). This sounds incredible, but on closer inspection, some of these prophetic visions at least seem to issue out of the unconscious perception of a sensitive and neglected child. Hurston writes: "I knew my fate. I knew that I would be an orphan and homeless. I knew that while I was still helpless, that the comforting circle of my family would be broken, and that I would have to wander cold and friendless" (*DT*, 42). It seems that Hurston had these visions at least because, as a young girl, she already felt at some level the tension that existed between her parents and especially a sense of betrayal and rejection by her father.

Though Hurston characteristically and philosophically downplays the pain of her father's abandonment of her at school and the demise of her family in her autobiography, her feelings about her father's rejection of her were clearly intense. At fifteen (by her count in *Dust Tracks*, but she may have been as old as nineteen), she got into a physical fight with her stepmother, which ended with Hurston throwing a hatchet at her. Hurston's first novel, *Jonah's Gourd Vine*, about a black preacher, is openly based on her father's life, and the daughter who corresponds to Hurston herself is neglected by her father from early on. When the girl Isis is sick with typhoid as a baby, her father, Pearson, flees town and takes up with the woman who will eventually be his second wife. The book's therapeutic value for Hurston is hard to miss: if *Their Eyes* is a hidden, even unwitting attempt to heal herself of her girlhood trauma, her first novel is hardly subtle in this regard. Importantly, she imagines the main character, who like her father is called John, going through the same sort of experience of desertion and betrayal that she herself went through *because of her father*. She also gets to imagine this reprobate father expressing remorse for his failings with his wife and family—something she apparently never got to see in reality. In addition, she invents a third, good wife who makes amends with John's children, both emotionally and financially. And finally, Hurston gets to kill this father off—violently—after he has yet another adulterous affair. It is difficult not to see this book as an attempt to reconcile herself with her father's behavior toward her, to understand her father—even to imaginatively punish him and almost redeem him, but not entirely—and to even the score and put things right.

It is worth noting that in *Jonah's Gourd Vine* Hurston implicitly dates her paternal neglect from before her mother's death, in fact from her infancy and even before, and this dating would explain the timing of her visions of loneliness from *Dust Tracks*, which likewise precede the demise of her family. Hurston's sense in *Jonah's Gourd Vine* of the hurtfulness of her father's self-involvement is dramatic. (It is not downplayed here in the same way that it is in her nonfictional account of her life. Hurston's fiction, partly because of a visionary or dream-like quality and partly because as fiction it involves at least some displacement, has a tendency to be more honest, and less guarded, than her autobiography.) According to the way Hurston depicts things, the father's emotional neglect of the mother and family (as he is off with another woman) affects the child Isis even in utero. The character Lucy, named for Hurston's mother, suffering the "cold feeling" of betrayal, comments: "Lawd lemme quit feedin' on heart meat lak Ah do. Dis baby goin' tuh be too fractious tuh live." And then again, "Lawd if Ah meet dat woman [the other woman] in heben, you got tuh gimme time tuh fight uh while. Jus' ruin dis baby's temper 'fo' it git tuh dis world" (*JGV*, 114).

Insecurity in intimate relationships is a theme that not only haunts Hurston's relationship with A.W.P. as she herself reports on it in *Dust Tracks* but also appears elsewhere in her life and writing. Just how alive in her psyche is this experience of rejection by her father is indicated by her emotional dramatics with Langston Hughes over their joint, failed theatrical project *Mule Bone* (1931). Hurston became absolutely furious with Hughes for his attempt to give their typist partial credit for the play (which was never put on because Hurston ended up vying with him for legal title to it). It seems that what happened in this instance is that Hurston's experience of rejection by her father in favor of a stepmother was reactivated by Hughes's apparent transfer of loyalties to their female typist (or Hurston's perception of such a transfer). Just as Hurston was with A.W.P. still living out all the intensity of her girlhood needs for affirmation of her looks, for playful adolescent romance, and for paternal care, Hurston was still living out all the intensity of her girlhood jealousies of her stepmother with Hughes.

Hemenway reports that in the years following the breakup of her family—and, thus, her father's abandonment—"she grew self-conscious about her looks, feeling that no man could really care for her" (ZNH, 17). The artistic apotheosis of this insecurity is the character of Arvay in Seraph, who, until the very end of the novel, is doubtful of her husband's love for her, though it is painfully apparent to the reader. While Hurston associates Arvay (in a letter to her editor) with men who felt inadequate with her, she also compares Arvay to herself in another letter: "Though brash enough otherwise, I got an overwhelming complex about my looks before I was grown, and it was very hard for a long time for me to believe that any man really cared for me" (ZNH, 310).

And indeed, Arvay experiences the other fear characteristic of Hurston in relationships, a fear that comes out in her account of A.W.P.—and a fear that, not unimportantly, seems hardly in character for the professionally nonambitious Arvay (who like Janie has no career or career aspirations): namely, the fear of being swallowed up by her husband and thus losing her individual identity and status. (For example, Arvay thinks "something must be wrong with her, for she knew that she could part with anything, even principles, before she could give up this man....That man's got me so that I'm just about as near nothing as anybody could be. Well, I just got to fight against it" [SS, 158–59].) One more striking psychological similarity between Hurston and Arvay is that both had older sisters who were favored by the father (and Hurston writes that the preference for the older sister "had done something to Arvay's soul across the years"). It has been suggested that Hurston wrote about whites in this novel perhaps because she wanted to prove herself a "universal" novelist (ZNH, 308) or perhaps because she was pandering to whites, but it might also be the case that Hurston was writing about something so personal to her that she needed to distance herself from Arvay, in the public view and perhaps in her own, by making her not only fictional, but white. Ironically, and despite prevailing critical notions, it may just be that Seraph—and not Their Eyes—is Hurston's most honest novel about herself.

There is one other, lesser, but nonetheless potent experience of weakness, failure, and shame connected with Hurston's youth and her mother's early death. It is an experience that Hurston recounts both in Dust Tracks and in Jonah's Gourd Vine, and her acknowledgement of its agony in her autobiography is part of the reason one might suspect it was less severe than the shame of paternal abandonment she downplays there. On her deathbed, her mother gave Hurston, a girl of thirteen (in her autobiography she says she was only nine), a task she was too young to carry out:

> I was not to let them take the pillow from under her head until she was dead. The clock was not to be covered, nor the looking-glass. She trusted me to see to it that these things were not done. I promised her solemnly as nine years could do, that I would see to it.
>
> What years of agony that promise gave me!...I was called upon to set my will against my father, the village dames and village custom. I know now that I could not have succeeded....
>
> My father was with the mores. He had restrained me physically from outraging the ceremonies established for the dying....[Mama] must know how I have suffered for my failure.
>
> But life picked me up from the foot of Mama's bed, grief, self-despisement and all....I was old before my time with grief of loss, of failure, and of remorse. No matter what the others did, my mother had put her trust in me. She had felt that I could and would carry out her wishes, and I had not. And then in that sunset time, I failed her. It seemed as she died that the sun went down on purpose to flee away from me. (*DT*, 62–65)

These passages in *Dust Tracks* conjure up some of Hurston's real pain, shame, and sense of ineffectualness as a child. No doubt if Hurston can be so direct and open here it is because she clearly experienced a pride in being singled out thus by her mother. In *Jonah's Gourd Vine*, Isis is told by her mother near the time of her death, "Youse mah chile 'bove all the rest" (*JGV*, 127). There is something appealing and even heroic about being the favored child who is put to the test prematurely by a loving parent. One wonders if some of the emotional drama of these passages isn't due to the other types of shame discussed here, types of shame that are in no way appealing and that Hurston, therefore, tends simply to deny.

Love and Imaginary Violence: *Their Eyes*

Intimate relations with men were thus threatening to Hurston on two scores: they could recreate the familiar humiliations of rejection and weakness and they could be experienced as obstacles in the way of the ultimate antidote for her deep-seated humiliation, namely, celebrity.

No wonder she continually fled them and more than once fled them for the rural poverty of the tropics: as a middle-class educated woman in the backwoods of Florida or, even better, in the shantytowns of Jamaica or Haiti, she was set apart as somebody special, an instant celebrity of a sort. And if writing fiction was for Hurston something like casting voodoo spells, an antidote for the weakness and shame she felt with men, then the regular pattern of violence against men in her work—for it doesn't stop with the death of John Pearson in *Jonah's Gourd Vine*—takes on a psychological significance.

Critical responses to *Their Eyes*, whether they ultimately see the book as feminist or not, have the odd tendency to elide the fact of— or at least the strange nature of—Tea Cake's murder. Again, the poetic and romantic Tea Cake is regularly seen as an alternative to Janie's first two husbands, who treat her more or less as property or chattel and suppress her process of self-development. But if one buys this reading, then the question arises: why must Tea Cake too be elimi- nated and left behind? Is it because he threatens the book's feminist message? Again, critics who cite the limitations to Hurston's feminism point out the ways in which Janie is subordinate even to the presence Tea Cake, her interior life is dominated by him, his violence against her is treated uncritically, and she does not speak for herself at key moments (*ZNH*, xiii–xiv). But even some of the critics who question Hurston's feminism in these regards (along with many who see Tea Cake more positively) ignore the fact that Janie kills him—though her murdering him would seem highly relevant to this question of Hurston's feminism. Perhaps more strikingly, the absolutely bizarre sequence of events that lead to Tea Cake's death—he is shot by Janie a few days after contracting rabies from a dog riding on the back of a cow, while trying to save Janie in a flood during a hurricane—almost always goes unanalyzed; these events are simply discussed on the level of plot, accepted as if Hurston were retelling actual events and not inventing them.[30] Of course, Janie's murder of Tea Cake can hardly be considered adventitious for the novelist, as opposed to the heroine (Hurston has purposely crafted the story, even the accidents), espe- cially when one considers that Hurston has had Janie play an arguably large role in the death of her former husband, Joe Starks. Joe takes to his deathbed shortly after Janie humiliates him in public and later dies as Janie shouts him down and finally expresses her pent-up anger at his years of suppressing her and her feelings.

It is striking that *Their Eyes* presents intimate male-female relation- ships ultimately as struggles of life and death. It is not an overstatement to say that the well-known misogyny of a Stephen Crane, a Henry Miller, a William S. Burroughs, or a Norman Mailer—the terror of and anger toward women reflected in their writings—is mirrored in the fear of and violence against men in hers. Hurston would criticize Richard Wright's *Uncle Tom's Children* in 1938 for its indulgence in racial hatred, for its "lavish killing" of white men, "perhaps enough to satisfy all male black readers" (SO, 80). Interestingly, Hurston's first two novels, *Jonah's Gourd Vine* and *Their Eyes*, could be similarly criticized for offering a fairly lavish killing of black men, even if the deaths are not always murders and the antagonism against men often seems overwhelmed by the romantic countertheme of ideal love.

In *Their Eyes*, it is true that Janie's first marriage, to Logan Killicks, does not end in a scene of confrontation and death, but, after finishing the book, the reader is likely to conclude that such a scene was in the offing had Janie only stuck around long enough. Killicks, whose very name smacks of murder, indeed threatens to kill Janie, after which she abruptly leaves. They are engaged in a battle of wills and egos over Janie's lack of submission to Killicks, who thus feels "low-rate[d]" by Janie. One of the last things he has a chance to say to her is, "Ah'll take holt uh dat ax and come in dere and kill yuh!" (*TE*, 30).

Of course, Janie's relationship to Joe Starks, more mutually promising at first, turns out to be just such a protracted, zero-sum struggle for dominance and finally for life. If Janie does not become unsympathetic when she verbally savages a dying Joe Starks, it is because Hurston has made us feel that if Janie, before he dies, fails to rebel against his two decades of suppressing her feelings and putting her down, she will be permanently crippled. In the world of the novel, emotional crippling can turn out to have fatal consequences: as in the case of Joe himself who has first of all suppressed his own emotional life in his all-consuming pursuit of wealth and prestige and second of all precariously built up his pride in part by controlling and humiliating his wife (Janie), and who, for both of these reasons, is thus vulnerable to an emotional and physical catastrophe when she suddenly rebels and publicly humiliates him.[31]

A vexing question in *Their Eyes* is why Janie's relationship with Tea Cake should likewise devolve into a battle for life, this time a quite literal one. For, of course, lower-class, vagabond Tea Cake is everything that Killicks and status-conscious Starks are not: alive to a world of feelings and pleasure, communicative and open with Janie, passionately in love with her, unconstrained by the pursuit of security, wealth, or prestige—and thus free to express and enjoy himself—and, most importantly, not interested in suppressing or dominating Janie. (Tea Cake is to former husband Joe Starks as Jack is to Cal the fiancé in *Titanic*.) Tea Cake seems quite explicitly to be the answer to Janie's life-long desire, which is, again, figured from girlhood in the now famous image of herself as a pear tree that needs to be pollinated. (Janie thinks of Tea Cake, soon after meeting him: "He looked like the love thoughts of women. He could be a bee to a blossom—a pear tree blossom in the spring" [*TE*, 101].) There is some jealousy on both sides and some violence in their relationship, but these reciprocal episodes are presented as issuing out of passion and bringing them closer (one of these violent episodes makes their marriage the envy of their peers on the muck), and the reciprocity seems to indicate the unusual equality in their relationship with each other. Neither seems to be in the process of being regularly subordinated and subdued—the reciprocal instances of violence even seem to be healthy in this sense— and, thus, no explosion of rebellion (as in Janie's first two marriages) seems to be on the horizon. Indeed, Janie's affirmation of their love, in the midst of the life-threatening hurricane into which Tea Cake has accidentally brought her, is absolutely unambiguous, is delivered in religious language, and occurs three times:

- "If you kin see de light at daybreak, you don't keer if you die at dusk. It's so many people never seen de light at all. Ah wuz fumblin' round and God opened the door" (TE, 151).
- "Once upon uh time, Ah never 'spected nothin', Tea Cake, but bein' dead from the standin' still and tryin' to laugh. But you come 'long and made somethin' outa me. So Ah'm thankful fuh anything we come through together" (*TE*, 158).
- "Ah jus' know dat God snatched me out de fire through you. And uh loves yuh and feel glad" (*TE*, 172).

It is safe to say that Janie does not want Tea Cake out of the picture. But the book does, and he will not be removed simply by an accidental death; Hurston will have her kill him. For, seemingly out of nowhere, comes a hurricane, a flood, a dog riding on the back of a cow, the dog's menacing of Janie, Tea Cake's protection of her and the bite he receives for it, his subsequent rabies and jealous madness, their showdown with guns, and his murder at point-blank range by Janie in self-defense. At the very least, the images of hurricane, flood, and rabies, in the context of their relationship, suggest disturbing associations between being in a love relationship and being swept away or possessed.

When a plot takes this kind of arbitrary and almost mystical twist, the reader's thoughts naturally turn from the characters' to the writer's motivations. In writing *Their Eyes* with her own relationship with A.W.P. on her mind, Hurston, it seems, was faced with a conflict between her own story (as she understood it) and that of Janie's. Because Janie, unlike Hurston, has no career or creative aspirations, Janie's relationship with Tea Cake was not a threat to Janie's self-realization, as Hurston's relationship *was* to hers. But to produce an ending that would affirm the autonomy, independence, and self-realization for which Hurston believed she was painfully sacrificing her love relationship, she had to have Janie alone at the end. At the same time, Hurston apparently wanted to idealize herself and A.W.P. (in Janie and Tea Cake), and so she removed those aspects of herself (career ambition and artistic passion) and of A.W.P. (desire for mastery and career) that would have explained the conflict in their relationship and thus its ending—but that would have made them less than unambiguously heroic and sympathetic. Also, the book does not want to investigate the long-term prospects of slumming and lower-class manual labor, just as slumming romance films do not. The result is that the book needs a deus ex machina to remove Tea Cake, thus putting Hurston and Janie back in sync (that is, each on her own) and severing Janie's sentimental ties to the muck. This comes first of all in the form of a hurricane, and Hurston had apparently encountered one in her travels in the South. But the process of removing Tea Cake has several subsequent steps, and here we leave the field of Hurston's experience and enter the realm of her imagination.

Or perhaps it might be more accurate to say the realm of her visions. Perhaps the flood, dog, and cow imagery of Tea Cake's wounding was not simply consciously crafted by Hurston, as a clever if bizarre or awkward way out of a novelistic dilemma, but rather *comes to her*, at least in part, because of her own recurring difficulty with love relationships. This imagery in *Their Eyes* might provide us with something like a partial blueprint of Hurston's conflicted psyche—or a picture of the "shadow" of her "cosmic loneliness" (*DT*, 43)—in symbolic terms. Or, to put it another way, the invention of this sequence might be imagined as akin to the mental processes of hypnosis, or dreaming, or an altered state of consciousness associated with the casting of certain spells in voodoo. And in creating and writing down this train of events, Hurston (in the form of Janie) takes a now justified revenge on A.W.P. (in the form of the mad Tea Cake).

This hurricane and flood scene, which provides the deus ex machina for Janie's release from an ideal love and out of which comes the title of the book, might also be seen as the return of Hurston's repressed, the surfacing of what has been subtracted from or "forgotten" about herself, in her creation of Janie. Hurston suggests that the scene be read on a supernatural level. She associates the storm itself with God. As the characters fearfully watch its initial progress, the reader gets the title of the book: "Their eyes were watching God" (*TE*, 151). God here seems to be those forces in the world that one cannot control. Again, Hurston also has Janie consider her relationship with Tea Cake an act of God. And as she explains to Pheoby at the end, one of the two things everybody has to do for herself is "tuh go tuh God" (*TE*, 183). The idea seems to be that one must relinquish security and make oneself vulnerable, both physically and emotionally. In leaving the town, her house, her status, and her money, Janie has made herself emotionally vulnerable to Tea Cake (and she must face her own jealousy and anger as well as Tea Cake's, their violence, and the possibility of rejection by him), and in going to the muck, which is in hurricane territory, she has opened herself up to physical risk. In this hurricane sequence, Janie's vulnerability reaches a dramatic climax, and the reader is three times reminded that the love relationship with Tea Cake has brought her into this predicament. But an even stronger connection between love and the storm exists in the book, and it is plausible to see Janie's string of physical vulnerabilities here—to the winds, the water, the dog, and, finally, to a rabid Tea Cake—as a kind of extended metaphor, an allegory, for the emotional vulnerabilities that a love relationship presents to Hurston.

The hurricane, and the flood it creates, figure for Hurston the storm of love, which importantly has emotional dangers that exceed those faced by Janie in her relationship with Tea Cake and which Hurston has "forgotten" in her depiction of an alter-ego (because, again, Janie is a streamlined, simplified, and heroic version of Hurston). At the end of the book, Janie herself will make an analogy between love and a body of water, which is interesting, since it seems that at some level Hurston has already made this association. Janie tells Pheoby, "Love is lak de sea. It's uh movin' thing, but still and all, it takes its shape from every shore it meets, and it's different with every shore" (*TE*, 182). What Janie undergoes physically in the hurricane sequence, then, might be thought of as a representation of Hurston's emotional experience of love. To put it another way, the hurricane scene continues the emotional drama of the love relationship—*by other means*. It is what loves calls up—on an emotional level and, thus, in a visionary way—not for Janie, but for Hurston. What Janie experiences here on the level of physical action (in the flood), Hurston experiences on a psychic level in the realm of love.

It is worth examining then how Janie enters this spontaneous sea and gets into mortal danger. When they first enter the "turbulent waters" (of love), "Janie could not hold up more than a few strokes at a time, so Tea Cake bore her up" (*TE*, 155). When they are once again on dry land, Tea Cake is worn out from helping Janie, and Janie responds by showing care in turn. When an exhausted Tea Cake can no longer walk on, still in the midst of the hurricane, Janie tries to protect and comfort him. In her effort to shelter him from the wind, she picks up a "piece of roofing" and is blown into the "lashing water" (*TE*, 156–57). This train of events is fitting so far: it is the instinct to love, to care for another—Janie's compassion for Tea Cake here and Hurston's feelings for A.W.P.—that brings on the (emotional) crisis.

The crisis comes first in the threat of drowning but is quickly compounded in the form of a "massive built dog sitting on [the] shoulders [of a cow] and shivering and growling" (*TE*, 157). So, we have two threats: the lashing water and the angry dog on top of a cow. These can be associated with Hurston's two distinct fears in love relationships, which seem both to issue from her childhood neglect: the fear of drowning in insecurity and the fear of loss of self. Consider the "lashing water." For Hurston, caring deeply for another is dangerous (and this danger helps explain the distance she almost always kept from love relationships, which is evinced most dramatically in her flight from the love of her life, A.W.P.): because she has the tendency to drown in a sense of being rejected.

What about the rabid dog? Tea Cake's advice to Janie on how to save herself from drowning is to grab hold of the cow's tail. This advice becomes psychologically comprehensible if we think of the cow as an image of female nurturing. In the face of Hurston's sinking into doubts about A.W.P.'s love—"the lashing water"—A.W.P.'s advice might have been to let herself be buoyed up by her own compassionate feelings. But if this bizarre scene is a blueprint of Hurston's psychic state in the situation of intimate love, then there is one more component: the dog that "stood up and growled like a lion, stiff-standing hackles, stiff muscles, teeth uncovered as he lashed up his fury for the charge" (*TE*, 157). This dog seems to be an image of Hurston's pride and ambition: thus the reference to the lion and also the reference to hackles, which refer literally to the hair on the dog's back, but unconsciously to a sense of being insulted (as in "to get one's hackles up"). Again, Hurston's childhood experience of neglect by her father had left her with a fear of loving another, since she feared his indifference and a repeated rejection (the lashing water). But this lack of love from her father had also created in her a psychic split—the Chimera of dog and cow—in which the compensatory and furious desire to be loved and admired (the dog) has subordinated and intimidated the desire to love, to give love (the cow). Interestingly, the dog stops short of plunging in after Janie because it "dreaded the water, somehow" (*TE*, 157). If most dogs do not dread water, dogs with rabies apparently do, and, fittingly as well, the dog of wounded pride—or shame—dreads the water of rejection and self-doubt. When Janie grabs hold of the cow (her compassion), the dog (her ambition) raises its fierce head and moves to attack her: Hurston's feminine compassion is experienced by her as a threat to her ambition because it ties her to a relationship that could hamper her career.

The rejection Hurston experienced in childhood led to the compensations of delusions of grandeur and a desperate drive for fame. Involvement in a love relationship—and especially care for another—must be imagined to have created intense anxiety for Hurston, an anxiety that her attention to someone else would take away from her own progress toward recognition and a resultant intensification of that very drive for recognition. Thus the dog raises its head in fury, its hackles up. Remember Hurston's own account of the primacy of her career concerns in relation to those of her love affair with A.W.P. (Hurston reports: "No matter how soaked we were in ecstasy, the telephone or the doorbell would ring, and there would be my career again. A charge had been laid upon me and I must follow the call" [*DT*, 188].)

The dog of career ambition attacks Hurston for grabbing onto the cow of compassion and care, but it is Tea Cake who is ultimately bitten. And it is the dog's bite that will transform Tea Cake into a monster of jealousy—a "mad dog" (*TE*, 178)—who will try to kill her, just as the bite of Hurston's "wounded pride" or "shame" will change A.W.P. in Hurston's mind into a monster of jealousy who seems to threaten her life's blood.

Given Hurston's furious drive and the male prejudices of the era, it is no wonder that she never found a lasting love relationship in which she could get past her profound insecurity about being loved (again, her three marriages lasted only a matter of months and another she was considering in her fifties never came off [*ZNH*, 297]). It is hard not to feel the pathos of her situation. We have to feel that she was indeed caught, as she puts it, in a "fiendish trap" (*DT*, 188) that was laid partly by her own insecurities and partly by the gender relations of her time.

Another deprivation we might imagine Hurston suffered because of her times was that of a lack of friends who could understand her decision to break off from "the perfect man" (*DT*, 190) because of her ambitions. It may not be insignificant that, in the matter of Tea Cake's murder, Janie is acquitted by an all-white jury of strangers while "the colored people" whom she knows "were all against her" (*TE*, 176). For a reason that the text does not make entirely clear, Janie considers "misunderstanding" by the all-white jury of strangers to be worse than a verdict of death (*TE*, 179). If Tea Cake's murder translates, for Hurston, into her ending her relationship with A.W.P., then perhaps it makes sense that a white jury acquits Janie and that Janie cares so much that they do: perhaps it was only her white professional contacts whom she could hope would understand her "call" and her decision to leave. We can imagine her sense of isolation must have been intense.

Color Consciousness

Consider Michael Jackson's plastic surgeries for another moment: they have not only or even principally preserved his youth; they have, by most accounts, made his skin lighter and given him more Caucasian-looking features. Hurston, again without recourse to plastic surgery of course, has done something analogous in the creation of the light-skinned and Caucasian-featured alter-ego, Janie, in *Their Eyes*. Hurston herself was not a light-skinned woman. What most critics have ignored about Janie's trajectory south is that it is not simply a journey "deeper and deeper into blackness," but at the same time, a progressive lightening or whitening of Janie's features. As Hurston has Janie enter a rural black culture of poverty and get involved with dark-skinned Tea Cake, the lightness of her skin and the whiteness of her features are insisted upon.

This theme of Tea Cake's darkness and Janie's lightness is developed through the obsessions of a character called Mrs. Turner. She is a despicably racist and white-emulating black woman who comes equipped with a political critique of Booker T. Washington, a sort of nightmare combination of progressive race politics and black bourgeois affectations. In a book that is largely silent on the issue of race relations and almost devoid of political discussion, the politically discursive Mrs.

Turner strikes the reader as another instance (along with the sequence of Tea Cake's death) of authorial heavy handedness. Mrs. Turner's politics are, up to a point, hard-line W. E. B. Du Bois progressivism; she criticizes Booker T. Washington for "'cut[ting] de monkey for white folks'" and her brother even presents academic papers on the subject: "'He didn't do nothin' but hold us back—talkin' 'bout work when de race ain't never done nothin' else. He wuz uh enemy tuh us, dat's whut. He wuz white folk's nigger'" (*TE*, 136).

But of course Mrs. Turner is no one to admire; she takes pride in her "white" features and believes lighter blacks "oughta class off" from darker blacks, whose cultural habits—"all dem loud colors, and whoopin' and hollerin' and laughin' over nothin'"—she blames for "holdin' us back" (*TE*, 135). She wants light-skinned Janie to dump dark-skinned Tea Cake.

Mrs. Turner is a fictional personification of a set of class and political attitudes Hurston would once again associate and pillory in an essay called "My people! My people!" in her autobiography. This refrain—"My people! My people!—she explains,

> is called forth by the observation of one class of Negro on the doings of another branch of the brother in black. For instance, well-mannered Negroes groan out like that when they board a train or a bus and find other Negroes on there with their shoes off, stuffing themselves with fried fish, bananas and peanuts, and throwing garbage on the floor....The offenders may be "loud talking" the place...in a voice that embraces the entire coach.

Hurston continues:

> Now, the well-mannered Negro is embarrassed by the crude behavior of others....He or she has set himself to measure up to what he thinks of as the white standard of living. He is conscious of the fact that the Negro in America needs more respect if he expects to get any acceptance at all. Therefore, after straining every nerve to get an education, maintain an attractive home, dress decently, and otherwise conform, he is dismayed at the sight of other Negroes tearing down what he is trying to build up. It is said every day, "And that good-for-nothing, trashy Negro is the one the white people judge us all by." (*DT*, 157–58)

These upper-class blacks also tend to make "the blackest Negro...the butt of all jokes" (*DT*, 164). Finally, in her essay, Hurston makes explicit the connection, in her mind, between this prejudice of "upper-class Negroes" (*DT*, 159) and the ideology of progressive race politics, which is given voice by "'the better-thinking Negro'":

> ...while they considered themselves Race Champions, they wanted noth-
> ing to do with anything frankly Negroid. They drew color lines within
> the race. The Spirituals, the Blues, *any* definitely Negroid thing was just
> not done. They went to the trouble at times to protest the use of them
> by Negro artists. Booker T. Washington was absolutely vile for advocat-
> ing industrial education. There was no analysis, no seeking for merits. If
> it was old cuffy, down with it! "My people! My people!" (*DT*, 169)

Hurston's hostility to both black bourgeois affectations and the progressive race politics of her day she associates with those affectations (and her hostility in particular to Du Bois and his notion of "the talented tenth"[32]) seems clear in the portrait of the woman she makes their spokesperson, but it is important to see that this caricature (in Mrs. Turner) is not simply an arbitrary slander of the class attitudes and politics Hurston dislikes. This portrait, rather, implies Hurston's belief that behind progressive race politics and black bourgeois affectations, and behind Du Bois's notion of "the talented tenth," is black self-hatred: a tendency to see black culture as unfortunate or pathological and thus to feel a hatred for that culture.

Meanwhile, Janie and Hurston seem on first glance to share an unqualified embrace of lower-class black culture: Janie, of course, *chooses* migrant agricultural work as a lifestyle (she is under no economic compulsion and leaves the job of storeowner in an all-black town to work in the fields for whites). This is a dramatic choice that Hurston has her heroine make; Janie, who has been brought up to admire Booker T. Washington, outdoes herself here in unconsciously living out a burlesque of his politics. It is no wonder that Richard Wright accused Hurston (in *Their Eyes*) of the same charge that Mrs. Turner levels at Washington, namely, that Hurston was writing to entertain white folks. Wright could not help but notice that Hurston almost totally elides the reality of white racism in *Their Eyes*, another aspect of the novel that links it with Hurston's later autobiography where, as Maya Angelou points out, "she does not mention even one unpleasant racial incident."

Hurston's studied obliviousness to "the race riots and other atrocities of her time"[33] could be chalked up to a refusal to sacrifice individuality in the interest of social responsibility and a dedication to the celebration of black traditions, but something more seems to be at play. Hurston's aggressive embrace of lower-class black culture and elision of white racism, when laid side-by-side with her assertion of individuality and her career ambition, might be considered to grow not only out of a common degree of pride but also out of a sort of terror of self-doubt. To explore the pervasive reality of white racism is to open up the possibility of admission that in some respects black culture—and thus one's own psychology—is reactive, self-defensive, and, thus, troubled: a possibility Hurston rigorously avoided. Such a terror of self-doubt or of self-hatred reflects the kind of vulnerability to shame that she developed in her traumatic childhood: and it is not hard to imagine that Hurston, with such a sensitivity to humiliation, would find the reality of racism in America to be nearly overwhelming, so potentially devastating that it must be largely denied.[34] To put it another way, if the profound injury to Hurston's sense of self is initially inflicted by her family, it is soon enough compounded by society at large: as a child she experiences not only her father's neglect and her mother's death and subsequent absence but also white—and black—society's color consciousness.

And if Hurston develops "an overwhelming complex about [her] looks" in her youth, racism no doubt also plays a role in this complex along with her abandonment by her father. These two "rejections" together create her sense of her unattractiveness. Hurston may have been spared a great deal of white racism as a child in an all-black town, but soon after her family dissolves she has to enter the larger society. Moreover, contrary to the myth of Alice Walker and others, in which Hurston develops a kind of "African" consciousness and an "easy self-acceptance" in her all-black hometown, as a child she is already aware of a black color consciousness that works against her: the tendency of blacks in her town, despite their regular talk of Negro superiority and equality, to value lighter skin. She writes in her autobiography: "If it was so honorable and glorious to be black, why was it the yellow-skinned people among us had so much prestige?" At the beginning of grade school, she has noticed the color prejudice: "The light-skinned children were always the angels, fairies and queens of school plays" (DT, 165). And this color prejudice does not favor her: she is not a light-skinned child.

Often early artistic works blatantly reveal an author's fears and compulsions, simply because early on artists have not yet taken much control over their materials: one of Hurston's first literary productions was the play Color Struck (1926), which Pierpont calls a "disconcertingly morbid document."

This brief, almost surreal play tracks a talented and very dark-skinned woman's decline into self-destructive madness, a result of her inability to believe that any man could love a woman so black. Although the intended lesson of "Color Struck" seems clear in the retelling, the play's fevered, hallucinatory vehemence suggests a far more complex response to color than Hurston's champions today can comfortably allow—a response not entirely under the author's control. (SO, 82)

In this light, Hurston's depiction of Mrs. Turner could be said to give us, to some degree, a portrait of her own psychic self-doubts. If with Mrs. Turner, she would like to reveal black Du Bois progressives and the black bourgeoisie to be self-hating, she is actually revealing that progressive racial politics are dangerous *to her in particular* because, if she were to entertain them, she would find activated her own self-hatred and shame—her own sense of inferiority inflicted by white racial hatred and black preference for lighter skin. That is, Mrs. Turner is Hurston's perhaps unconscious projection of her own sensitivity and shame onto black politics and black bourgeois behavior. In other words, Hurston's linking of black bourgeois attitudes or progressive politics with self-hatred tells us more about Hurston than about these black politics or bourgeois attitudes. Mrs. Turner is in this sense another instance of the return of Hurston's repressed content in this novel: not this time her vaulting ambition and the underlying shame of her father's neglect (that Janie does not share, despite the fact that she too has no father), but the shame that racism and color consciousness has inflicted upon her (that Janie is also spared).

In fact, it might even be said that when the novel reaches the Everglades with Tea Cake, Hurston's alter ego splits in two, producing a fantastically light-skinned Janie and a darker, self-hating Mrs. Turner (who resembles in obvious ways the character in *Color Struck*). Janie, the consistently sympathetic hero, is happily oblivious to Mrs. Turner's obsession with looks and politics. She is spared Hurston's consciousness of color prejudice among blacks, and she is also spared Hurston's complex about her looks, of course in part at least because she looks white.

In much the same way that Hurston lets the reader of her autobiography know at the very beginning of the chapter on "My Folks" that her father was "mulatto" (*DT*, 7), she insists on Janie's lightness. Hurston's making Janie light obviously conflicts with Hurston's penchant in *Their Eyes* for the culturally "black" and in particular Tea Cake, who is disliked by Mrs. Turner because he is dark. But this claim to lightness, like the embrace of lower-class black culture, can be seen as another salve against the shame of color consciousness. Hurston wants to believe that black culture has not been twisted in any way by white racism; likewise, a consciousness of the mixture of the races is meant to take Hurston, as it were, out of the direct line of racist fire. Thus we also have Janie, "sincerely mystified by Mrs. Turner's tirades" (SO, 86), saying, "We'se uh mingled people" (TE, 135). (And we have Hurston apparently telling an anthropologist at Barnard that, as he put it, she was "more white than Negro in her ancestry" [SO, 83].) It is not that Hurston is exactly proud of being of mixed race; it is rather that she is relieved by anything—including the genetic mixing of black and white—that allows her to dilute or deny her experience of color consciousness and repress her humiliation by it.

But there is another important and a more disturbing aspect to the theme of Janie's lightness or Caucasian features. And that is the apparent need for Hurston to separate Janie—by an assertion of her lightness—from the darkness of Tea Cake and the "cultural blackness" of her surroundings in the Everglades, just as she is embracing them. No such distancing from Tea Cake was necessary back in the town where Janie had the distinction of being the mayor's widow who lived in the biggest house. Her exalted status was in place. In the Everglades, on the muck, without her money, out in the fields, Janie is "in danger" of being indistinguishable from the other lower-class, dark-skinned blacks. She is saved from this fate of submersion by the entrance of Mrs. Turner and a narration that emphasizes and develops her lighter features. The fact that Janie doesn't care about her "whiteness" may further ennoble her, but the development of this theme makes Hurston something other than a Black Nationalist.

What is at issue here is more than the fact that Hurston uses the traditions of black cultures of poverty for her own "empowerment" as a fiction writer. It is that Hurston is not finally comfortable identifying herself with these cultures and their blackness. Here is the key point that critics have somehow managed to overlook: Hurston's embrace of black culture is partial, provisional, sentimentally slumming. For every embrace, there is also a distancing. This is the same dynamic that is played out in Hurston's visits to Jamaica and Haiti; she is distinguished from the mass of Caribbean women: Hurston is of course not suddenly white-featured, like Janie, but she is American, middle-class, and educated.

Julia Kristeva, the French psychoanalyst and critic, has an "Essay on Abjection" that sheds light here.

The one by whom the abject exists is thus a *deject* who places (himself), *separates* (himself), situates (himself), and therefore *strays* instead of getting his bearings, desiring, belonging, or refusing....Necessarily dichotomous, somewhat Manichaean, he divides, excludes, and without...wishing to know his abjections is not at all unaware of them. Often, moreover, he includes himself among them, thus casting within himself the scalpel that carries out his separations....For it is out of such straying on excluded ground that he draws his juissance [joy]. The abject from which he does not cease separating is for him, in short, *a land of oblivion* that is constantly remembered.[35]

For Hurston, black rural cultures of poverty are such excluded ground, reminiscent at some level of her consciousness of the rejection and dejection she felt as a dark-skinned child living in a color-conscious community and abandoned by her father. She does not merely identify with the backwoods of Florida, New Orleans, Jamaica, and Haiti; she visits them and at the same time distances herself from them. Likewise, to remain a Hurston heroine and alter ego, Janie cannot go to the muck with Tea Cake unless she can at the same time be distinguished from those around her, including Tea Cake.

That Janie's adventure in the Everglades ends with her desperately desired acquittal by a white jury on a murder charge deserves, in this context, another look. Here is another way in which Janie is lifted out of the black community that she had temporarily associated herself with. In her deep wish for the understanding of the white jury—stronger than her concern about a verdict of death—we might even associate her with Mrs. Turner, who yearns for general acceptance from the white community. In any case, the special understanding of the white jury, in contrast to a black community that was "all against her," does something other than spare her from a death verdict, which might have been achieved in the novel by any number of means. It might have been achieved, for instance, by "the colored people" (*TE*, 176) rallying around her and hiding her from the law. What this recognition by the white jury does is distinguish her, yet again, from the excluded community she has joined. In this context, it makes perfect sense also that Janie would leave the muck at the end of the novel, though its black people have embraced her again and she has forgiven them, and that she would return to the upwardly mobile town she had hated and that viewed her with suspicion after her disappearance with Tea Cake. Janie, like Hurston, cannot belong to any group, but she needs greater distance from excluded or impoverished groups (that she celebrates) than from a middle-class community.

Moreover, Hurston yearns for recognition from the middle class she leaves behind on her research ventures and implicitly criticizes in *Their Eyes* as small minded because impoverished in experience and thus "parched up from not knowing things" (*TE*, 183). This desire for recognition is partly why Hurston turns down an offer from a great voodoo doctor to stay in New Orleans and work with him as a partner until his death (*TMH*, 205). Her career is always directed at a middle-class audience. To say that Hurston was dedicated only to art or writing is to forget that she also imagined celebrity for discovering the medical secret of the zombies and later a lost Mayan city. Hurston desired the validation of celebrity—as an iconoclast to be sure (again, she did not want to be too closely identified with any group, the middle class included). And this same desire is partly why Janie returns to Joe Starks's middle-class town: even as she shocks most of its cowardly and opinionated residents, who are at bottom jealous of her, she will also be directly validated in telling her story to Pheoby, who is openly in awe. The other reason is that Hurston had to have Janie at the end absolutely separated from the socially excluded of the Everglades.

Voodoo

It is only in the context of Hurston's profound and hidden sense of shame or abjection that we can fully understand her experience with voodoo—with the dead, with animal sacrifice, and with the supposedly "undead." In the Caribbean, Hurston was not merely collecting folklore or watching demonstrations or dances staged for her benefit but also was being initiated into *obeah* and voodoo.

In Jamaica, Hurston took part in two "Nine Night" rituals, ceremonies whose purpose was to keep the spirit of the dead—the "*duppy*"—from haunting the living. As her biographer, Hemenway reports, "one of these ended in a naked, orgiastic dance climaxed by the sacrifice of a goat" (*ZNH*, 230). In a funereal ceremony in Haiti, a chant is repeated, and "the body of the dead man sat up with its staring eyes, bowed its head and fell back again..." (*TMH*, 142).

In Haiti, she also regularly participated in animal sacrifice. She describes the killing of a goat:

> The next day..., the male and female goat were sacrificed. The male goat was brought under the tonnelle in its little flowered cape, but he was most unwilling. We chanted, we sang, and effort was made to lead

the goat gaily about the center pole but he balked and had to be pushed every step of the way in the procession. The red-clad Ogoun bestrode him and the crowd yelled and pushed and pulled but the goat was emphatic in his desire to have nothing to do with the affair. The crowd sang and shouted exultantly but I could hear the pathetic, frightened bleat of the goat beneath it all, as he was buffeted and dragged to make a grand spectacle of his death.

She also describes the ritual killing of a dog: "That ceremony was the same except that the dog was not killed so soon in this instance. Only part of one of his ears was cut off by the priest. Then an assistant pulled the teeth of the dog and finally he was buried alive. The god had indicated that he desired his food thus" (*TMH*, 172–73). In one ceremony, in which a chicken was being sacrificed, the bird had leapt in its death throes and touched Hurston. "My heart flinched and my flesh drew up like a tripe" (*ZNH*, 247).

Hurston also pursued the mystery of zombies. She writes in *Tell My Horse*:

> I saw the broken remnant, relic, or refuse of Felicia Felix-Mentor in a hospital yard....
>
> I had the rare opportunity to see and touch an authentic case. I listened to the broken noises in its throat, and then, I did what no one else had ever done, I photographed it....So I know there are Zombies in Haiti. People have been called back from the dead....
>
> [The Zombie was] cringing against the wall with a cloth hiding her face and head....Finally the doctor forcibly uncovered her and held her so that I could take [a photograph of] her face. And the sight was dreadful. That blank face with the dead eyes. The eyelids were white all around the eyes as if they had been burned with acid....The sight of this wreckage was too much to endure for long. (*TMH*, 179, 182, 195)

Hurston's fascination with voodoo—with rituals of the dead, with animal sacrifice, with zombies—may seem less than comprehensible until we recognize, with Kristeva, that "Abjection accompanies all religious structurings....Abjection appears as a rite of defilement and pollution in the paganism that accompanies societies with a dominant or surviving matrilinear character."

Hurston, in her continual straying on excluded or marginal territory, stumbles upon and finds herself drawn to ancient, pagan rites of defiling and "*purifying* the abject." Of course, "the corpse, seen without God and outside of science, is the utmost in abjection."[36] Cutting the dog's ear, pulling out its teeth, and burying it alive defile the dog, make the animal more abject. Chants said and food prepared in ceremonies for a dead man, the cape put on the sacrificial goat and the singing that accompanies the slaughter: these are rituals for purifying the abject object. The Nine Night ritual addressed to the spirit of the dead to keep it from returning from the grave enacts the separation of the abject being from the living. Hurston, with her sensitivity to shame or abjection, had a desire to be near excluded beings or abject things and to separate herself from them—they died, or were sacrificed, and buried; she survived, walked away, and returned to the world of the living. And she was not only drawn to these rituals but also was able to describe them in a way that delivers up some of their primal cathartic quality. So beneath the chanting for the goat she heard the animal's "pathetic, frightened bleat." And the touch of the dying chicken elicited a vivid description of elemental repulsion.

One wonders in this context if Hurston's experience of the death of her mother—in the house when Hurston was a child of thirteen—did not play a role in her seemingly compulsive involvement with the dead in Haiti. No doubt her father's neglect gave her the sense of dejection that would make such an indulgence in death joyful if also threatening; perhaps her mother's dying gave her a first, traumatic, and shameful experience of death that stayed with her.

Her encounter with the supposed zombie, the most dramatic portion of *Tell My Horse*, underlines her vulnerability to this fascination and flirtation with the abject. She was ready to believe that she was encountering a creature who had been turned into a zombie—a being brought back from the dead and deprived of will and speech—with a secret drug. Particularly interesting from the point of view of the shame theorist is the fact that the supposed zombie, when left to herself, assumed a position of fear and shame: cringing against a wall, hiding her face with a cloth. Clearly fascinated, Hurston saw her as the "refuse" or "wreckage" of a person. Hurston also registered her repulsion here—she could not endure the sight for long—and then her separation: she and the doctor "went to a more cheerful part of the hospital and sat down to talk" (*TMH*, 195–96).

It is perhaps only after considering Hurston's investment in voodoo ritual and zombie lore—and glimpsing the dynamics of her abjection—that the peculiar and violent demise of Janie's relationship with Tea Cake becomes fully intelligible. For, of course, Hurston could have chosen to remove Tea Cake in any number of ways in order to restore Janie to complete independence at the end: he could have died without first being transformed into a sort of monster and he could have died without Janie killing him. But Hurston had left A.W.P.—thus taking an active role in finishing the relationship—and she had clearly perceived in him a dramatic threat to her career and independence, and thus, apparently, Hurston was true to her sense of her actual relationship in the depiction of the fictional one in *Their Eyes*.

A question perhaps remains, though: why must Tea Cake become "some mad dog" (*TE*, 172)? This issue can be considered at a couple of levels: First, Hurston wanted to preserve the ideal quality of the love between Janie and Tea Cake, and, therefore, everything that happens after the dog bites Tea Cake could be bracketed off from their relationship. Second, Hurston's angry pride or shame, which took the form of the rabid dog in the novel, caused a metamorphosis both in A.W.P. and in Hurston's sense of him. But one can also integrate into this account Tea Cake's blackness and his migrant-worker, lower-class standing—which apparently both attracted and repelled Hurston because at some level she projected onto these lower-status qualities a sense of her own shame and rejection. (Remember her complex about her looks and the play *Color Struck*.) In other words, Tea Cake's reduction to an abject being—a mad dog that must be killed—is not at all accidental or a matter of bizarre plotting. When Janie begins to "fear this strange thing in Tea Cake's body" (*TE*, 173), Hurston was delivering up some of the repulsion that she herself is vulnerable to in sexual relationships, a vulnerability that had everything to do with her experience of abjection or shame. This experience of profound shame or abjection involves a coming close to and then a violent separating from people and things that are somehow marked with the stamp of exclusion. It is disturbing, but sensible, that Janie eliminates Tea Cake much as Mrs. Turner would have her do.

Hurston's Self-Mythology in Her Autobiography and Fiction

Despite the claims of critics who want to construct a heroic younger Hurston by dismissing her later work and politics, Hurston's career and oeuvre shows the consistency characteristic of compulsion. It might be said that in her later work and political positions, Hurston did not become *out of* character, but rather hardened *in* it. She did not reverse her views; she became extreme in them. It might also be said, more specifically, that under the pressure of poverty, neglect, and poor press, she became obsessed with preserving her own self-confidence and thus terrified of and rigidly hostile to any admission whatsoever that might smack of self-doubt or shame: including any political position that could be said to admit that the black community had been in any way harmed (by systematic racism). "Negroes Without Self-Pity"—the title of one of her articles in the 1940s—was, as Pierpont puts it, "her life's theme, and she sounded it all the louder as two new novels [after *Moses, Man of the Mountain* (1939)] were rejected, her poverty went from bohemian to chronic, and her health gave way" (SO, 88).

Hurston's *pride* is by now legendary: later in life she took menial jobs rather than appeal to her family or friends for help; Walker cites a niece of Hurston's who reports that "her aunt was so proud that the only way the family could guess she was ill or without funds was by realizing they had no idea where she was" (*ZNH*, xvii). But perhaps *shame* is the better word here: for this fantastic pride is, of course, a compensation for intense feelings of dejection and abjection.

The writers and critics who subscribe to the Hurston myth—of the all-confident and iconoclastic Black Nationalist and feminist—have essentially bought into the myth she fabricates about herself, in her autobiography and through her fiction, a self-mythology achieved through repression and fantasy.

To recapitulate, this myth of herself centered around a fantasy of her exemption from the usual human competition for power and prestige coupled with a sense of a personal mission that transcended this competition. What one notices in looking at *Their Eyes* along with Hurston's other fictions is that Janie's search for a selfhood, a mate, and a locale, *removed from the concern with status*, rehearses a fundamental Hurston theme that runs through most of her work. Her fiction is in general populated with "little" people,[37] preoccupied with their own sense of importance, and thus devoted to putting other people down. (Sometimes this preoccupation is a source of comedy, say in the short story, "The Bone of Contention"; at other times it is dangerously serious.) *Their Eyes* has not only Starks and Killicks and Mrs. Turner, but also Janie's grandmother and the ubiquitous porch sitters, who make up a kind of chorus of such "small-minded" voices that are from the start of the novel in the business of mocking Janie for her iconoclasm. *Jonah's Gourd Vine* has the members of John Pearson's congregation who wish to bring him down, many of whom simply resent his being in a position superior to theirs. In *Seraph*, it is the main character who is conspicuously (and perhaps tediously, following Alice Walker) paralyzed by self-doubt and resentment—and who eventually triumphs over this paralysis. *Moses* is absolutely exhaustive on this theme: the ten plagues of Egypt are explicitly delivered in response to the Pharoah's pride, and Moses's most consistent task in dealing with the Hebrew people is to handle the resentful egotism of its leading men and women.

Meanwhile, Hurston created characters who are exempt from this curse of egotism and who, because of this exemption, stand out as "unambiguously heroic" (*TE*, xiv)[38] characters: Janie and Moses, most importantly, but also their sidekicks (Tea Cake, and Mentu, Jethro, and Joshua). Both of these heroic protagonists importantly give up wealth and position in the process of discovering their true callings, both are wrongfully held suspect by the "mob" for doing so, both go into a kind of "exile" in the process, both discover soul mates among a lower class, and both are temporarily fulfilled and aided by spouses whom they eventually must put aside in pursuit of their destiny. (It is worth adding, then, that much about Janie's quest for self-realization was apparently not for Hurston particular to women.)

Clearly, this repeated imaginary trajectory is central to Hurston's sense of or fantasy about herself. In regard to the pursuit of her career, her conflict between the career and her love life, her travels to the South and to Jamaica and Haiti, her association with the poor on these "research" ventures, and her initiation into voodoo, she sees herself as a type of Janie or Moses. Or, rather, Hurston's character of Janie and her quite particular twist on Moses issue from this fantasy about herself. The fantasy went something like this: her exile among the poor and the pursuit of her art were considered purified of the ubiquitous striving, or pursuit of status, that she had supposedly left behind in the middle class. She blinded herself to her own desperate pursuit of recognition and fantasy of fame and also to the special status she acquired as a visitor or exile among a lower class. And she imagined herself capable of living without intimate ties to the opposite sex.

Hurston was deeply revealing—about herself—when she wrote at the beginning of *Their Eyes*: "Now, women forget all things they don't want to remember, and remember everything they don't want to forget. The dream is the truth" (*TE*, 1). Her repressions were central, then, to the construction of her self-mythology or dream. Like a male writer such as Crane who compensated for weakness and shame with a supreme toughness, Hurston consciously practiced a sort of heroic stoicism that shades off into a repression of self-understanding. And as with Crane, there was a sort of terror of vulnerability. As Hurston acknowledges bluntly at one point in her autobiography, "I do not choose to admit weakness" (*DT*, 202).

Hurston "forgets" her great need for recognition, her problems with intimate relationships, and the injuries she suffered from racism; she also represses her neglect and abandonment by her father. For although Hurston writes a whole novel based upon her father and within that novel seems to glimpse the damage he did to her even while she was still in utero, she also tends to downplay the pain of her father's neglect in her autobiography. For example, she denies missing her father's affection: "It did not so much matter to me that Sarah [her sister] was papa's favorite. I got my joy in other ways, and so, did not miss the petting. I do not think I ever really wanted it" (*DT*, 73). And though Hurston viciously excoriates her stepmother, and has a violent fight with her, she indulges in no diatribes against her father.

Hurston detested bitterness and fantasies of personal importance (that are the flip side of bitterness), mocked them in her fictions, and did not allow herself to indulge in them: "I take no refuge from myself in bitterness. To me, bitterness is the under-arm odor of wishful weakness. It is the graceless acknowledgement of defeat. I have no urge to make any concessions like that to the world as yet" (*DT*, 205). So her grief and anger were always contained—and stylized. Hurston's claim in her autobiography, for example, that she has "been in Sorrow's kitchen and licked out all the pots" (*DT*, 205)—a phrase, by the way, she had already put in the mouth of the character based on her mother in *Jonah's Gourd Vine* and that would return almost verbatim in regard to the white heroine of *Seraph*[39]—was typical of her manner of handling her pain in print. She admits suffering, but only abstractly, at some distance from it; moreover, though she speaks of suffering here, the formulation is so clever and homey that it seems to belie the meaning. This was a characteristic Hurston device: to admit the reality of a pain (like her father's neglect) or an injustice (like racism) and to declare herself nonetheless immune to it in the same breath. Another notable example of this abstraction and stylization of grief may be the very title of her autobiography. "Dust Tracks on a Road" seems an abstract image of loneliness or abjection, which is not exactly in keeping with the confident voice of the narration, and is also hardly very personal.

She saw her loneliness as ultimately "cosmic" rather than familial. This seems to be another instance of the same self-protective abstraction. And though it is true that Hurston seemed to approach the familial sources of her pain, she ultimately shied away from them and could not acknowledge them fully. She did write an autobiography and did recount her childhood suffering, if at a remove; she did write a novel openly based upon her parents' lives. And yet the ultimate intention seemed to be to assert a mastery over what had happened: to heal, or, rather, to prove herself unhurt by a show of control.

If Hurston's self-mythology in her autobiography is principally a matter of the suppression and repression of her shame and pain in the interest of creating an image of boundless self-confidence, in her fiction it is a rather more complicated matter of the "alchemical" transformation of this dejection into a badge of uncanny distinction.[40]

II

Class and Status Trauma

3

Nauseating Indie Films

"Let's do it. Let's hurt somebody."

—*Chad in* In the Company of Men

Consider the plots, or subplots, of two sets of 1990s independent films. The first is a group of trauma films set among the lower classes.

Kids (Larry Clark, 1995) describes a white, hip-hop, streetwise New York City boy's quest to con relatively innocent young girls into sleeping with him so he can be the one to take their virginity; meanwhile, the boy, Telly, is unwittingly spreading the AIDS virus, and the subplot of the movie is a search by one of his sexual victims, a less-degraded white girl named Jenny, to find and confront him. She never quite does. She finds him at a party in bed with a new virgin, and she retreats to a body-strewn living room. She collapses on a couch, high and exhausted, and is raped by the boy's best friend, Casper, whom the viewer must assume has contracted HIV in turn.

In *Clerks* (Kevin Smith, 1994), Dante, a convenience store clerk in suburban New Jersey, attempts to get back with his snooty ex-girlfriend when he learns from the newspaper that she is engaged. Their reunion date is interrupted when she mistakenly has sex with an older man who has died while masturbating in the lightless toilet of the convenience store, believing she has encountered an already-prepared Dante. She is carted away in a state of shock by paramedics when she learns she has been the victim of rape by a dead man with rigor mortis.

Gummo (Harmony Korine, 1997) surveys the physical and psychic devastation of a small, working-class town in Ohio in the wake of a tornado. There is hardly a plot, but the main story line involves the killing of cats and the torture and sale of the dead cats by the male protagonists, Tumler and Solomon. This killing and torture eventually includes that of a beloved home cat, who belongs to the two female protagonists, Dot and Darby.

Requiem for a Dream (Darren Aronofsky, 2000) follows the relentless degradation and humiliation of four increasingly marginal characters, including a young white woman who becomes a sex slave to a black drug-dealer in exchange for heroin.

Next, consider a pair of trauma films set among the upper classes.

Welcome to the Dollhouse (Todd Solondz, 1996) humorously chronicles the unending abuse that a girl, Dawn Wiener, receives from her suburban junior high school peers. And it tells the story of her doomed romances with two cool boys, a middle-class high school rocker who is unaware of her romantic feelings and a lower-class junior high troublemaker, Brandon, who never makes good on his somewhat touching threats to rape her. But though they never quite unite, she and the poor boy, Brandon, begin to develop a relationship that is caring rather than abusive. He is the single character who comes to treat Dawn with respect and affirmation.

In the Company of Men (Neil LaBute, 1997) describes a plot by two big-city corporate men to seduce and dump the most vulnerable woman they can find so they can enjoy her abasement; they decide to target a deaf, working-class woman, Christine, while on temporary corporate assignment in a smaller city. Not only does their plan work; it turns out that the woman's humiliation was part of a larger and also successful plot by one of the men, Chad, to get ahead of the other man, Howard, his friend and coworker. But Howard, meanwhile, has developed something heartfelt for the innocent, honest Christine; however, a relationship is impossible given Howard's collusion in her humiliation.

Trauma films with lower-class settings are inversions of slumming drama movies. That is, in trauma films set in the social depths, the domains of poverty, of low life, or even of mild social marginality, far from being utopias of compassion and freedom, are imagined to be zones of degradation, where everyday, regular encounters and transactions are brutal and degraded, devoid of what the middle class calls humanity. Almost every encounter is governed by the rule of degrade or be degraded. These films can be called "class traumas" because the depicted communities are traumatized by their class inferiority. Here the low-life male is not a liberator but a victimizer. A common plot is the traumatic humiliation of a weak, vulnerable, naive, or relatively innocent character, usually a female, at the hands of a more socially degraded male. This is, of course, Stephen Crane's narrative in *Maggie*.

Meanwhile, in trauma films set at the social heights, it is the middle and upper classes that are zones of mutual degradation, and these films might be called "status traumas" because the depicted communities are traumatized by competition for status. In terms of their classploitation content, as opposed to their genre style, these films are akin to slumming dramas. These films contain a romanticization of the lower classes similar to that of slumming dramas: the domains of the lower class are again imagined to be more honest and decent. But here the focus is not on romanticized lower-class domains that have the power to liberate. Rather, the oppressive upper-class domains are dominant and predatory, and the plot involves the vulnerable lower-class character being harmed by his or her encounter with brutal higher-class enclaves.

Trauma films set in the lower classes share a radical departure from movies of every familiar genre: there are hardly characters in these films with whom the audience can sympathize. Or, rather, sympathy with characters is short-circuited. This is not because most or all the characters are despicable or repulsive; it is because they are not imbued with the kind of consciousness that the middle class imagines for itself and is used to finding in its movies and books. In essence, these movies verge on proposing a different notion of human personality. Traditional characters appeal to middle-class viewers because of an aspect of what is called their humanity: not simply their ability to suffer, but their ability to transcend their humiliation.[1] Like Crane's, the characters in these class trauma movies cannot rise above.

The protagonists of the films at issue here sometimes suffer, but most of them hardly have consciences or, more often, simply lack the will to overcome their humiliations. Of course, melodramas of various genres contain remorseless villains, but these movies differ in two ways from melodramatic Western, crime, and action films. First of all, the bad guys here are not stopped and do not experience comeuppance; second, the potential good guys have only the most rudimentary consciences themselves or have little or no ability to fight back.

Telly in *Kids* and Chad in *In the Company of Men* appear at first to be classic villains of melodrama. Telly shamelessly cons young girls into letting him have sex with them, merely faking care and love for the fifteen minutes or so it takes to get them into bed. Afterward, he shows absolutely no interest in the girls and no remorse; rather, he feels only contempt for them. Immediately after exiting the bedroom of the girl he deflowers in the first scene, he spits luxuriously on the family's expensive coffee table from the floor above (in their magnificent New York apartment), and moments later he is referring to the girl as a "bitch" in conversation with his friend Casper. Chad in *In the Company of Men* actually stays around to savor the moment of humiliation. He doesn't merely abandon the woman he deceives and move on; he lingers in order to watch his victim suffer the exquisite pain of rejection.

But neither Telly nor Chad turn out to be the familiar bad guys of melodrama because neither is stopped. At the end of *Kids*, HIV-positive Jenny has failed to confront Telly. Not only does she arrive too late to prevent another virgin from being "fucked" and infected; she doesn't have the will to interrupt his sex act. He goes on with his predation. Chad meanwhile is wholly victorious. Howard's attempt to derail his assault on the deaf Christine by confessing the men's plot blows up in his face. Christine doesn't want to believe that they have set her up, and so Chad still gets the pleasure of dumping her and watching her suffer. Moreover, he takes over Howard's position at work and retains his unwitting girlfriend Suzanne, whom he continues to lie to through the very end. The last we see of Chad is his chest and belly as Suzanne kisses her way down his body, presumably heading for his groin. He is not punished but rewarded on every level.

Of course, there are some if not many traditional books and movies in which evil triumphs and good is defeated—*Braveheart* (Mel Gibson, 1995) might be an example—but the movies at issue here depart even from that less usual formula. First of all, in a movie such as *Braveheart*, good is not entirely defeated, it is temporarily set back; there is reason for hope, and a postscript even assures the audience that good will triumph later. In these trauma films, on the contrary, good never quite gets going.

The potential good guys in these films never really develop into full-fledged sympathetic characters. They are more pathetic than sympathetic, because they can hardly stand up for themselves and sometimes, in addition, because they are hardly better than anybody else in the degraded community.

Dawn in *Welcome to the Dollhouse* is a constant victim; what prevents her from being sympathetic is that she has let her suffering make her mean like everybody else in her world. She is hateful of her little sister and comically complicit in Missy's kidnapping because she purposefully holds back a message from the little girl. There is also a devastating—and not funny—sequence in which Dawn takes out her frustration on her one loyal friend, someone who has never hurt her, a young boy in the neighborhood with whom she shares her clubhouse. With Missy holding the phone for her to take, Dawn shouts abuse, finally yelling, "I hope he rots in hell." In short, she treats her friend no better finally than all the victimizers at school have treated her. Dawn doesn't finally desire to be good, to transcend the mutual torture of junior high; like everyone else, she simply wants, as she says at one point, "to be popular." When she dreams of saving her sister Missy, the dream centers on the familial love and peer acclaim that will shower on her as a hero.

Howard in *In the Company of Men* is the prospective hero of a Cinderella romance who, like Dawn, never in the end rises above the status of vindictive victim or ineffective victimizer. Howard does tell Chad near the end of the film that he felt "lousy" about revealing their cruel plot to Christine and thus hurting her and that he'd never "done anything like that" before. He does seem more concerned about hurting Christine than being demoted at work. And he has tried to apologize to her, telling her he's "so sorry" and that he's a "fuck" and a "bastard." These are all the marks of a man of conscience, who has done wrong but has come to his senses and restored the correct priorities.

But Howard's apology to Christine and his expression of guilt to Chad are both undercut and ultimately overwhelmed by base and selfish currents in his behavior to her. As he confesses to her their plot and apologizes, Howard also tries to set himself apart from Chad, claiming that Chad is her real enemy, and that he, Howard, truly loves and deserves her. Completely undermining his apology, he goes so far as to say at one point, "What did I ever do to you? Can't you see I'm the good person?" And he doesn't stop there in his self-promotion. He not only attempts to win her over, away from Chad, but he also tries to humiliate her yet again when she naturally resists his half-hearted apology for the cruel game they have played on her. When she throws away his proffered engagement ring, he yells, in his perhaps most brutal moment, "You are fucking handicapped!…You think you can choose? Men falling at your feet?" Howard's final approach to Christine in the last scene of the film, after his expression of remorse to Chad, shows little more sensitivity. When Howard confronts her at her workplace and she refuses to respond to his demand to listen to him, he begins screaming, loudly and more loudly, with growing desperation and anger, "Listen to me." A silent shot of his venomous, screeching face—from Christine's soundless point of view—ends the movie.

In a similar way, the child-molesting therapist in another status trauma film by Todd Solondz, *Happiness* (1998), fights a losing battle against the "monster inside," and succumbs to his lust for boys. In trauma movies, the inner (and outer) bully carries the day: there is no transcendence.

When not downright monstrous, these potential heroes turn out to be merely pathetic. Like Howard at his best, Dante in *Clerks* is wishy-washy. He is also a whiner. Though the audience doesn't exactly embrace his trickster friend Randal, he does seem to have Dante's number. In regard to Dante's ambivalence about his present girlfriend and his longing for his past one, Randal chides, "Don't pine for one and fuck the other." At the end of the movie, he maintains that "you [Dante] blame everybody else" for your own weaknesses and problems. Dante's own account of his humiliating passivity is along the same lines. He explains, "When I was three, my mother told me my potty lid was closed; instead of lifting it, I shit my pants."

Jenny in *Kids* is a relatively sympathetic character in a class trauma film, and this is because her membership in the demeaned teenage street community is not total—her social distinction or superiority is invidiously suggested by her race (she is the lone white girl in her group) and indicated by her demeanor. She seems an innocent compared to her tough-talking and promiscuous girlfriends and she has only slept with one boy, Telly, who promised not to use her and then never spoke to her again. The audience is made to feel the injustice of her infection with the HIV virus. She has only been tested in order to provide company for her dark-skinned friend, Ruby, who is rightfully worried about having HIV; Ruby has had unprotected sex a number of times including anal sex without a condom at least twice. But Ruby's test comes out negative and Jenny is positive. What makes Jenny in the end something other than a familiar sympathetic character is her maddening ineffectiveness and passivity. Though she at first feebly refuses barbiturates from a boy at a club, she gives in with little prompting, setting herself up to be victimized once again. Perhaps her failure to confront Telly when she finally finds him makes a kind of tragic if defeatist sense: she is too late as Telly has already made his way inside another girl. But from the moment of her tearful and drugged collapse on the couch, she becomes something other than a tragic heroine defeated by fate. She joins the community of the prone

and unconscious boys and girls strewn around the room and unconsciously passes on the virus to Casper. Of course, she is raped but she
also has become a passive agent of infection.

By contrast, in status trauma movies, the sole or unusual lower-
class character can be fully sympathetic. Such is the case eventually
with Brandon in *Welcome to the Dollhouse*; it is also the case with
Christine, the deaf woman in *In the Company of Men*. She is a truly
decent person, who expresses heartfelt remorse and concern when she
realizes she has led Howard on while falling in love with Chad. When
he takes her away for the weekend and he starts to declare his love for
her, she apologizes, "I've let this go too far. I should have told you
before. I love someone else. I made a mistake...I didn't want you to
feel that [I didn't care for you]...But it was wrong for me to come
here." Her face reveals her real compassion and she goes on to confess
her own frailties and vulnerabilities in explaining her mistake. "It's my
fault...You both should have known about this. When you don't date
for a while, you wonder if you're attractive or interesting. You let
things get out of hand, first chance you get. That's what I did."

Working-class Christine is importantly outside the upper-class corporate community of the demeaned from which Howard and Chad
hail. They are executives in a big firm in a big city; she has a secretar-
ial job in a more humble establishment in a small city that Howard and
Chad consider outside "civilization." She doesn't have their college education or their slick, ironic way of talking. She has not been poisoned
by their dog-eat-dog corporate world, and—according to the familiar
slumming outlook—this is precisely why she can still be a decent, sympathetic person. Not only her small-city experience, but her working-
class status and disability as well have apparently served to lock her out
or protect her from involvement in their brutal world. (At least until
Howard and Chad come along.) The last shot in the movie seems to
drive home the insulation from a degraded world that her deafness can
still provide her. Suddenly we get Christine's point of view of Howard's
loud, aggressive screaming: nothing but a silent, twisted face.

It is Howard's breakdown at Christine's hands that insures this is a
status trauma film (with a certain romanticization of the working
class), in which Chad represents a class and community ethic, rather
than a sort of horror melodrama, in which Chad would simply be an
eccentric, demented monster. For though Christine is outside the
upper-class community of the demeaned at the beginning of the film,
she has certainly been touched by that community, if not fundamentally inducted into it by the end. One can wonder if Christine hasn't

become colder and less trusting as a result of her abuse by Chad and Howard; we only see her shutting out Howard at the end, in justifiable repulsion and self-protection; we don't see her interacting with those in her small-city community. Nonetheless, she is acting in a manner toward Howard at the end that would have been unthinkable for her before the two big-city corporate men entered her life. Previously, in the most painful sequence in the movie, after Chad gleefully admits he seduced her as a game to hurt her then cruelly asks her how she feels and finally leaves, we have seen her break down and collapse into a fetal position.

In short, we see Christine *traumatically humiliated*—and then Howard humiliated as well. She is unmistakably traumatized by her contact with members of the brutal, upper-class community, and then, like Jenny in *Kids*, she participates in passing on trauma (to someone who is by no means innocent, but nonetheless is still capable of being further damaged). This scene of Christine's traumatic humiliation is central to Chad's sadistic plan and central to the movie *In the Company of Men*; scenes of traumatic humiliation are in fact at the heart of all of the movies under discussion here. It is for this reason that I am calling this genre of story a trauma tale. In the more familiar genre of the drama, good and evil confront one other as people struggle with each other and within themselves. In this genre of the trauma, good cannot, or can hardly, struggle with evil because it has been traumatically degraded and paralyzed by evil. Crane's *Maggie* stakes out this territory: Maggie is lavishly rejected (over and over again), and she is rendered speechless before her tormentors, unable to talk back and protect herself verbally.

This sort of traumatic humiliation explains the good, honest, lower-class Christine's inability to fight back against the Machiavellian Chad; it also explains Howard's virtual inability to struggle within himself and deliver a true, heartfelt apology to Christine. Chad has obviously humiliated and demeaned Christine, leading her on to believe that he loved her only to inform her cruelly that he could never love someone like her. More subtly, Howard's internal struggle is also governed by the defeat of goodness by humiliation. His attempt to apologize and express compassion toward Christine is thwarted by his own sense of humiliation. Howard feels demeaned by Christine's rejection of him in favor of Chad and so puts her down to protect his own ego. Just this sort of humiliation likewise seems to explain Jenny's inability to confront Telly when she finally finds him and her crying immediately afterward: she is once again humiliated by coming upon Telly in the act

f having sex with another girl; after all, he had promised Jenny that
e cared for her and then never called her. Without even looking to see
hat it is Jenny who has entered the room, Telly yells, "Shut the fuck-
ng door." She weakly turns away and collapses in tears.

Heroes in dramas often retreat to solitude to gather strength; close-
ups of their faces in such moments suggest their moral or spiritual
apacities, their interior dimensions. In trauma films, by contrast,
characters in solitude or isolation have either been rejected or have
staggered off to hide themselves. In either case, their interiors are filled
with nothing but shame and despair. Jenny retreating to the couch
after being shouted away by Telly; Christine crumbling on the motel
bed after being psychologically savaged by Chad; Howard's twisted,
screaming face seen in the distance of silence by Christine: this is the
traumatic isolation of rejection and defeat. Casper's traumatized final
look and utterance in *Kids* is surreal, as he wakes up naked and alone
after raping Jenny to ask himself, "Jesus Christ, what happened?" He
cannot possibly know that he has perhaps contracted the AIDS virus,
but the film does, and *Kids*, like these other trauma movies, wants to
dramatize traumatization and stigmatization and prefers to end with
a shot of a traumatized face. In *Requiem for a Dream*, all four of the
principal characters are progressively degraded and traumatized, and,
with a self-consciousness approaching the formulaic, the script has all
four end up in fetal positions.

The comedies here also hinge on primal scenes of humiliation—
even if those traumatic scenes are humorous in their exaggerated, fantastical quality. *Clerks* builds to the climactic humiliation of snooty
Caitlin when she accidentally has intercourse with a dead, perverted
old man with a rigor mortis erection and initially considers it the best
sex of her life. She is clinically traumatized and must be carted away
to the hospital. "Shock trauma," the paramedic casually comments in
regard to Caitlin; "She'll need years of therapy." Dawn Wiener's experience in *Welcome to the Dollhouse* is hardly more than a string of
outrageous humiliations; in the climactic one, she is giving a speech to
the entire school about her sister's kidnapping when she is interrupted
by the crowd's chants of "wienerdog." Though ordered by the principal to continue after he quiets the crowd, Dawn can hardly speak.

The comedies naturally tend toward base bodily humiliations. So
Dawn undergoes a shaming that violates the privacy of her body just
as Caitlin in *Clerks* does. When Brandon's tough girlfriend encounters
Dawn in the school bathroom, she forces Dawn to defecate in front of
her. "You came in here to take a shit," the girl menacingly insists when

Dawn tries to excuse herself. She pushes her back into the stall. "I want to see it with my own eyes." The coda to this sequence is a shamed moment of solitude. We see Dawn panting alone at the school fence, in traumatic need of a place to hide temporarily from her tormentors.

Indeed, it might be said that traumatic or shock humiliation is the key interior or personal experience in this genre, replacing the moralistic drama's epiphany of conscience, the romantic comedy's epiphany of love, the horror movie's epiphanies of terror (and resolve), and the slumming genre's epiphany of freedom and self-discovery. In *Happiness*, a woman writer plagued by artistic and personal self-doubt actually rues the fact that she has missed this experience of traumatic humiliation: "If only I'd been raped as a child. Then I would know authenticity." Her recourse in adulthood is to pursue sexually an obscene phone-caller who she obviously hopes will humiliate her now and fill the "void" of trauma that she laments in herself.

Communities of the Degraded

"They're the most fucked up bunch of kids I've ever seen in my life."

—Mike, a cop, in Freeway

These trauma movies not only depict the traumatic humiliation of individuals but also present traumatically humiliated communities— of the upper or lower classes—whole communities of people that have undergone, and continue to undergo, traumas of humiliation. And included in these communities are the films' active victimizers as well as their victims. That sort of community depiction was also part of Crane's agenda in the unprecedented *Maggie*.

Indeed, the bizarre *Gummo* presents a multiply humiliated small-town community and tries, unlike the other class trauma movies, to capture trauma itself in moving pictures (and at times in the degraded production values of the film itself, in the blurriness of voices and images): its inhabitants are not only suffering from the humiliating effects of parental neglect, absent husbands, child abuse, and cancer but also their degradation has been topped off by the visitation of a tornado that has razed buildings and left dead animals laying around. Thus *Gummo* spends time showing the funnel cloud itself.

The action of these movies is the spread of degradation, the circulation of cruel humiliation, much as disease spreads and circulates. These movies should not be mistaken for revenge movies such as *Unforgiven* (Clint Eastwood, 1992) or *Sleepers* (Barry Levinson, 1996). There is payback in these trauma films, but the payback is indiscriminate and the initial injury or injustice to the protagonists is diffuse and often not depicted.

Nor should these trauma films be confused with dramas and comedies that reveal or revel in the destructive pursuit of pleasure or freedom, such as *Fear and Loathing in Las Vegas* (Terry Gilliam, 1998). Nor should these films be classed with films that expose reckless and dangerous greed, such as *Wall Street* (Oliver Stone, 1987).

In short, in the communities imagined in these movies, the cruel encounters between people are governed not so much by a single-minded pursuit of revenge, pleasure, or money as by the desperate need to avoid or discharge shame by humiliating others. The victimizers' seemingly gratuitous indifference or sadism comes out of a desperate quest for respect or status.

As Chad explains to Howard in *In the Company of Men*, the seduction and dumping of a "vulnerable as hell" and "disfigured" woman will "restore a little dignity" to their lives. It will give them some psychic capital to draw on later. "No matter what happens after it: jumped over for promotions, wife runs off with a biochemist, who knows what; we'd always have this to fall back on. [We'd be able to say,] they never got me like we got her. I think it would be refreshing, therapeutic." *American Psycho* (Mary Harron, 2000) ratchets up the desperation of the lead character's quest for status; for Wall Street broker Patrick Bateman, it is not enough to humiliate women and trounce his fellow employees because he can't get a reservation at New York's most chic restaurant or because a colleague's business card outshines his. He resorts to brutal murders with axes and chainsaws. The "gimmick" of the movie, perfectly fitting for the trauma film centered on humiliation, is that he can get away with a killing spree precisely because his colleagues have so little respect for him or barely seem to be aware of him: he is regularly mistaken for one business associate or another, and, when he confesses his multiple murders to his lawyer, the man simply dismisses the idea that Patrick Bateman would be capable of such crimes, not because he's a decent person, but because he's a wimp.

Likewise, Telly's constant pursuit of sex in *Kids* is not ultimately about pleasure. His obsession with deflowering young virgins in *Kids* gives the lie to his claim that "fucking is what I love." To deflower a virgin is to take something away from the girl that cannot be restored. As he says to his friend Casper, "If you deflower a girl, you're the man...no one has the power to do that again." Of course, that power for Telly is one of defilement and pain, since he thinks in terms of "purity" and "skank" and recounts the degradation the girls go through in the act. "That bitch was so clean," he tells Casper after the sexual triumph that initiates the film, "I kept thinking how much I wanted to put it in her ass." As for the pain he causes, he gloats, "I think I saw her bite down on a pillow." Casper makes it clear that Telly's "addiction" is no less than a stab at fame: "It's like getting fame, yeah...fifty years from now all the virgins you fucked" will remember it and tell their grandkids. Telly is more honest and accurate when he explains the stakes of his sexual ventures: "Take that away from me," Telly says of his pursuit of sex, "and I really have nothing."

Money is only part of what motivates the cat-killing boys in *Gummo*, and of course, they use the money to buy glue to obliterate their general psychic discomfort. Their need to whip already dead cats suggests a need to purge themselves of a sense of powerlessness, as does the spontaneous, almost ritual destruction of a chair by a group of young men, which is accompanied by the hoots and cheers of both men and women. One man actually spits on the lifeless chair after its dismemberment.

Clerks concludes with a flat analysis of the clerks' attitude by Randal. He says to Dante: "You work in a convenience store, and badly I might add. We like to make ourselves feel so important and look down on the people who come in here....If we're so advanced what are we doing working here?"

Demeaning others is essential to the characters in these films because they are attempting to function in zero-sum games of esteem—where everybody in the degraded community has a deficit or is threatened with one. Each assertion of individual worth has to come at the expense of another person. Again, Crane's *Maggie* invents this zero-sum dynamic.[2]

This zero-sum game explains the common use of degrading profanity in addressing almost everyone else. It explains *Kids*'s generic male use of the term "bitch" in talking about girls and in talking to boys. Degraded, lower-class white kids in *Gummo* casually use the n-word in referring to blacks. In *Welcome to the Dollhouse*, the zero-sum game explains the torrent of expletives that greet Dawn in the course of her school day, most prominently "lesbo" and "wienerdog." This zero-sum game also explains the video clerk Randal's seemingly gratuitous rudeness to his customers in *Clerks*, which the convenience store clerk Dante begs him to curtail. At one point, he actually goes so far as to spit a mouthful of water on a customer who is merely commenting about the tabloids. Dante is scandalized and so is the audience, but it is in keeping with Randal's consistent though usually figurative spitting on his customers.

The knee-jerk reflex to put others down is constantly operative in Chad's behavior in *In the Company of Men*. A moment of comic relief in the film comes when, in a meeting, Chad studies a booklet of personnel and expresses distaste seemingly for every person pictured: "I hate this guy, that guy too...oh man, I despise that dude...major fucker, a new breed of fuck, a new strain of fucker." After a colleague enters the room, exchanges some friendly words with Chad and then leaves, Chad comments, "I hate that prick." And of course Chad's misogyny is hard to miss. Speaking at the beginning of the movie of Howard's fiancée who has called off the wedding, Chad concludes, "If we were living in India, you could burn that fiancée on a pyre." His antifemale humor is savage: "I don't trust anything that bleeds for a week and doesn't die," he cracks. "What's the difference between a golf ball and a g-spot? I'll spend twenty minutes looking for a golf ball."

The demeaning of relatively innocent victims for one's self-promotion always threatens to become a disturbing spectacle, and so comic trauma films must make the humiliation funny by exaggerating it or detaching it from human agency. *Welcome to the Dollhouse* relies largely on the first strategy; Dawn Wiener's degradation is so universal, extreme, and constant that it is unbelievable. The profane graffiti on her locker continues on up to the ceiling; she is trounced by students, teachers, and parents alike; she goes from one humiliation to another with hardly a respite.

Clerks also indulges in marvels of humiliation, but a central ploy here is to make Caitlin's devastation accidental. If Randal and Dante had purposely set her up to have sex with a dead man in a dark toilet, the audience could hardly find the event funny. However, the accidental nature of her humiliation, necessary to the maintenance of comedy, should not make us conclude that the zero-sum game has broken down. Part of the audience enjoyment of Caitlin's "shock trauma"—its poetic justice—comes from the facts that she is somewhat stuck-up and had not only previously dumped Dante but also, as he learns in the course of the film, had cheated on him and thus humiliated him in front of their entire high school when they were going out. There is cosmic payback involved, if not by Dante then for him, and for Veronica, his current, more down-to-earth, and less economically privileged girlfriend. The element of payback doesn't stop there. Dante is made to feel sick at the beginning of the film when he learns that Veronica has given blowjobs to no less than thirty-six previous lovers. One of them is derogatorily called "Snowball" because he likes to have his own ejaculation spit back in his mouth. "Every time I kiss you, I'm going to taste thirty-six other guys," Dante laments: the film goes out of its way to plant the notion that Dante has been "snowballed" and not with his own ejaculation. Insofar as Dante has been humiliated at the beginning of the film by learning the "truth" of his past kisses with Veronica, Caitlin's realization that her just completed sexual experience was in fact rape by a dead old man comes as Dante's psychic payback against women. Again like Dante, Caitlin too reports feeling sick and nauseous, before she passes into shame shock and is carted away by paramedics.

In such communities of the demeaned, compassion is an invitation to be or feel humiliated and fairness is for suckers. Apology involves too much self-abasement. Compassion, fairness, and apology become untenable; their pure expression is too dangerous, too harmful to the embattled pride, and characters begin acting in discordant or schizophrenic manners. Thus, Howard can't simply apologize to Christine and accept her deserved rejection but must also try to plead his superiority to Chad and insult her at the same time.

This resulting schizophrenia is an opportunity for humor in the comic trauma films. In *Welcome to the Dollhouse*, Brandon's only safe romantic and sexual approach to the outcast Dawn is under the cover of rape. He is truly drawn to her, and his sympathy for her may issue out of his own outsider status as a lower-class kid at a middle-class school, but he cannot admit his emotional need to himself and his attraction to her and his classmates. Thus Brandon comes up with such howlers as "you better get ready because at three o'clock I'm going to rape you" and "same time, same place; you get raped; be there." And Dawn not only shows up to the invitational rape but also asks, "Are you still going to rape me?" when the time is getting late. The audience understands that the knife Brandon holds now and again to Dawn's neck is no physical threat; rather, it is a psychic prophylactic, protecting him against the appearance of—and the humiliation implicit in—sexual interest in Dawn, who is considered ugly and almost universally ostracized for it, and—worse—emotional interest in anyone.

The ethic of a fair fight or "picking on someone one's own size" is lost because the characters who inhabit these demeaned communities feel that they are facing enormous, unfair odds. Though most do not, some of these trauma movies directly discuss the diffuse injury, injustice, and humiliation that the characters feel and wish to revenge themselves upon. *In the Company of Men* is indeed structured like a revenge film and begins with Chad's and Howard's description of the "crime": the unfair rules operating in the corporate workplace. Chad asserts that women are given all the advantages; he complains about new corporate titles being created to accommodate them. Meanwhile, "we [men] can't even crack a joke in the workplace; we need to put our foot down pronto." In addition to the preferences given to women, Chad claims he faces inhuman pressures in the corporate world. "Vultures," he calls his bosses and coworkers. "I get low numbers two weeks in a row, they're ready to feed on my insides." Howard agrees: "It's work, women, getting out of balance." There is no trust in the system or in authorities; as with *Welcome to the Dollhouse*'s parents and teachers, the bosses here are not experienced as fair and just, as authorities to be respected; they are simply humiliators and victimizers with unassailable power.

All of this felt injustice—and the knowledge that the injustice will continue—sets the stage for the Chad's desire to victimize someone weak, "vulnerable as hell," and in fact "disfigured." Because he feels besieged, Chad feels the right and the need to attack whomever he wants. He targets the weakest victim possible because there he will meet the least resistance and thus produce the most injury. The powerful will be defended and hard to get at; they may very well hurt him. The bosses are beyond his reach. Maximum injury is his aim—at no risk to himself. Payback or revenge here is not about justice, or redressing an injustice, it is about creating a victim who can always be remembered as more pathetic than himself, no matter what humiliation he must undergo in the future. *Gummo* likewise is very explicit about the humiliating traumas that beset the small town of Xenia, Ohio, and *Gummo* too stages disturbingly unfair assaults: boys with BB guns hunt down and kill cats.

Though *Kids* doesn't explain the injury or humiliation that the characters have undergone, this film too is based on unequal predator and prey—in fifteen-or-sixteen year old Telly's assault on a girl barely in her teens. The film unmistakably renders Telly's sexual behavior as ultimately brutal. He not only deceives the virgin girls with promises of care but also hurts them physically in the act itself. He promises a painless experience only to ignore their cries of "it hurts" as he thumps away at them in the sexual act.

Kids also portrays a drastically unfair fight. Telly and Casper's entire assembled gang of more than a dozen kids descends on an older black youth who gets into an altercation with Casper. They badly beat the man, Casper finishing him off with a skateboard across the face and Telly by dropping a mouthful of spit on the bloody and unconscious face, much as he spits on the coffee table in the first scene.

Welcome to the Dollhouse also shows the besieged or the weak lashing out at the weaker. The movie opens with a small boy being beaten up and made to call himself a "faggot"; when Dawn tries to extend a helping hand afterward, he rejects her in turn: "Leave me alone, wienerdog." When Dawn gets home, she applies the same terms of abuse to her little sister that the girls in school heap on her. When Missy approaches her, she responds, "Drop dead, lesbo."

In fact, *Welcome to the Dollhouse* highlights a theme that is subtle or implicit in many of these films: the desire by the humiliated to degrade the innocent, especially the innocent young. In *Kids*, there is not only Telly's desire to "fuck" young girls who look and act like children (he comments on a picture of one of his victims painting an Easter egg and on watching another eat watermelon). There is also the inclusion of young boys—perhaps ages ten to twelve or even younger—in drug and sex parties. These boys participate in smoking dope and kissing girls and calling them bitches. Casper specifically contributes to their corruption by asking about their preferences in girls (whether black or white and how old) and asking one if he's ever had a "blowjob." As a comedy, *Welcome to the Dollhouse* can hardly show Dawn's grade-school sister Missy seriously corrupted at Dawn's hands, so the movie has Missy, thanks in part to Dawn, abducted by an adult pervert who doesn't do anything but photograph the girl in her leotard. *Clerks* participates in the theme without sickening the comedy audience by reducing it to absurdity: Randal sells cigarettes to a four-year old (and hapless Dante is tagged with a five-hundred-dollar fine for selling tobacco to a minor). Chad deprives Howard, not exactly of childhood innocence, but of the innocent and childlike conception Howard holds of himself as a decent person. After they have played their game on Christine, Chad pointedly asks his friend (and, not accidentally, uses a childhood-sounding nickname), "So how does it feel, Howie, to really hurt someone?"

Welcome to the Dollhouse also explains this persistent corruption of the innocent more fully than the other films do: the desire by the humiliated to degrade the innocent is based on jealousy, a desire to deprive them of a happiness that is lost to the victimizer. Providing a silly visual and vocal counterpoint to the demeaned community of middle-class teenagers in the suburbs, Dawn's little sister Missy essentially dances through the film *Welcome to the Dollhouse*, a tiny pink-suited ballerina accompanied at times by "The Dance of the Sugarplum Fairies" on the soundtrack. Between cursing her and wishing her ill, Dawn also observes at various times that Missy "has got it so easy" and is "so lucky."

Class Traumas vs. Status Traumas

Class traumas and status traumas are films with opposing outlooks on the poor, and they have different etiologies of the social drift to community degradation. Class trauma movies depict communities degraded by poverty and other social devastations and tend to imply that the degradation spreads out from the lower classes to middle-class individuals, for example, through youth culture. The class trauma film *Gummo* depicts poor families and touches on the social pathologies of lower class rural life. In the urban *Kids*, Telly and Casper have black and Hispanic friends who are not from the white middle class; a group of them are living communally in a tenement apartment. Telly and Casper have presumably learned from them the speech and profane slang (the use of the "n-word" between the two white boys seems to confirm this transfer), the dress (especially the low-riding pants), and the attitudes about sex and violence of inner-city culture.

Kids, which offers little in the way of understanding Telly's general state of humiliation that inspires his brutality (we see his nursing mother who refuses to give him money, but not exactly evidence of poverty or parental misuse), implies by default of any other explanation that the street ethos is simply drifting—as hip subculture—from lower-class kids of color to white kids (and back). Jenny, the white kid among a racially diverse group of girls, is by far the most chaste and modest among them. This is not to say that *Kids* is inaccurate when it shows middle-class white kids aping the talk and dress of inner-city blacks and Hispanics or depicts "ghetto style" spreading to the better neighborhoods; the point is that *Kids* provides little explanation for that aping or that spreading.

Meanwhile, status trauma movies depict degraded upper-class communities and identify the germ of corruption, not in poverty and class humiliation, but in consumer- and corporate-society competition for wealth and popularity. Dawn in *Welcome to the Dollhouse* dreams of popularity among her peers but instead experiences rejection, and *In the Company of Men* begins with a recounting of workplace competition and wrongs.

Welcome to the Dollhouse, which is set primarily in an upper-middle class suburb but includes the lower-class Brandon, seems to directly challenge the class profiling that *Kids* indulges in. We see Brandon's lower-class origins in the slightly degraded condition of his house and the gruff manner of speech and dress of his father. The movie in fact implies that because Brandon is lower class, he alone among his drug-dealing friends is punished by the authorities with suspension from school. Likewise, he alone among his friends is excluded from a popular girl's birthday party, and again the issue seems to be one of class. "How come I wasn't invited?" Brandon asks the birthday girl, and when he proffers a cookie, she responds, "But Brandon, this didn't even cost anything."

Lower-class Brandon's exclusion by some of his peers and his expulsion by the school authorities, then, is based on an ideology or logic that the class trauma movie seems to endorse: namely, that the corruption or ethos of cruelty or humiliation at the center of these films originates with the lower classes and trickles up, infecting the higher classes. The school principal's solution to the drug problem in *Welcome to the Dollhouse* is to exclude Brandon; his middle-class friends are not likewise punished. *Welcome to the Dollhouse* explicitly challenges such class profiling; Brandon complains of his unjustly being blamed for the drug dealing, and he takes Dawn to task when she seems to assume he is guilty. "You're just like everyone else," he exclaims.

Freeway (Matthew Bright, 1996), like *Welcome to the Dollhouse*, seems to reject the notion that the sickness spreads out from the lower class neighborhoods like an infection. In this odd, combination slasher-trauma film, the serial killer Bob's psychotic solution to social problems—to eliminate the "garbage people"—follows the class-profiling logic of the principal's treatment of Brandon in *Welcome to the Dollhouse*. But, as the lower-class "heroine" Vanessa says, Bob is a "hypocrite." Of course, Bob, the upper-middle-class professional, is worse than anything Vanessa has encountered at the social bottom.[3] Though he has no social agenda like Bob, similarly psychotic and upper-class Patrick Bateman from *American Psycho* sometimes targets the socially marginal, seemingly out of a need to assert an absolute distinction from them. In a memorably disturbing sequence, he murders a homeless African American man, after announcing that he has "nothing in common" with him.

Likewise, *Welcome to the Dollhouse* shows Brandon's wealthier peers as more brutal in their degradation and humiliation of others than he is. In a similar vein, socially privileged Chad in *In the Company of Men* humiliates a black intern whose cultural and class origins are pointedly suggested by a use of black English that Chad mocks as well as by Chad's references to affirmative action. In a highly discomfiting scene, Chad gratuitously humiliates the young man by browbeating him into pulling down his pants and proving that he has "the balls" to do the job.

Status trauma movies, meanwhile, like slumming movies, romanticize lower-class individuals—such as the vulnerable, honest Christine in *In the Company of Men* or the sensitive Brandon in *Welcome to the Dollhouse*—and they are seen as more noble in part because they have (as yet) been excluded from this brutal status competition. The traumatizing of these lower-class victims by upper-class victimizers in status trauma movies is uncomfortable and painful. The audience is appalled by the abuse of Christine, and viewers can sympathize with Brandon's running away to New York City to escape the class-profiling, middle-class junior high school world.

Though class trauma movies do not, conversely, romanticize the upper classes, the humiliations in these films can also be disturbing because of the gender vulnerability of the victims. We feel sorry for Jenny in *Kids* because she is a naive, almost innocent girl. Of course, the humiliation of the socially privileged—in either type of trauma film—can also be comic or even gratifying. We do not feel too sorry for Caitlin in *Clerks* or Howard in *In the Company of Men*: in being savaged, they seem to get tastes of their own medicine.

Trauma across Classes: *Being John Malkovich*

Meanwhile, trauma narratives set mainly in higher-class communities need not be lower-class privileging in their outlook: *Being John Malkovich* (Spike Jonze, 1999) is one such movie that seems to explain the drift to social degradation at all class levels in terms of economic and social competition. Thus, the main character, Craig, is an unhappy and humiliated bohemian artist—not a free-spirited bohemian indifferent to economic success and recognition (such as Jack in *Titanic*), and not an honest and decent person. The movie opens with the neglected and despairing puppeteer, Craig, whose humble career playing street corners for change is contrasted with the made-for-television spectaculars of one Derek Mantini, who moves his gigantic multistory puppets with cranes. That is, the film immediately establishes Craig's diminished sense of himself in terms of the celebrity puppeteer he cannot escape because the rival, who is on television, is all but ubiquitous. Because of Mantini's high profile, Craig cannot even console himself with the typical lament of the self-pitying bohemian artist, "Nobody's looking for a puppeteer in today's...economic climate." All Craig can do is turn to the chimpanzee he lives with and remark, much as Dawn in *Welcome to the Dollhouse* says to her kid sister, "You don't how lucky you are being a monkey." Here bohemian or lower-class exclusion is not enough to protect one from the capitalist status struggle: nothing short of literal dehumanization might make one immune to the brutal competition for recognition and acclaim in which most are left wanting.

Craig will be a good deal more demeaned before he hits on the bizarre solution to his status problems, which combines elements of the trauma film and the sci-fi flick. He will be physically demeaned at work: he will be beaten up as a pervert by the irate father of a little girl who watches one of his street-corner shows that involves pelvic thrusting by the puppets. He will join an office community on floor seven and a half, whose low ceilings allow no one to stand erect. He will finally be repeatedly and callously rejected by a woman, Maxine, whom he falls for.

She enjoys humiliating him, making him declare his sexual and romantic interest in her, only to shoot him down. Here is a typical exchange:

> Craig: "I don't know what it is about you."
> Maxine: "My tits."
> Craig: "No, your energy...."
> Maxine: "Are you a fag?"

Eventually, she shames him into saying, "I love your tits, I want to fuck you," only to shoot back at him, "Great, now we're getting somewhere; not a chance." When Maxine eventually rejects Craig for his wife, he retreats in vacant-eyed defeat to his bed, a familiar tableau of traumatic humiliation.

But there is a deus-ex-machina deliverance for Craig. His fortuitous solution to his status washout and sexual-romantic humiliation is to occupy the body—in a sci-fi manner—of film celebrity John Malkovich. As already-famous Malkovich, he can launch an instantly successful career as a puppeteer; he can also win Maxine's Machiavellian heart for his newly revealed ability to play, not just with dolls, but also "with people." The film makes clear that, Craig, like victims of humiliation in other trauma films—such as Dawn in *Welcome to the Dollhouse* and Howard in *In the Company of Men*— is hardly different from the humiliators who make him suffer. Far from evincing a compassion for others that might win audience sympathies, he ends up pulling a gun on his wife, tying her up, and locking her in a cage with the chimp when he finds himself in competition with her for Maxine. He realizes he has become a "monster" but that doesn't stop him from leaving her in the cage and in addition gagging her with tape. Likewise, once Craig finally figures out how to take complete and permanent possession of Malkovich's body and voice, he savages the celebrity as well. When Malkovich feebly struggles for control of himself, Craig tells him, "Shut up, you overrated sack of shit," and later he humiliates Malkovich by making him do his puppet "dance of despair and disillusionment" for Maxine's viewing pleasure.

The film registers not just Craig's desire to leapfrog into fame but also a general desire to occupy the body of a celebrity, if only for the proverbial fifteen minutes. That's how Craig and Maxine start out exploiting Malkovich's status: they sell tickets to Malkovich's "portal," and the reference to Warhol's fifteen minutes of fame is hard to miss. When Maxine informs a potential customer who has come "to be someone else" that he can be Malkovich, the man, on the verge of tears, wants to share his long-suffering sense of degradation and now sudden relief, "It's perfect; my second choice, but it's perfect; I'm a fat man...."

Maxine cuts him off. She isn't interested in relieving the suffering of the demeaned; she's interested in the two hundred dollars. In fact, what gives Maxine power in the world imagined in the movie is that she is not a worshipper of (mid-range) celebrities; she is ignorant of them. She is moved only by her own desires for power and pleasure. She sneers at Craig when he tells her about the metaphysical "portal" he has discovered: "Who the fuck is John Malkovich?" She only becomes interested in Malkovich when she realizes he's a celebrity whom others will pay to get near (or inside); indeed, she eventually plays Malkovich for a sucker just as she takes advantage of his fans. "I'm a great admirer," she tells Malkovich, in the process of her successful attempt to seduce him—and have sex with Craig's wife, Lottie, with Malkovich as male medium.[4]

The Trauma Film and the Horror Film

The trauma film might be said to be a sort of inverted revenge film, in which the stronger tend to take out their "revenge" on the weaker, the guiltier on the more innocent. But the analogy only goes so far because the inversion involved in the trauma film makes its ethos so different: in the trauma film, there is no vindication, no reestablishment of justice, no hero to root for, no deserved punishment, no healing of wounds, and even a more indiscriminant vengeance than the above inversion implies. There is rather the fairly wanton spreading of wounds, of punishment, of injustice, of humiliation—again, much as sickness spreads.

Still, as a first approximation, it can be said that whereas revenge dramas involve an equalizing of the abusively powerful and the initially humiliated, trauma films increase the differentials between the strong and weak. Revenge dramas begin with humiliations and degradations and then restore the wounded characters as they bring down the victimizers; trauma movies tend simply toward extremes of degradation and humiliation.

In effect, the familiar revenge genre closest to the trauma film may be the horror movie. Trauma films could be said to be haunted with images of abject humiliation (such as representations of the physically disfigured and socially untouchable), just as horror/slasher movies are haunted with images of abject terror (such as representations of torture and dismemberment). And like horror movies that are inflected with terrified faces and with terrified screams, trauma films are punctuated with faces of breakdown, with sobbing, angry screaming, vomiting, or catatonic stares.

Like vampire movies and certain other types of horror movies, such as *Invasion of the Body Snatchers* (Don Siegel, 1956), trauma movies are haunted by the threat of infection by corruption. Chad and Howard feel to the audience like carriers of the humiliation germ, taking it outside the big city corporation into small-city office life. AIDS is both an issue and an eerie metaphor for stigmatization in *Kids*, just as the tornado in *Gummo*—directed by *Kids*'s screenwriter Harmony Korine—is both a reality and a symbol of humiliation. Like the AIDS virus itself, the trauma of stigmatization that accompanies AIDS and the trauma of humiliation in general spread in *Kids* to the guilty and innocent alike. Telly's pursuit of virgins, likewise, is focused on a "purity" that is at once physical and psychological. "No diseases, no loose-as-a-goose pussy, no skank," goes his praise of virgins. He of course wants to avoid AIDS, but he is also avoiding the humiliating implication of "looseness" and the demeaning and nonclinical "skank" that Dante must endure in *Clerks* when he discovers that Veronica has so much previous sexual experience.

It is no coincidence that all of these movies picture or discuss the mentally and physically disabled and several of them broach the issue of sex with the disabled. The genre has this peculiarity from the start: Crane's *Maggie*, my "ur-trauma text," involves an outing to see "meek freaks" and their "deformities" (*M*, 26).[5] The physically disfigured have experienced the traumatic humiliation of social stigmatization; meanwhile, the mentally disabled are also stigmatized, but their disability itself can protect them from experiencing the full force of the stigma. *In the Company of Men* is unusual as its plot actually centers on the further humiliation of someone already stigmatized by disability; Chad explicitly intends to prey upon a woman to whom, because of her disability, "a full healthy sexual life…is lost…forever." The motif of sex with the disabled or disfigured, though, is actually commonplace in these films. In *Kids*, we hear about a cousin of Telly's who has "a thing for handicapped girls"; "he went into the handicapped bathroom and fucked her….The leg braces were scratching him…" Tumler and Solomon in *Gummo* both pay to have sex with a mentally retarded girl, and an unnamed young man attempts to initiate sex with a male midget who rejects him.

Disability is also fairly important In *Welcome to the Dollhouse*; there, both of Dawn's romantic relationships are weirdly mediated by derogatory use of the word "retard." One of Dawn's few joys in life is her "special people" club and the attendant clubhouse. The high-school rocker whom Dawn idolizes and who for most of the movie does not at least join in her abuse, finally rejects her invitation to join her club and insults her by informing her that "special people" means "retarded"; "Your club is for retards," he cruelly tells her. Meanwhile, Brandon's brother is actually mentally "retarded," and his "retardation" has much to do with the attraction that Brandon develops to Dawn, an attraction that alone contradicts the otherwise universal rejection that Dawn receives from her schoolmates for her being "ugly." Brandon too does nothing but insult and terrorize Dawn until at one point she shoots back that Brandon is a "retard." From that moment begins Brandon's interest in Dawn; she has touched a nerve. Her insult has hit home: in the comic trauma film, effective insult and the resulting injury does not only sever bonds; it can create them. Dawn has pierced Brandon's defensive armor, reaching an open family wound by a fortuitous accident. Indeed, Brandon touchingly confesses to Dawn on their first uninterrupted "rape" rendezvous in a vacant lot that his brother is "retarded," then reflexively—and comically—covers up his familial vulnerability a bit by adding, "He's a tough kid; he could beat you up if he wanted." (We finally get a glimpse of Brandon's brother at the end of the movie; he offers Dawn a piece of his donut with an innocent generosity that sets him apart from the mentally "normal" in the film.) But the very discussion of mental disability opens up an almost sacred space in this trauma film: in this sequence in the abandoned lot (a locale of abjection, not accidentally), Brandon and Dawn share a nonironic, intimate moment. Their exchange is moving and the audience sympathizes with them: this is the stuff of a slumming drama or, indeed, any other romantic drama.

The mentally disabled actually occupy a unique place in the trauma film: they are utterly stigmatized and often treated in degrading ways, but, because they are presented as unaware of this treatment and, thus, have no reason to be hostile and feared (Brandon's brother wouldn't *want* to beat up Dawn), they can stand magically outside the community of the demeaned. They either cannot be traumatically humiliated or are very resistant to such humiliation. Thus, the girl in *Gummo* who is being pimped out by her father or brother, and whose face has been made up in bright, streetwalker colors, doesn't seem to understand the nature of the transaction into which she has been impressed. She treats her tricks with gentle and ingenuous affection, asking them, "Do you love me?"—and because of her unique status and behavior in fact elicits some tenderness from the cat-torturing Solomon.

Nonetheless, this scene of coerced prostitution is hardly, of course, a tender one. The pathos of the innocent young girl's degradation is extreme here; to add insult to injury her father or brother watches her prostituted sex from a window above the door. The larger point here is that trauma movies tend to be littered with talk, images, or tools of the disabled because they are haunted by extreme images of the humiliated, stigmatized, and rejected just as horror/slasher movies are littered with the symbols and apparatuses of pain and death, such as human bones, graveyards, ghouls, razors, knives, and chainsaws.

In *Kids*, then—seemingly gratuitously but with purpose—Telly and Casper encounter a man with no legs, who cruises through a subway car on a skateboard singing, "I have no legs." Likewise, *Being John Malkovich*'s trauma film pedigree is manifest in its several apparently arbitrary—but generically routine—visual and verbal references to mental and physical disability. The degrading floor seven and a half was originally designed, legend has it, to make comfortable a woman of "miniature" stature, whom we see in an orientation film for the job

Craig takes. When Malkovich at one point enters his own portal and encounters a world populated by male and female clones of himself, we glimpse a couple of Malkovich-faced midgets. Malkovich is portraying a hunchback (presumably Richard II) in one of his rehearsals. And, finally, a fan congratulates Malkovich for his rendition of "a retard" (apparently his portrayal of Lenny in the film version of *Of Mice and Men* [Gary Sinise, 1992]).

Gummo, seemingly incoherent at first, is actually governed by a logic of abjection. The film is little more than a string of grotesque if sometimes comical images of rejected things and objects: A half-naked boy in pink bunny ears is on a highway overpass, alternately sitting alone in shivering dejection and pissing and spitting through the fence on the traffic below. Solomon bathes in dirty brown water while eating spaghetti and a chocolate bar (which he must fish out of the bathwater when he drops it), his hair in a white lather. Another mentally disabled girl shaves off her eyebrows. A black midget rejects a homosexual man's advances, the homosexual man meanwhile whines about his rejection by his parents and his loveless state, and finally pours beer over his own head in miserable self-denigration. A little boy tries to adjust a picture hanging askew only to reveal a colony of bugs while older kids get high on glue on a nearby dilapidated couch. Rain-soaked boys whip dead, hanging cats. A boy and girl pet each other in a junked car with a broken windshield, a burning garbage can visible though it; the boy stops when he feels a cancerous lump in the girl's breast. Most of these are images of the socially rejected rejecting something else (the stigmatized black midget rejecting the whining homosexual, the abandoned boy pissing on the traffic, the mentally disabled girl getting rid of her eyebrows, a boy in a junkyard rejecting a tumorous breast) or at least of a superabundance of rejected objects and beings. *Gummo*, of course, is a sensationalist film, and perhaps most of all it inspires repulsion and even nausea.

Like horror films that represent as well as inspire terror, these films represent as well as inspire nausea. In these movies, nausea is a physical manifestation of humiliation, but it marks a state of humiliation short of trauma. Dante and, of course, Caitlin each feel sick over their sexual debasement in *Clerks*; in the end, Dante regains his composure and Caitlin passes into shock. Howard is vomiting over his degradation near the end of *In the Company of Men* before his final rejection by Christine that seems to leave him absolutely broken. In fact, these trauma movies in general might also be thought of—in comparison with horror movies—as repulsion or nausea films.

A Spiritual Autopsy of Stephen Crane

Not a Slumming Drama

Stephen Crane is often credited with inventing the modern myth of the bohemian writer, or, to look at it a bit differently, Crane has been integrated into the mythology of the slumming drama: he lived fast and furiously, spurned the middle class, associated with the poor and lowlifes, and died young. But instead of Crane's famous, romantic, masculine adventure seeking—supposedly in revolt against a feminized, middle-class Victorian culture—the shame theorist would find a host of psychological symptoms and defenses generated by an identity formed in the shame of parental neglect: an anxiety near panic, paranoia, and thus a need for terribly exciting distraction (such as the battlefield allows); delusions of grandeur, a drive for fame, and a world seen through the lens of shame or self-esteem; claustrophobia, alienation, and misogyny; anger, self-hatred, and thus a self-punishing stoicism.

Crane was the last of fourteen children; his father died when he was young, and his mother was often away from home. As a child, he was already spinning tales of her neglect; he would later create monstrous maternal figures in his writing. He craved notoriety among the class he was ostensibly rejecting, but the achievement of dramatic fame with *The Red Badge of Courage* (1895) put him in a public eye he found threatening. Nor was his alienation resolved by his cohabitation with an unconventional, bohemian woman (the former madam of a brothel), partly because she thrived on social gatherings. This relationship allowed Crane to relive his childhood sense of neglect, and he eventually fled it for the Spanish-American war. Despite Crane's reputation as the ultimate bohemian adventurer who died young from taking too many risks, it was after his return to domesticity that his health precipitously declined. And he died, not in the slums, on the battlefield, or out West, but in a fashionable sanitarium.

The bohemian or slumming myth of his very active life and his death from tuberculosis at twenty-eight has been constructed in a number of slightly different ways. In one version he was a reckless bohemian spirit, and his recklessness eventually caught up with him. He left behind all secure sanctuaries; he left his family, college, his religion, the middle class, his country. His fierce adventuring took him into war zones and other dangerous climes—the slums, Mexico, and Cuba. His biographer, R. W. Stallman, tells us that "reckless Crane paraded up and down in his white raincoat" while Spanish riflemen fired at him (*SCAB*, 393)[2] and that he came down with a fever in Cuba that he never fully shook; in one of these wild places he came in contact with the tuberculosis bacteria. In another version of Crane's end, he was world weary and ready to die—a more recent biographer, Christopher Benfey goes so far as to say that "he seemed to plan his death."[3] Having sucked out the marrow of experience with a frenzied hunger, Crane exhausted what life had to offer him and became indifferent to everything. In a third version he was simply a bright light that burned intensely for a short time and then went out.

But in all of these tales of Crane's bohemian life and death there is the idea that he went too far or too fast—and one is left with a mixed feeling. He was the lone, heroic rebel who breathlessly threw off the constraints of a repressed society and pursued life in its rawest incarnations; but alas, it is these constraints that protect us from terrible diseases and premature deaths. "Compared with the extremist Crane," Richard Chase writes, "Hemingway is a prudent, peace-loving citizen."[4] We are awed by Crane, but we do not envy him; we live well past our twenty-ninth year, and we do so through moderation. "Crane...established the modern legend in this country of the literary bohemian," Chase tells us[5]—and part of this legend is of course the mortal danger of such rebellion.

The problem with these at once thrilling and self-satisfying stories of Crane's demise is that they leave out the death itself. Of course it is well known that Stephen Crane died of tuberculosis, but this is hardly a full explanation; not everyone who contracted tuberculosis in the late nineteenth century died of it—or died so quickly. Some recovered. Crane first collapsed, not in a tenement or a tent or in isolation, but in his English manor after a perhaps lavish, but hardly dangerous, party. And, again, he died in a sanitarium in the mountains of Germany a few days after arriving for something called the "Nordrach treatment," which involved chaise lounges, cod-liver oil, and mountain air.[6] He was accompanied in both cases by the woman he referred to as his wife, Cora Taylor, who had in fact engineered both the party and the treatment. Crane may have lived a short, happy life of solitary, antisocial adventure; he may have been, just the year before, so hard to track down that Cora had to employ the American Secretary of War to locate him in Havana, but he died in the busy arms of his wife, pursued by creditors, reported on by newspapermen, and about to receive the latest medical treatment for tuberculosis.

Thus, it is possible to argue—against the bohemian and slumming myths—that it was hardly immoderation that brought Crane down: the opposite might be closer to the truth. Perhaps the woman he lived with was not legally his wife, perhaps she was a former nightclub owner and not a debutante, perhaps his manor was in England and not the United States, perhaps he attempted to pay off his debts by writing and not by working in a brokerage firm. Still, the last year of his life resembled in its outline the sort of existence he had originally tried to escape at top speed. The man who wrote a few years earlier the uncanny note, "I cannot help vanishing and disappearing and dissolving. It is my foremost trait" (SCAB, 421), was in fact at the end of his life a sitting duck. That foremost trait was nowhere in evidence, except in his disease itself. One might perversely suggest that when Crane abdicated his own compulsion to vanish, the tuberculosis took over the job. Crane's death would not then represent the revenge of nature upon a wild soul who has gone outside of all social bounds. His death would be the revenge of a troubled soul upon a successful man who has forced upon himself social bounds he was deeply uncomfortable with. His death would come about because he attempted to ignore his extreme discomfort and bind himself to a domestic existence.

The lesson we have taken away is comforting: if only Crane had been less the bohemian and more like the average man in the street, he would have lived to a ripe old age, produced a larger oeuvre informed by his characteristic vision, and died in a hospital bed. The lesson we might actually take away is less comfortable: Crane's bohemianism and slumming were strategies for dealing with his psychic unrest—his shame—and either he abandoned those strategies to his peril, or the strategies stopped working for him. He either stopped listening to the impulses that told him to flee and settled for certain bohemian trappings and a wife who was not someone he could develop an intimacy with. Or else he could no longer stand to be so solitary, but he despaired, in late nineteenth-century America, of finding the soul mate he longed for, and so he committed himself to a marriage and a married life he likewise could not bear.

It is possible to detect in Crane's life interconnected patterns of illness and emotional conflict. There is a clear disease pattern, in which sickness again and again followed upon his captivity in or a return to the domestic. Crane was torn between, on the one hand, a desire for solitude and excitement that led him away from his family, his admirers, and later his wife, and took him to places like the slums and the battlefield, and, on the other hand, a countervailing fear of absolute alienation and of consequent madness and also an ethic of duty that led him to return to his domestic life. Crane's home life with Cora, thus, involved an intense claustrophobia with her (and the crowd she brought to their home), a suspicion of her intentions, and a despair for the future that apparently led to the acceleration of his illnesses.[7]

Slumming Trauma Poetry and Class Trauma Novels

Crane left no journals or memoirs, but his poetry is revealing about his inner experience. His first book of poems, *The Black Riders* (1895), though greeted mostly with bafflement at the time of their publication, and still today,[8] can be read as chronicles of Crane's inner struggle, of a personal conflict he experienced between the demands of others and his own impulses or intimations. Unlike his novels, which open up the class trauma genre, Crane's poems are often in a slumming mode, though still traumatic and not sentimental. That is to say, his poems assert a mystical individuality associated with deprivation and do so in a manner that does not shy away from defilement and self-destruction. There is his well-known poem about a self-cannibalizing "creature, naked, bestial" "in the desert" who "held his heart in his hands, / And ate of it." When asked, "Is it good, friend?" this creature oddly replies,

> "It is bitter—bitter," he answered.
> "But I like it
> "Because it is bitter,
> "And because it is my heart." (Poem 3)[9]

Other poems are set in the mystical desert of solitude:

> I walked in a desert.
> And I cried,

"Ah, God, take me from this place!"
A voice said, "It is no desert."
I cried, "Well, but—
"The sand, the heat, the vacant horizon."
A voice said, "It is no desert." (Poem 42; 1314)

Crane imagines the conflict between his social obligations and his radical individuality as that between two warring gods: "The god of many men" and "the god of his inner thoughts," the first hostile and "fat with rage," the second sympathetic and "lit with infinite comprehension" (Poem 51; 1317). The poems record a spiritual battle between faith and fear. At times Crane trusts his inner god, no matter if the only nourishment he can offer himself to eat is his own bitter heart (Poem 3; 1299), no matter if everything inside of him other men call "sin" (Poem 33; 1310), no matter if other men call him "a toad" (Poem 47; 1315), no matter if his "new road" leads him "into direful thickets" where he will eventually die "alone" (Poem 17; 1304). At times like these he says to the "Blustering God" of many men, "I fear you not": "there is one whom I fear; / I fear to see grief upon that face"; "Ah, sooner would I die / Than see tears in those eyes of my soul" (Poem 53; 1318). At other times, he doubts himself. His path seems to him "a desert" (though the voice of his inner god tells him "It is no desert") (Poem 42; 1314). The "great light" that allows him to see "the wishes of [his] heart" is too much for him, and he prays to be in "the darkness again" (Poem 44; 1314). Or, again, he "hesitated" to follow "in the far sky...a radiance / Ineffable, divine" because "sometimes it was not" there; he loses the "vision" and, "in despair," asks the "thousand voices" of society for guidance (Poem 49; 1316). In *The Black Riders*, although the conflict is always there, always wrenching, one has the feeling that Crane's inner god is winning out: he is sticking to the lonely, solitary path his "soul" is setting out for him, though it is often hard even to see.

But Crane's "god of his inner thoughts" would not carry the day. After *The Black Riders* it would be given little medium. There was a reason Crane stopped listening to his inner demands for solitude and disappearance and self-revelation, and that was because he began to attend to other demands upon him, social demands for service and sacrifice and for an art that celebrated them. These demands became more personal and compelling when he met great success as a war writer; the "thousand voices" of other men became voices of praise, and they were harder to resist. As he wrote to one admirer: "You delight me with your appreciation and yet it makes me afraid. I did not bend under the three hills of ridicule which were once upon my shoulders but I dont know that I am strong enough to withstand the kind things that are now sometimes said to me" (*SCAB*, 194). He apparently was not. His fame proved irresistible; it swallowed him up. "I am engaged in rowing with people who wish me to write more war-stories. Hang all war-stories," he wrote to his love, Nellie Crouse, in 1896[10]—and then went on to write dozens more.

All of Crane's prose heroes are men who make sacrifices for others, certainly out of vital compulsion and not hollow form, but sacrifices nonetheless. There is Henry Fleming in *The Red Badge*, whose anger drives him on to risk his life and become a heroic soldier; Dr. Trescott in *The Monster* (1899), who, despite the ostracism of his town, is compelled by unspeakable gratitude to stand by the mutilated man who has saved his son; and Timothy Lean, in that chilling late story "The Upturned Face" (1900), who insists on burying his fallen comrade while under enemy fire. These are men who stand and do not run—regardless of loss of reputation and love, or threat of death.

Crane looked for situations like these all his life, both in his writing and in his experience. He stuck it out in the Bowery, through poverty and misery, to be a real writer. He once testified for a prostitute despite the warnings of the police and friends and was all but hounded out of New York for it. He tried to enlist in the Spanish-American War but was rejected as physically unfit; he ended up covering it as a war correspondent.

At the same time, Crane was a man relentlessly on the run. He often felt cornered, and his self-proclaimed vanishing is evident throughout his life. He left his family home in New Jersey to frequent the Bowery. He quit college one day and moved to the Lower East Side of New York. He left New York and went out West and to Mexico. He returned to New York City but soon dashed off to his brother's place in Hartwood to escape the attention of his new fame. He went south to Florida (where he met Cora), attempting to get to the Cuban war. He was shipwrecked and never made it, so he went off with Cora to Greece and the Greco-Turkish war. Then he went to England with her when the war was over, and then back to Cuba without her. All of this happened in a decade.

Crane sought out situations that could satisfy at once his compulsion to disappear and his need to serve. The Spanish-American War was perfect: after a year in England with his wife he was anxious to get out and deliriously excited to get to Cuba. (Joseph Conrad noted that "nothing could have held him back. He was ready to swim the ocean.") The received idea on Crane's involvement in the war is that it was a mortal folly: he probably already had tuberculosis; in any case, the reckless trip to the tropics bought him a fever that fatally weakened his health. Stallman argues that "his going to the war in Cuba was the beginning of the end" (*SCAB*, 348). It seems the exact opposite might be true: his leaving Cuba was the beginning of the end. His much-discussed Cuban fever came on more than two months into his war reporting—it came on, in fact, when all signs pointed to the war's finish and his obligation to return home. Again, Crane's disease pattern is fairly unmistakable: when the excitement stopped, when the promise of action and movement ended, when he was faced with captivity in the mundane, the civilized, and the domestic, he got ill or his disease accelerated.[11]

Indeed, Crane was practically a casualty of the winding down of hostilities in early July 1898. It was during negotiations for a cease-fire and surrender that he "caught a fever," as he put it (*SCAB*, 402). The same thing had happened at the *end* of the Greco-Turkish war; only the physical symptoms were different. A few days after the armistice, Crane was in Athens; it was then and there that he got dysentery, one evening when he was supposed to go to a dinner party—not on the battlefield in the thick of the war (*SCAB*, 294).[12] By the time of the Cuban ailment, it seems, Crane knew his patterns of illness well enough to make a spiritual diagnosis: he said that his sickness began with "a languorous indifference to everything in the world" (*SCAB*, 404).

Luckily for Crane, the Spanish-American War resumed in a Puerto Rican campaign, and he joined in again; his illness apparently subsided enough for him to miss nothing of the final phase of the conflict. And he seemed to have learned something from his bout with depression and fever on the eve of the cease-fire. When the war ended for good the next month, he had apparently worked something out in his own mind: he was preparing to disappear. He cabled his wife from Key West, then slipped into Havana illegally, posing as a tobacco buyer.

Crane stayed on in Havana for months after the war with no further word to his wife or family; in addition to dispatches, he wrote a set of love poems called *Intrigues* that expressed doubt about Cora and expressed love for a former lover. "The three months he spent in Havana...was one of the happiest periods of his life," says Stallman (*SCAB*, 425). Crane called a book of poems he worked on in Havana, *War Is Kind* (1899), and though the title was sardonic, there was a deeper truth to it: war was certainly a tonic for him. Above the action and the danger, above the inspiring displays of courage, war gave him a lot of freedom—irreproachable freedom—and it gave him communion with people somewhat like himself.

But Cora hunted Crane down with the help of the Secretary of War: another liability of his fame was the attention he attracted, among even the highest powers. There were already nasty rumors flying around that he had abandoned Cora (*SCAB*, 416). Once he was located, he delayed and dallied, stopped off in New York, and apparently debated with himself about whether to go back, but he eventually returned to his wife and home in England—where his health would fatally deteriorate.

Though he stopped breathing six months later, Crane first collapsed with a lung hemorrhage at a party celebrating the New Year, 1900. One might take some poetic license and imagine the mental darkness that could have overcome Crane at that Christmas-New Year's Party at his home with Cora, Brede Manor, in late December 1899. Crane had always hated crowds and mobs, both friendly and unfriendly. In college he had pulled a revolver on a group of fraternity boys who broke down his door in a prank. He had shown up at the New York courthouse pale and trembling to testify for a prostitute named Dora Clark who was arrested in his company (he was ostensibly talking to her for his research). He had hated the party that the Society of the Philistines had thrown for him to toast his book of poems *The Black Riders*, and in the end he fled New York entirely and hid out at his brother's house to avoid the adoration that it and *The Red Badge* were bringing him. Crane had already felt poorly in Brede in September 1899—he had an abscess in his rectum—and he made a connection, though perhaps unconsciously, between his health and the crowd of guests at the Manor: "The clockwork is juggling badly," he wrote to George Wyndham; "I have had a lot of idiotic company all summer" (*SCAB*, 493).

And here he was again besieged in his own home by lots of friends and hangers-on—on the verge of a new century that promised nothing but more of the same. He was mired in debt. Here he was facing an endless expanse—of obligation to his wife, of writing for hire to support the expenses of the manor, of being surrounded by others. There was no war to run to. Where else could he find that rare combination of freedom and community? He might have felt as though he had run out of escape hatches. What could pose a more intimidating expanse of time than the advent of a new century? For Crane, entering this century must have been like entering a dark tunnel without light at the end. The weight of a century of crowds and service, a hundred years of claustrophobia, must have fallen on him all at once. This time Crane did not flee; he stood fast. Still he panicked—not outwardly; but his being, which loved freedom and disappearance, went into panic. Crane's tubercular body—long the battlefield of his inner struggle—had already laid the groundwork for a crisis. He had a hemorrhage in his lung and collapsed.

In the name of chivalric duty, in the name of human goodness, Crane gathered around himself conditions that he hated: crowds, immobility, accountability. In fact, Crane had inklings—and perhaps more than inklings—of the "honorable" demise he had set up for himself. During his last months, after his New Year's collapse, Crane wrote a troubling autobiographical tale called "The Squire's Madness," in which the squire and his wife, after ten years of "incomprehensible wandering," settle down in a Hall called "Oldrestham," a place that rings of weariness. The squire begins a poem about a woman who has poisoned her lover: "The garlands of her hair are snakes / Black and bitter are her hating eyes / A cry the windy death-hall wakes / O, love, deliver us. / The flung cup rolls to her sandal's tip / His arm—" But the squire cannot continue the poem and describe "a writhing lover...dying at the feet of the woman." The squire's wife, meanwhile, begins to insist that the poet is ill, though he asserts he is fine; he begins to wonder if he is mad. Just as the squire cannot finish the poem, he cannot countenance its unconscious insight and accuse his own wife: "Did this thing of the poisoned cup...—and her eyes, her hating eyes, mean that his—no, it could not be." (It was Cora who had insisted on the expensive manor in England, she who was constantly inviting guests there, she who then failed to respect or recognize Crane's need for solitude and who pushed him into debt, causing the need to churn out his writing like a machine.[13]) But in the end, it turns out that she is mad—the squire-poet is not ill.[14]

Crane's Personal Trauma Myth

Many commentators have looked behind the romantic bohemian or slumming myth and commented on Crane's psychological compulsions. John Berryman finds "the ghastly reign in his work of...the Emotion Fear" (*SC*, 297–98).[15] Chase senses in Crane an "almost mystical attraction to war and extreme individual terror."[16] Mark Van

Doren suggested that the compliment to be paid to Crane "will take the form of an analysis of his need to live, at least as an artist, in the midst of all but unbearable excitement" (*SC*, 297–98). Michael Fried detects in Crane's compulsive repetition of images of disfigurement a repressed "fear of writing."[17] It is also hard not to notice that Crane lives out with Cora, to use Nina Baym's phrase, "a melodrama of beset manhood."[18] An analysis of Crane has perhaps to synthesize these observations and to understand how these various compulsions are connected.

The general action of Crane's stories and novels might be described as a zero-sum game for admiration or self-esteem: characters engage in a continual struggle for self-promotion.[19] The little theatrical contests between Crane's characters are often comic. But what is even more striking, in this context, is that Crane's famous irony on this subject often turns to something gruesome. Of his four acclaimed longer works, two—*Maggie* and *The Monster*[20]—are trauma tales, in which a weaker character is stigmatized and discarded, or nearly discarded, and three—*Maggie*, *The Monster*, and *The Red Badge*—confront the terrifying prospect of universal rejection. The new recruit Henry Fleming contemplates the intolerable nature of being rejected by his peers as one of the unfit and spends a day in terror of the possibility of being "thrust out" from "all the vast lands"[21]—but only a day. The other two short novels—his first and last artistically acclaimed novels—are at their heart trauma tales of ostracism. Maggie Johnson will experience systematic rejection—by her family, her lover, a priest, and later, as a prostitute, her potential clients—to the point where she is suicidal and ready for nonceremonial, anticlimactic, offstage slaughter. Henry Johnson (no relation to Maggie Johnson, except in Crane's mind), who starts out black, and thus a species of social outcast, will become, as a result of a fire, a faceless, mindless monster whom the community would gladly banish, or even kill. In *The Monster*, then, Crane also stakes out as central themes the motifs of disfigurement and mental disability, which are staples of today's trauma films. From the beginning to the end of his career, Crane's oeuvre is haunted by the specter of traumatic ostracism of the weak.

Now, Johnson is a name that Crane used in the pseudonym he fashioned for the first publication of *Maggie*, and it was an apt name as he was the son of a Jonathan; so one might be on the lookout to understand the relationships these characters named Johnson have to Crane; Berryman has called them "Crane masks" (*SC*, 193). What links these characters, though, beyond their names, are their self-sacrificial kindness and the adversary that eventually destroys them. First of all, both Maggie Johnson and Henry Johnson start out as creatures that are kind to children. Maggie is an exception in her brutal slum world. Maggie, as a child, tries to protect her little brothers, Jimmie and Tommie, from their abusive mother, and Henry is mutilated trying to save a child, also named Jimmie, from a fire. Secondly, Maggie's mother later all but destroys her by putting her out of the house and damning her in front of the entire community; meanwhile, the fire that all but kills Henry, and leaves him disfigured and mad, is twice described as a "lady" (*TM*, 338). This is peculiar. The stories, on their faces, are hardly comparable—one is ostensibly about a girl of the slums, the other about a doctor in the suburbs—but they figure this same mythic kernel.

In *Maggie*, this myth Crane is fashioning, consciously or unconsciously, is hardly disguised. As Berryman has noticed, the Johnson family is, in many respects, the Crane family transposed to the slums (*SC*, 310). As in Crane's family, the mother is dominant, the father dies when some of the children are quite young (Crane was nine when his father died), and, most blatantly autobiographical, the mother's first name is Mary (as was Crane's mother's). In the novel, the mother abuses the children and, later, viciously banishes the vulnerable child, driving her toward suicidal feelings and essentially sending her to her death. Meanwhile, of the two brothers, the younger one dies very young, and the older becomes "a young man of leather" (*M*, 13). One of the most striking things about this novel on first reading is the depiction of a family all but devoid of affection. The plot outline of *Maggie*—the fall of a slum girl and her death—was indeed a familiar tale in literature, but the demonic role of the mother in the story is a Crane innovation. Given the potential impact on his family, it is hard to imagine that Crane could have given this monstrous woman his mother's name. But he had left the Crane home in New Jersey, dropped out of college, and moved to the Bowery—*and*, perhaps most importantly, his mother had just died.

The Monster rehearses the same myth, but with greater compression and symbolism—and perhaps less awareness on Crane's part. The demonic mother is gone and has been replaced by a terrible fire, flames that are referred to as "a fairy lady" and "a sapphire lady." The fire does much the same work on the black man, Henry, as Mary Johnson does on her daughter. It is the "fairy lady [who] with a quiet smile…blocked his path and doomed him and Jimmie," and then catches him with her "talons" and knocks him down (*TM*, 338–39). Jimmie is saved, but Henry is left disfigured and insane; he, like Maggie, ends up despised and untouchable, as well as mentally broken.

Berryman has thoroughly and creatively elucidated these two novels in terms of Crane's recurring fantasy of rescuing the desired and hated mother, a Freudian complex (called "love for a harlot") that was manifested in Crane's life as well as his work: namely, in his attempts to rescue a prostitute named Dora Clark, for whom he testified, and the nightclub owner, Cora Taylor, whom he married (*SC*, 298–99). Berryman connects this complex to the conception of *Maggie* immediately upon Mrs. Crane's death: "It gave him a chance for rescue, he could show Maggie the way out." Likewise, Berryman associates the writing of *The Monster* with Crane's settling in England with Cora: he was rescuing her, and he imagined he would be punished with scandal and further accusations of madness for doing so (*SC*, 304, 192–96).

Though Berryman's account explains Crane's choice of a love object, it does not explain why his works are haunted by the terror of ostracism. Berryman rightly points out that, again and again in *The Monster*, rescue is punished. Interestingly, here, the central punishments are the same: out and out ostracism. In addition to Johnson, there is the father of the boy, Dr. Trescott, whose subsequent protection of the mangled Johnson leads to the town's ostracism of the entire family. The last image of the story is of a table still set for the weekly tea party of fifteen guests at the Trescott home, to which only one woman came.

Furthermore, the rescues that Crane enacts in these stories are not *of* the mother, but *from* the mother. It is the boy child, in both cases named Jimmie, who is being rescued—and then, later in the latter story, it is the monster. Now, it seems reasonable that both of the Jimmies were (more or less unconsciously) versions of Crane himself as a child. They are, of course, little boys. Jimmie of the slum novel is not saved from his mother by Maggie, his childhood protector, and he becomes "hardened at an early age": "a young man of leather...[who] never conceived a respect for the world, because he had begun with no idols that it had smashed....[and who] clad his soul in armor" (*M*, 13). All of this fits well with what we know about Crane as a young man (raised by an older sister) and beyond. When Crane wrote this frightening and unprecedented miniature psychological portrait of the hatching of a Bowery tough in chapter four of *Maggie*, he was not borrowing from the slum reporting of his day, and he did not need to; he was certainly drawing on his own experience in suburban New Jersey. As for the other Jimmie—in *The Monster*—he too can be connected to Crane as a boy. He has a father who in the first sequence of the novel reminds us of Crane's father, the Reverend Jonathan

Townley Crane: Dr. Trescott is—oddly enough—"shaving this lawn as if it were a priest's chin" (*TM*, 324).

The implication makes sense; in his stories and his actions of rescue, the person Crane wants to rescue is himself. He wishes, it seems, in the perhaps unconscious language of his myth, to rescue the boy before he is scarred and hardened and embittered—traumatically shamed. The portrait of Jimmie in *The Monster* is of an infinitely sensitive and vulnerable little boy. In the opening chapter, he is guilty and wretched for destroying a flower, and a mild scolding from his father makes him feel "disgraced" and "gory from unspeakable deeds." Even more telling, he considers his father "the moon" and himself "the victim of an eclipse"—this is an image of being cast out from the light, rejected by the heavens. Jimmie voluntarily removes himself from his father's heavenly presence, out of a "desire to efface himself" (*TM*, 326, 325). The language here is apt: Jimmie effaces himself, and Henry, after the fire, will be described several times as having "no face" (*TM*, 344). (The father's rejection is a pale reflection of the violence that the female can deliver up, just as the moon is a wan reflection of the sun. In Crane's personal if unconscious *mythology* here, the conventional heavenly polarity is reversed; the father is the moon, the female is fire.) Henry's literal loss of face echoes Jimmie's figurative one and suggests that Henry's actual facelessness is a figuration of shame.

What is the obscure crime for which these characters—Maggie, Jimmie Trescott, Henry Johnson, Dr. Trescott—are being punished? Indeed, there are no real crimes to speak of, there are merely sins of self-assertion in the interest only of gaining attention and receiving love. Maggie is guilty of dressing up and going off with the young tough Pete, the first person who has shown interest in her. Jimmy Trescott is guilty of playing train engine with his cart and accidentally destroying a flower (the full significance of this event that opens the novel—and Crane's personal myth—is not yet clear). Henry Johnson is, like Maggie, guilty of dressing up and, in addition, strutting through town doing a cakewalk. Dr. Trescott is guilty of showing off his medical skill by saving Henry's life. Moreover: in all cases, the characters' goodness is overlooked. Maggie is the only person in the novel to show genuine affection; her mother fails to recognize her kindness and damns her as a harlot, a woman gone to the devil. What Dr. Trescott does not know when he reprimands his boy is that Jimmie has just attempted to "resuscitate" the flower with no success; nor does the father applaud or at least acknowledge Jimmie for confessing his mistake (*TM*, 324–25). Henry Johnson is initially lauded for his heroism in the fire, but, once his wounded condition is made clear, his deed is forgotten and he is despised. Finally, Dr. Trescott's act of loyalty to his groom and the savior of his boy is greeted with hatred by the townspeople.

The shame theorist might propose, then, that this repeating story is for Crane a myth of personal origin and development, as well as a symbolic representation of a wish. Jimmie Trescott is wounded—not so much because of his father's sternness (it is easy to imagine Crane's minister father as a good deal more stern), but because of his own profound sensitivity, or, perhaps, his father's inability to recognize this sensitivity.[22] What Jimmie does next is quite telling: after slinking from his father's presence, he goes to find solace with the black man, Henry, Dr. Trescott's groom. Now, the black man on the 1890s America scene was certainly an outcast, and Crane, in fact, makes it clear that in this town the blacks for the most part live separately from the whites, "in the suburb of the town." Crane in his own life made a move similar to Jimmie's. In college, he began to frequent the Bowery slum, a zone of outcasts, and he eventually dropped out of college and moved there. Jimmie does in fact find solace with Henry: "these two were pals"—"fraternal"—and Jimmie feels better in the company of Henry, who has also committed household sins or "committed similar treasons" against the doctor. In fact, "in regard to almost everything in life they seemed to have minds precisely alike" (TM, 326). Likewise, Crane, it seems, was confident enough that he understood the subjective experience of the members of social outcast groups to rewrite the psychology of the slum dweller in Maggie and George's Mother (1896).

Now, in The Monster, the myth gets somewhat less transparent. Jimmie is only outcast during his sojourn to Henry; the eclipse of his father's affection will end, and he will return to grace. Meanwhile, Henry is always, at some level, an outcast. And so, we might imagine, was Crane, mentally, by the time he was living in the Bowery and both of his parents were dead. There was no going home again. If Jimmie can stand in for Crane as little boy, Henry might stand in for him as young man. There is the name Johnson, which Crane identified with himself a few years earlier. There is also the fact that Henry is a groom and Crane's love and fascination for horses is well known. The boy and the young man are both in this story perhaps because their psychologies are both alive in Crane.

And their psyches, though "alike," are not identical. "There were points of emphatic divergence," the narrator says, and the point he brings up is that of pride. "For instance, it was plain from Henry's talk that he was a very handsome negro, and he was known to be a light, a weight, and an eminence in the suburb of the town,...and obviously this glory was over Jimmie's horizon" (*TM*, 326). That is, Jimmie and Henry differ in two basic and related ways: Henry is permanently an outcast and—consequently, or in defense against this shame, one might say—his pride has assumed magnificent proportions.

Then, in the scene of fire and mutilation, we seem to get a replay of the myth but with certain key elements changed. In fact, we may be seeing the replay and the further elaboration of this early trauma in Crane's psychic life. For now there is an attempt by the proud outcast to rescue the boy. This could be, again, Crane trying to rescue his childhood self—his sensitivity, vulnerability, openness, his bitter heart, his "soul" "clad...in armor" (to borrow from Crane's description of the other Jimmie's spiritual clothing [*M*, 13]). But what we have not yet explored is that the result of the attempt is just a further ostracism and mental alienation. Why does the rescue turn out that way? Perhaps because the rescue attempt of the boy Crane is an approach to the female—an attempt at love.

The fire is twice referred to as a lady and several times given a feminine pronoun. It is presented as at once visually fascinating and delicate but also vicious. On one hand, the fire is attractive like multicolored "flowers," and precious stones of all types ("emerald," "sapphire," "jewels"), and it is also "delicate, trembling"; on the other, it is violent in the manner of an "animal," "a panther," "eagles," a "serpent," a "snake," and it "seemed to be alive with envy, hatred, and malice." The "fairy lady," in particular, seems sadistic: she smiles quietly as she traps Henry and Jimmie (*TM*, 338–39).

And at this point it is possible to make more of Jimmie's accident that opens the story; apparently, it is not adventitious but works with the same mythic symbols as the fire sequence. Like Henry acting as a fireman, Jimmie is "playing" train engine and encounters flowers—associated later with the fire woman. Both Henry and Jimmie are pitting themselves against natural objects associated in the story with the feminine. Given that the real firemen in the story are beloved of the town for their prowess and every act of self-assertion in the tale is an occasion either for admiration or mockery, it might be said that, symbolically here, both Jimmie and Henry are seeking love in approaching the female, in more or less vulnerable positions. It is interesting to note that upon Johnson's entering the fire to save Jimmie, the first thing that happens, rather arbitrarily, is the destruction of an engraving commemorating the Declaration of Independence, as if to say, upon approaching the female, independence is the first casualty. Jimmie's destruction of a peony, his act of "deflowering," is then an attack on the female, and one wonders if this is, in fact, an accident. It would appear not to be an accident, whether conscious or not, on Crane's part. Jimmie could be expressing aggression against a female, which, along with his huge sensitivity, might explain his profound sense of guilt for the seemingly minor sin. In his run in his toy engine, Jimmie is angrily seeking female love, presumably from his mother, presumably because she is not giving him enough (this is perhaps for now too much conjecture, but we can say that Mrs. Trescott is mostly absent from the story, and her appearance at the end seems to suggest a selfishness on her part). The myth here of psychic origin perhaps begins with this lack experienced by the boy, this angry seeking and the subsequent guilt. Here, of course, the flower is pictured as only delicate and weak; when we next meet flowers, they are the "delicate" (*TM*, 338) but dangerous blooms of the fire. We have an impression of revenge. At some level, one speculates, Crane experienced his mental torture at the hands of women from whom he sought love as punishment he has earned.

We are not done with the fire. Crane's hallucinatory vision of a sort of female Chimera, which tempts with its beauty and vulnerability and then maims out of jealous hate and with pleasure, is all the more disturbing because one finds, in the middle of this lengthy, wildly overwritten description of the fire, the incredible sentence, "there was one blaze that was precisely the hue of a delicate *coral*" (*TM*, 338, my emphasis). This allusion to Cora, the woman he was at the time living with in England, may again be unconscious, but seems hardly accidental; before the story is finished, there will be three references made to a gossip monger named Mrs. Howarth who spreads a damaging story about Dr. Trescott all over town. Cora's maiden name was Howorth (*SC*, 194).

Berryman, who reads the monster's story as Crane's fear of more scandal and more rumors of his madness, concludes: "So Stephen Crane 'rescued' Cora....He pretended to marry—and nothing happened. Not a word of scandal seems to have got into print; his family would not retort for nearly forty years" (*SC*, 196). No doubt this story of Henry Johnson is, at some level, a myth about Crane's persecution by the larger social world. Henry, the cakewalker and braggart, like Crane, gets his wish for fame from the world, but in a twisted, horrible way that leaves him much worse off than before. He becomes not only famous, but notorious; he is not loved or recognized, but made fun of and ostracized. If Crane has won wide fame for his work by the time of the writing of *The Monster*, he has also been mocked for his "obscure" poems and essentially hounded out of New York by the police on account of his having testified for the prostitute Dora Clark.

But this fire scene, it seems, is not only about Crane's reputation but also cuts closer to the bone. It is about nonrecognition in the most intimate of arenas. American society may be full of beauties and riches, hatred and envy, but it is not female. The fire unmistakably is. Crane's latest and most serious attempt to rescue himself was with Cora. Yes, he was attracted to prostitutes and women on the fringes of society and desired to save them, perhaps because he experienced himself as a social outcast who needed rescuing. But in trying to gain salvation through a woman—through Cora—he had to negotiate the beautiful and terrible fire that Henry Johnson encounters.

Berryman says Crane rescued Cora and nothing happened but he might be wrong about this. Something happened; Crane, like Henry, got caught, and he was wounded—again in the same place. Henry went from black face to no face, from partial outcast to total outcast, and (on a figurative level) from tortured pride to abject shame; Crane, we might imagine, experienced a similar intensification of his feelings of alienation—because now he experienced alienation not only from his family and from middle-class America, but also from the outcast woman who was supposed to save him as he had saved her. (I am imagining that Crane entertained a combination slumming/Cinderella fantasy along the lines of the reciprocal salvation recently staged in the movie *Pretty Woman*: a successful, accomplished man rescues a prostitute from her life on the social margins and the prostitute meanwhile, as she puts it, "rescues him right back," emotionally.) Henry lost his mind; Crane perhaps felt crazy in the same way that someone does who feels he cannot be understood. Crane's dissatisfaction with Cora seems almost incomprehensibly savage and terrified in a poem that, according to critics, he wrote about her a year after *The Monster* while hiding from her in Cuba.

> Thou art my love
> And thou art a storm
> That breaks black in the sky
> And, sweeping headlong,
> Drenches and cowers each tree.
>
> ...
>
> Thou art my love
> And thou art a priestess

> And in thy hand is a bloody dagger
> And my doom comes to me surely.
>
> ...
>
> Thou art my love
> And thou art a skull with ruby eyes
> And I love thee
> Woe is me....[23]

Cora appears in this poem, to say the least, as dominating and insensitive. Crane's alienation here would seem to include a sexual anxiety: Cora's sexual domination and insensitivity or Crane's fear of impotency or castration is perhaps registered in the already "bloody dagger" but fairly unmistakably in the image of Cora as a "storm," which "sweeping headlong, / Drenches and cowers each tree."

Romance and Misogyny

Why were women so dangerous for Crane? One comes back, of course, to Crane's relationship with his mother. Much has been made of Crane's apparently rebellious relationship to his minister father, who preached and wrote against many of the vices Crane would develop and who died when Crane was not yet nine. But interestingly, the fathers in Crane's novels, with the exception of the kind Dr. Trescott, tend to get less attention; they are already dead (as in *George's Mother* and *The Red Badge*), or are weak and die soon (as in *Maggie*). Less has been said about his relation to his mother, who was also a public voice against vice. To begin with, one can imagine he was rebelling as much against her as his father when he took up smoking, drinking, cursing, gambling, and sex. In fact, she was probably the greater antagonist for Crane after age nine, given that she was alive. Crane's general misogyny is not hard to spot. He attacked society matrons in his stories; in *The Monster*, a character asserts that "'it's the women'" who are the "very thoughtless fools" and are demanding Henry be gotten rid of (*TM*, 377). Then there are Crane's angry depictions of mothers in particular: Maggie's mother is a fiend; George's mother, in the book by that name, is an overbearing and overprotective woman, who, like Crane's mother, "was helpetin' around' the' country lecturin' before W.C.T.U.'s an' one thing an' another."[24]

What little we know of Crane's early years appears to indicate that he did not seem to get much mothering at all—certainly not from his mother. Mrs. Mary Helen Crane was deeply involved in the temperance movement and other charitable enterprises even before her husband's death. Again, Stephen was the last of fourteen children (the four children just previous had all died), and, by the time he appeared, she had left the running of the household and the raising of children to an older sister, Agnes. Jayne Anne Phillips says that "Crane was first taught loneliness by his parents, stern, kind people, whose demands were high."[25] Mrs. Crane's sternness has often been noted. Supposedly— though this may be apocryphal—even when Crane was a very small child, she did not want him to cry or show feelings of weakness. Berryman reports that around the age of four "Stephen was held on a white horse which he remembered twenty years later as a savage beast. But it was no part of Mrs. Crane's theory that a child of hers should be afraid of anything. He was told to stay on the horse and not to be scared" (SC, 321). What has been less remarked—and is certain—was Mrs. Crane's frequent physical absence from the family. When Stephen was eight and his father was still alive, Mrs. Crane was apparently openly chastised by the ladies of her husband's congregation for neglecting her duties at home and instructed by them to take care of her family instead of making so many speeches.[26] Now, one might suspect this accusation of revealing more about sexist attitudes of the 1890s than about Mrs. Crane, but we get corroborating details about Mrs. Crane's absence from a playmate of Stephen's, who later recalled:

> His mother was…[an] active woman,… an ardent temperance lecturer. You could not be a temperance worker then and be much at home. His sister Agnes…mothered the family, but the brood was too much for her. Steve was just grown out of "knee pants": small, under-nourished, coming home from school or play…to find no supper. He would then range the neighborhood for food and companionship, telling tales to the other children of the various mothers—mine was one—who often sewed on his buttons.[27]

If this was not a faulty memory then it is possible to say not only that Crane's mother was not very available to him but also, more importantly, that he was already at a young age telling stories about her neglect.

In this regard, it is worth noting that Crane attacked Christianity in his letters (in one letter he acknowledges that he is not very friendly to Christianity as it is practiced around town) and in his stories (two priests in *Maggie* are ridiculed; one priest is actually the last person

Maggie turns to for help—in vain). One can speculate that these attacks are in part an index of his feeling that it was Christianity that had drawn away his mother and deprived him of her. "After my father died, mother lived in and for religion," Crane once commented.[28] And, of course, Crane was not merely a social critic of the practice of Christianity. Considering his well-known existentialist or atheistic doubts, it might be said that, in Crane's writing, private neuroses blended into metaphysical fears. Crane the neurotic boy was haunted by his "absent mother"; Crane the thinker feared that God was "absent" or at least uninterested.

When Crane chose a wife, he seemed to have had a double agenda. He was apparently not only choosing a woman who resembled himself (in her outcast status) but also selecting a woman who resembled his mother. By the time Crane hooked up with Cora, he already had an abundant history of showing interest in, almost worshipping, older women: Helen Trent, Mrs. Munroe, Mrs. Chaffee, Mrs. Sonntag, Amy Leslie, Mary Horan (SC, 304). And Cora was not merely older than Crane (five or six years older [SCAB, 240]); this Florida nightclub owner seemed to resemble Mrs. Crane in another way as well. Though their professional activities obviously put them on opposite sides of the fence in terms of vice, they were both active women, both enterprising, and both engaged in public activities. This may seem like a small similarity, but if Crane's childhood experience of maternal preoccupation had attuned his personality to the shame of neglect, then Cora would be a fine candidate to play the role of humiliator.

And she evidently played the role of betrayer in the melodrama that Crane was psychologically poised to experience. When Cora settled with Crane in England, she became mistress of Villa Ravensbrook and later Brede Manor, and enjoyed the position. She was frequently inviting and entertaining guests and running up expenses they could not afford; she was often involved in activities that took her away from intimacy with Crane—and perhaps put her in league, in Crane's mind, with the enemy. H. G. Wells noticed that Cora pursued her social program with excessive vigor. Again, we know Crane disliked crowds and he complained to his friends about the "idiotic company" Cora was keeping at Brede (SCAB, 493–94). Another man might have been bemused or irritated; Crane, one can imagine, experienced betrayal. His "Intrigue" poems register that feeling: "And I doubt thee," he wrote.[29] Their talk of "death" and "doom" seem hyperbolic or mad until one imagines the mental stakes being wagered in his relation to Cora, and until one remembers, of course, that his health would rapidly decline after he came back to Cora from his hideout in Cuba and that he would be dead within a year and a half after his return.

Crane, it seems, would compulsively play this game out to the end, and in order to win the game, apparently, he had to win the attention and love from Cora that he had never felt from his mother. Interestingly, Crane started a short story—"His New Mittens"—just after leaving Cora for the Cuban war (Stallman speculates that he actually began it at sea during the Atlantic crossing from England [*SCAB*, 350]) that concerns a boy's perceived rejection by his mother, a story that was set in the same town as *The Monster* and was included with the novel when it was published. In the story, a young boy named Horace is reprimanded by his mother for soiling his new mittens, just as Jimmie Trescott is reprimanded by his father for destroying a flower. As in *The Monster*, the boy exiles himself; however, in this story, he is not seeking solace with an outcast, but revenge through his own degradation. He first attempts to gain sympathy from his mother by refusing to eat his dinner; when this tactic fails, he decides: "He would run away. In a remote corner of the world he would become some sort of bloody-handed person driven to a life of crime by the barbarity of his mother. She should never know his fate. He would torture her for years with doubts and doubts and drive her implacably to a repentant grave."[30]

In this context, it should be mentioned that Crane had already written a whole novel on this theme a couple of years after his mother's death; in *George's Mother*, George essentially drives his overbearing mother to death with his carousing and drinking. Once again, Crane's anger as well as guilt over his perceived rejection by his mother seems to be evident.

Jimmie's rejection by the father in *The Monster* is experienced as entirely deserved; Horace's rejection by the mother here likewise involves some sharp guilt (over soiling his mittens), but it is felt more intensely, and, importantly, it also leads to a fierce criticism of her. One cannot help but wonder after reading this story if Crane was involved—perhaps unwittingly—in carrying out a tactic similar to Horace's. The object here would not have been to rescue the boy child from the barbarous mother before she shames and hardens him, as Maggie attempts to do in *Maggie*, or to rescue the girl child from the same mother before the mother banishes her and sends her off to her death, as George imagines doing in *George's Mother* (both written soon after Crane's mother's death), but to rescue the boy by the reformation of the mother (probably begun as Crane left Cora for the

Spanish-American War and finished in Havana, after the war ended, when he thought about returning to her). And "His New Mittens," unlike *Maggie*, ends happily. Horace is returned home by the butcher; he gets to see "his mother lying limp, pale as death, her eyes gleaming with pain," and he runs into her arms with a "grief and joy" that she shares. His mother manifests her love, and, safe in this knowledge, he lets down the barrier of tortured pride (that was permanent with Jimmie Johnson of *Maggie*) and allows his own feelings to pour out in a "prolonged wail."[31]

After the Cuban war ended, Crane did not return home to Cora, in part, to be sure, because he had grave misgivings about his relationship with her and was seriously considering never going back. But once Cora found out where he was and got a message to him in Cuba, he did go home, as though he had been testing her love for him as well as running away from her, as though he had wanted to see if she would track him down. One can imagine that Crane was enacting—or at least wishing for—a scenario not unlike the one he had just finished writing for Horace. In any case, the identification for Crane, at least unwittingly, of Cora and his mother seems irresistible. In Cora, Crane seems to have found or experienced again the distant, socially active mother who had brought him so much pain, and he evidently kept hoping for a transformation in her that would allow him to release his soul from its armor—heal his shame—and thereby be saved.

But Crane's return apparently did not work the magic that Horace's does; Cora, it seems, was not transformed in his estimation. If Crane felt betrayed by her social habits, then it is significant that life at Brede Manor was clogged with guests and Cora now played the socialite hostess on a grand scale. Indeed, several stories attest to Crane's continued alienation from Cora. One is another Whilomville tale of the Trescott family called "The Angel-Child," in which a little-girl cousin named "Cora" comes with her parents to visit the Trescotts. The town immediately learns that Cora—ironically called "the angel child"—has a "high and commanding" voice; the children "at first feared, then admired, then embraced [her]; in two days she was a Begum" (a Muslim woman of rank). She is also referred to as "their queen." "All day long her voice could be heard directing, drilling, and compelling those free-born children." Jimmie Trescott and the other children do not feel "oppression," but rather are eager to show "loyal obedience."[32]

Crane's ambivalence to Cora is not only registered in the heavily ironic tone of the narration but also in the two characters who stand in for him and have very different relationships with and reactions to the little girl Cora and her mother who resembles her (like her daughter, she is also "quick, beautiful, imperious"). On the one hand, there is the boy, Jimmie, who is captivated by her and, as is made explicit in a subsequent story, "The Lover and the Tell-Tale," falls in love with her. On the other hand, there is the man, her father, "a painter of high degree [and]...national reputation," who feels misunderstood and not respected by both daughter and wife: "Her...father was never energetic enough to be irritable unless some one broke through into that place where he lived with the desires of his life. But neither wife nor child ever heeded or even understood the temperamental values and so some part of him had grown hardened to their inroads." Little Cora comes to her father clamoring for money, and, like Crane with Cora one imagines, the father dishes it out mechanically. With the five dollars he gives her, she gets several of the children in the town in trouble, and, eventually, it is the father who is blamed by his wife, who cannot find fault with her "'angel child.'" "He was the guilty one—he!" The story ends with a telling summary of Crane's situation with his wife Cora: "Attached to them [his wife and daughter] was a husband and father who was plainly bewildered but still more plainly vexed, as if he would be saying, 'Damn 'em! Why can't they leave me alone!'"[33]

This is a Crane story that seems to require very little interpretation; like some of his "Intrigue" poems, it reads at one level almost like a diary entry. Crane's audacity in calling the girl "Cora" might perhaps be a measure of his exasperation—and desperation—at this point, after his return from Cuba. It is one thing to call Maggie's horrible mother by his own mother's first name; his mother had just died. Cora was very much alive and likewise the wife in the story is "a veritable queen of health"; perhaps it was Crane's declining health that incited him to forego the least displacement. In any event, the husband, like the story's author, is "of a most brittle constitution." One wonders if Cora read this story, and, if she did, whether she took it as genial ribbing. The irony here seems obviously bitter at points. Crane's pillorying of Cora in this way without her taking it seriously would, in any case, only be further evidence for him of the serious problem between them, which he apparently blamed on her and which the tale would seem to state quite explicitly: "neither wife nor child ever heeded or even understood the temperamental values" of the father. This seems to be what Crane wanted from Cora; this seems to be what he felt he needed in order to be in an intimate relation with a woman and thus rescue himself: to be understood. And this is what he evidently felt he did not get. Instead, he ended up again like Jimmie Johnson at the hands of Mrs. Johnson: "*hardened* to their inroads." He still lived essentially alone, holding others at bay from "that place where he lived with the desires of his life."[34]

In "The Angel-Child," the boy is in love and under the thrall of the beloved; the man is vexed and bewildered but compliant. Here we have perhaps another emblem of Crane's split psychology. Because Crane as a boy never felt understood, and, as he grew older, continued to feel not understood, the boy does not entirely change into a man and disappear. He remains, and Crane's *visions* continue to contain boys and their psychology. Alfred Kazin aptly described Crane the man as "an old child." He was always the wounded, even traumatized, child, and, as Kazin says, "In the end he seemed to be mocking himself with the same quiet viciousness with which, even as a boy, he had mocked the universe."[35] It makes sense that his Whilomville tales— often centered around boys—should be written during his marriage with Cora, a relationship that seems to recapitulate his childhood experience. Maybe Crane's remarkable "maturity" as a writer is based, in part, on the remarkable "immaturity" of his psychic life—his apparent inability to recognize and move beyond his childhood habit of experiencing humiliation and neglect.

But to come back to the first and longest Whilomville story, *The Monster*. Unlike *Maggie*, *The Monster* does not finish in complete despair and destruction. There is certainly ostracism; the story ends first with Dr. Trescott standing up to all the town leaders, who tell him he is ruining his practice by keeping Johnson in the town and who suggest a public institution for "the monster," and then with Mrs. Trescott crying over the unattended tea party. But the story does not have the desolation of the slum tale. Maggie is rejected by everybody and dies in utter isolation, but Henry Johnson, though faceless and an idiot, does not die, nor is he committed. Dr. Trescott first saves his life by pulling him out of the fire, then saves his life again on the operating table, and finally refuses to abandon Henry to save himself. *The Monster* even seems a corrective to *Maggie*: though horrible, there is hope. That hope is lodged in the father.

The last scene not only gives us a taste of the Trescott family's ostracism by the town but also shows us where the mother's priorities lay. Dr. Trescott's medical profession is, like Mrs. Trescott's Wednesday social, already suffering, but he has remained focused on Henry. The mother, Mrs. Trescott, it would seem, is most of all concerned with her own social life. Dr. Trescott is associated with Crane's father by a seemingly arbitrary reference to a priest's chin on the first page.

Crane's older brother William was a doctor and thought Crane had him in mind when he created Trescott (*SCAB*, 477). Trescott is also connected to the horse and buggy in which Henry Johnson drives him on his house calls; the Reverend Crane likewise used a buggy on professional trips to nearby towns (where he preached), and he sometimes took Stephen along with him. He was apparently partial to his youngest son.[36]

The Monster, then, seems to express resignation and a painful longing. The attempt to save the boy from the fire ends in disaster, but not total disaster. The female fire that the mature Crane apparently braves in an attempt to restore himself emotionally only leaves him further damaged; afterward, he cannot be restored to the health and sanity that would return him to the community, but he can be protected. If love from the mother—or the potential savior/saved woman—is impossible, and one must live faceless and in shame, or without essential recognition and human communion, and insane, or in painful mental withdrawal from the rest of humanity, one can at least be protected by the father—or older brother—from the hatred and derision of society. This mythic wish, if it is indeed Crane's, is all the more painful for its being unlikely or hopeless at this point in his life. If this was a longing for his father specifically, then we must be reminded that Crane was doubly wounded. Not only had his mother been absent, detached, and self-concerned but also his father had died when he was young. Twenty years after the Reverend Crane's death, Crane remarked with angry sadness that he had forgotten "not a damned iota, not a shred" about the day his father died.[37] This longing might have been in part satisfied by an older brother—Crane had earlier taken refuge with his brother William when he felt besieged by social calls after the publication of *The Red Badge* brought him his initial fame—but part of the pathos here is that Crane could no longer live in the United States where his brothers were. Stephen and Cora were living in England to avoid the scandal of their not being married, and they could not be married because Cora's husband would not divorce her. Her situation was in part responsible for his isolation. If Dr. Trescott is another representation of Crane himself, or, rather, if Crane tried to make himself into a man who behaves like the implacable Dr. Trescott (most publicly in the Dora Clark court case), one has a sense of the difficult psychic task that faced Crane. He would have been at once Jimmie Trescott/Johnson, the supersensitive child, smarting from his parental rejections, and Maggie/Henry Johnson, whom the mother/fire-woman turns into a spiritual and social pariah and mental outcast. Thus, he would have been in need of making himself into a Dr. Trescott who could be the protective father he lacked and desperately needed.

Shame Syndrome

Consider the famous but bizarre image from Crane's *Black Rider* poems of a creature who eats his own bitter heart from his hands out in the desert. Perhaps after this discussion it is not so strange. The desert figures isolation. The exposed heart, held in the hands, signals vulnerability. The creature must eat his own heart because no other emotional nourishment—no love—is available. The heart is bitter because he has been harmed in love, humiliated, rejected. He likes the heart because, though injured, it belongs to him—it is all he has, and he must like it despite the fact that others have rejected it. Finally, he likes the bitterness because he is also self-hating, and he treats himself with the same cruelty he has felt from others.

An anxiety near panic; a huge egotism, a drive for fame, and a world seen through the lens of self-esteem; claustrophobia, alienation, misogyny, and adventure seeking; stoicism, self-hatred, anger: these are all one syndrome. The context is a psyche formed in the experience of rejection and shame. Crane is from the start detached from others. Neither his mother, who is detached and busy outside the home, nor his father, who is stern and dies early, answers his emotional needs, nourishes him spiritually, or recognizes his mental life, and all of this leaves a tremendous humiliation that he cannot reveal to anyone, hardly even to himself.

Crippled with self-hatred in response to his perceived rejection, one imagines, he pulled away early from his family. Already smoking cigarettes and drinking beer before the age of seven, he rebelled.[38] And he was driven, unwittingly and compulsively, to seek compensation for missing love and proof of his worth in fame. Crane's departure from family, college, and middle-class society, and his slumming move to the Bowery would make sense; with a psyche formed in shame and thus hypersensitive to rejection, he preempted any possible further criticism and tried to heal himself by rejecting nearly everything and imagining himself superior to the worlds he left behind. His hatred for gossips and self-appointed moral and social judges would also be a function of this vulnerability to criticism. His solution was to remove himself from his own class, take up residence in a lower one, surround himself with people of his own class who felt as he did, and thereby put himself directly into an unchallengeable position of superiority—certainly as a writer. As Crane says of Jimmie the Bowery tough, "He himself occupied a down-trodden position that had a private but distinct element of grandeur in its isolation" (*M*, 14–15). Or, as Crane says of Henry Fleming after he runs from battle in *The Red Badge*, "There was a melancholy grandeur in the isolation of his experiences." And if Crane can likewise imagine Henry Fleming's grandiose ideas of prophethood[39] and George's wild fantasies of kingship in *George's Mother*, it is because his move to the Bowery allowed him to indulge in a secret fantasy of fame that no one around him could challenge: that he would be a great and famous writer. In this way, Crane avoided the uncomfortable phase of apprenticeship—and the obligatory criticism that goes with it—that he had small doses of as a student at college and a staff reporter for a newspaper.

Crane's strategy for publishing *Maggie* shows the same desire to protect himself from rejection. Crane explained his use of the pseudonym "Johnston Smith":

> I hunted a long time for a completely commonplace name....I think I asked [a friend] what he thought was the stupidest name in the world. He suggested Johnson Smith and Johnston Smith went on the ugly yellow cover by mistake. You see, I was going to wait until all the world was pyrotechnic about Johnston Smith's "Maggie" and then I was going to flop down like a trapeze performer from the wire and, coming forward with all the modest grace of a consumptive nun, say, I am he, friends.[40]

After having escaped the social judgment of his own class, Crane was going to submit himself to it again. Yet he would hide behind a name that was not only a disguise but also a commonplace, even a ridiculous one. If his work were rejected, only he would know of his failure; he would keep himself out of the drastic public eye. If he succeeded, he would reappear in middle-class view, again with an unassailable superior status. Incidentally, Crane's bizarre and seemingly arbitrary image—of "coming forward with all the modest grace of a consumptive nun"—might also issue out of his obsession with exile and ostracism.[41] Consumptives and nuns, apparently unrelated, have this in common: they are both divided off from the rest of the community. Meanwhile, consumptives are quarantined because they are diseased and contagious, and nuns reject the social world out of moral purity and choose to sequester themselves. "A consumptive nun," then, is someone who both rejects the community and is ostracized from it: perhaps an apt, if partly unwitting, description of Crane's sense of himself, a sense of self that was at once proud and anxious. Perhaps this also explains the cryptic, but nonetheless obviously ironic comment about "modest grace"—Crane as the rejected exile was neither modest nor graceful, but rather proud and awkward. As for the gender of a nun (he might have chosen the word "monk"), one might even imagine that Crane was embarrassed by the cowardly nature of his pseudonymic ploy and perhaps was disparaging his manliness.

Crane again and again depicted and pilloried tender and bloated egos because he had one himself. He was aware of it and he hated himself for it. He discussed it in his letters: "When I reached twenty-one years [before any fame, then] and first really scanned my personal egotism I was fairly dazzled by the size of it. The Matterhorn could be no more than a ten-pin to it."[42] Such "personal egotism" was a tactical defense against the shame of rejection—his primal self-hatred. It was compensation and protection. His pain was buried beneath. But this narcissism also locked him away from other people. And his quest for notoriety turned out to be a trap; though he indeed achieved the dramatic fame he was looking for, it did not remove the tendency to feel shame. Fame did not bring Crane what he longed for. "Now that I have reached a goal," he wrote (to a young woman he loved) after the success of *The Red Badge*, "I suppose that I ought to be contented; but I am not. I was happier in the old days when I was always dreaming of the thing I have now attained" (*SCAB*, 325). In fact, the experience of fame seems mostly to have intensified his distance from others—as well as stripping him of the illusion that it would save him.

His nearly continuous anxiety, bordering on terror, might have come from a sense of being absolutely alone. He did not exist in the web of relationships that makes one at home in the universe, and so he felt himself always dangling above the abyss that he imagined Maggie tossed into. His characters are notoriously flat, lacking the emotions of traditional literature,[43] perhaps because Crane himself had little access to his own emotions. His affects other than shame were undeveloped, crippled, numbed. A need for adventure was concomitant to this numbness because "unbearable excitement" (which was sometimes pure terror) was not just one of the few things he could feel, along with bitterness and pride, but perhaps the only feeling strong enough to take him out of himself, engage him in the world, and stop the general monotonous anxiety, bitterness, and narcissism of his disconnection. On the battlefield, he might have gained something else as well; he would no longer have been a solitary freak because everyone felt the mortal terror that he could feel practically anywhere.

He searched for a love that could save him from being an outcast, and so he apparently chose an outcast woman whom he could save—and who also resembled his mother. But, if he was subject to this terror of isolation, he was also vulnerable to the repulsion of claustrophobia. To put it as Nina Baym might, he was caught between a melodrama of being rejected and a melodrama of being besieged. Proximity to another could always replay the experience of rejection: closeness without intimacy. Thus, in his marriage with Cora, he felt anxiety, mistrust, humiliation, and disgust, and he had a propensity for illness. A poem in *The Black Riders* characterizes a general horror of coming back from his solitude to the world of other people:

> Behold, from the land of the farther suns
> I returned.
> And I was in a reptile-swarming place,
> Peopled, otherwise, with grimaces,
> Shrouded above in black impenetrableness.
> I shrank, loathing,
> Sick with it.
> And I said to him,
> "What is this?"
> He made the answer slowly,
> "Spirit, this is a world;
> This was your home." (Poem 29; 1308–9)

As the ancient Greeks believed, the sin of alienation is punished with sickness; the sickness occurs when closeness is defiled by alienation, or vice versa, isolation is defiled by social invasion. Crane was in tremendous pain, and he knew he needed a love, wrote about it openly, sought it obviously. But he was doomed to closeness without intimacy, to the sickness of alienation, unless he took the leap of faith necessary in order to show, express, even in a way transmit his pain and shame, of which he was in turn ashamed. Crane evidently knew what he had to do by the time he was hiding out in Cuba:

> Once I saw thee idly rocking
> —Idly rocking—
> And chattering girlishly to other girls,
> Bell-voiced, happy.
> Careless with the stout heart of unscarred womanhood
> And life to thee was all light melody.
> I thought of the great storms of love as I knew it

> Torn, miserable and ashamed of my open sorrow,
> I thought of the thunders that lived in my head
> And I wish to be an ogre
> And hale and haul my beloved to a castle
> And there use the happy cruel one cruelly
> And make her mourn with my mourning.[44]

The female love object is figured as happily oblivious to suffering; she is not scarred in love, and so for her it is light. Her obliviousness would torture Crane by making him feel alone in his pain, which he experienced in approaching love, and by making it that much more difficult to reveal his suffering to her. So, in defense and in revenge, he imagines himself a cruel ogre. But the last line is not entirely angry or sadistic; it is not just a vengeful urge to brutalize and defile the happy, innocent, distant woman; it is also a sad yearning for communion with her.

Crane knew what he had to do but he apparently never managed to do it with Cora. The humiliation and suffering, one suspects, stayed hidden. Perhaps Crane had chosen a woman truly incapable of or uninterested in understanding him, like little Cora in "The Angel Child" or her mother. Yet one cannot help but speculate that, like his character George in *George's Mother*, who can never so much as approach the dream girl he would like to rescue (Maggie Johnson) because she might laugh at him, Crane was at the same time ashamed and terrified to show his "open sorrow" and thus make himself so vulnerable to a woman, so vulnerable to further humiliation.

Writing was evidently Crane's primary means of healing himself, at least temporarily: the fantasy of fame as a writer was *supposed to* undo the shame of rejection; in the meantime, the strange catharsis of writing, of poetry especially, could record what he saw, allow him a means of expression, give him a spiritual connection to the universe, and quiet the anxiety. This therapy would explain why he wrote furiously, compulsively, and sometimes like a man entranced. Writing for Crane, one guesses, was a form of meditation that could give him practically his only calm, partly because it allowed him to turn away from his pain. And this would also explain why Fried finds surfacing in his prose a "repressed" fear of "the deathliness of the blank upward-staring page."[45] After all, the act of writing could also bring him up against the very isolation, disconnection, and emptiness that it was supposed to repress and relieve him of. Such an analysis also explains, perhaps, "the burden of Crane's animism," as Fried puts it.[46] Like the act of writing in general, it might be a feverish attempt to counteract the terrifying emptiness and deathliness that Crane perceived and experienced in the world.

Still, repression seems to be only part of the calming effect that writing has for Crane; repression is something other than creative inspiration. Crane called his poems, sardonically, but oddly, "pills." Berryman rightly compared Crane, as a poet, to a medicine man in the act of casting "primitive anti-spells" (SC, 273). This final aspect leads to a mystery that one can only cite—and in regard to which one can only turn to Crane for corroboration. In the terror of isolation and the depression of self-hatred, some, like Crane, seem to be vulnerable to what is called creativity or artistic inspiration. Crane was writing his *Black Rider* poems when he was terribly depressed over *Maggie*'s universal rejection by publishers, and he wrote his "Intrigue" poems in the desperate solitude of Havana. With Crane, dreams, visions, poetry came into his head: "they came and I wrote them," he explained to a friend, "that's all" (SCAB, 88). Some of the poems he said he did no more than transcribe; stories and other poems he crafted, using the raw materials that came to him.

Crane has figured this mystery of creativity in a poem that is unusually cryptic and dense even for his notoriously esoteric collection of poetry:

> There is a grey thing that lives in the tree-tops
> None know the horror of its sight
> Save those who meet death in the wilderness
> But one is enabled to see
> To see branches move at its passing
> To hear at times the wail of black laughter
> And to come often upon mystic places
> Places where the thing has just been.[47]

Crane, of course, is a famous and obsessive colorist as well as an animist (one need only think of the titles of some of his most renowned works: *The Red Badge*, *The Black Riders*, "The Bride Comes to Yellow Sky," "The Blue Hotel"), and no doubt his colorism performed a function similar to his animism: a sally against depression. This poem is peculiar, and telling, because it takes us directly into the gray—the bleak realm of the colorless, the feelingless. The horror of this thing in the trees is precisely that it has no feeling, or rather, the gray thing is the horror seen only by one who is numb to all feeling. That mood of emptiness is the horror one finds shot through Crane's oeuvre, the gray terror of isolation, ostracism, or rejection unto death, figured here as "death in the wilderness." Perhaps it is located in the tree-tops because, in this state, one looks up desperately to the heavens, and one sees instead the gray thing. "But one is enabled to see"; there is a compensation for this pain. The experience of this gray horror, this abyss in the tree-tops, this depression, gives one insight, vision, access to "mystic places." Yet, this is here hardly a romantic notion. Perhaps most uncanny of all in this poem, unmistakably Crane's, is the idea that the insight one receives is an insight into none other than the gray thing itself and its effects. Yes, one can hear what others presumably cannot, but what one hears is by no means comforting; "the wail of black laughter" sounds like the exclamation of bitter irony. There is compensation for this horrible alienation; it is painful perception and entrance to mystic places: connection, if there is any, to others who have been visited by this pain, and to their art—and also to the universe. The poem ends with a seemingly brutal tautology: mental pain allows one to encounter mystic places, and mystic places are precisely places that have been touched by this mental pain. However, the "horror of its sight" (the feeling that the gray thing gives) is different from the insight that the horror gives. It is not, of course, that one is cured of the pain and horror, but that one can mystically see and articulate them, and this experience brings a sort of temporary solace. One is consoled by a connection to something mystic, to a mystic source of creativity. When the gray thing departs, it leaves in its wake inspiration—about itself. This poem, then, is a trace of "the grey thing." This poem is a place "where the thing [had] just been." And so was the mind that created it.

III

Slumming Trauma

The Cult Film *Fight Club*

The stark polarization between blockbuster sentimental slumming dramas and sardonic independent traumas is only part of the profile of contemporary class-crossing cinema. Between the slumming fantasy film and the class trauma movie stands a sort of hybrid genre, what might be called the slumming trauma. Between the sentimental slumming hero Jack in the Hollywood blockbuster *Titanic* and the humiliated and humiliating degenerate Telly in the indie art film *Kids* stands Tyler Durden in the cult movie *Fight Club*. This third type of classploitation story tends to produce underground or cult sensations, and the film *Fight Club* is indeed a recent prime example of the genre: it had a mediocre showing in the theaters, but developed a cult following with video and DVD.

Trauma as Therapy

Like Lester Burnham in *American Beauty*, the Edward Norton character and narrator in *Fight Club* (who goes by various names, including Rupert, Cornelius, and Jack) is in the process of rejecting his corporate and consumer identities and discovering a deeper, more vibrant and authentic self (in the persona of his alter ego, Tyler Durden). Tyler appears on the scene to end the narrator's "slave[ry] to the Ikea nesting instinct" as well as his slavish conformity at work. He begins by blowing up the narrator's high-rise apartment and eliminating all his possessions. He subscribes to the radical slumming notion that "only when you've lost everything are you free to do anything." Like the romantic bohemian hero Jack in *Titanic*, played by heartthrob

Leonardo DiCaprio, Tyler "look[s] like you [the narrator] want to look" and is "free in all the ways that you [the narrator] are not"; he is played by sex symbol Brad Pitt. And like Jack in *Titanic* or Shakespeare in *Shakespeare in Love*, who liberate the women they become involved with, Tyler Durden is a sort of free agent of liberation, spreading freedom, vitality, and authenticity to others, including the narrator of course, but also his slumming girlfriend Marla Singer, random individuals he accosts on the street, and men at large.

He helps Marla in her quest to "hit bottom"—Marla, like the narrator, has been attending a wide variety of support groups for the seriously ill in search of authentic emotional expression and connection. (Slumming trauma films share with trauma movies a penchant for disfigurement and disease, but they treat these themes differently.) In one scene, Tyler pulls a gun on a convenience store clerk named Raymond, asking him "what did you want to be?" and threatening him with death if he doesn't pursue his discarded dream of becoming a veterinarian. "If you're not on your way to becoming a veterinarian in six weeks, you'll be dead." As the terrified but liberated Raymond runs off, Tyler yells after him, "run, Forrest, run," a mocking reference to the sentimental slumming film *Forrest Gump*. He also, from time to time, splices porno shots into "family" films, forcing the bodily realities of human existence onto a sentimentalizing and Puritanical culture.

Tyler's largest achievement of liberation and authenticity, of course, is his invention of the Fight Club, which as the narrator indicates, was what men deeply desired and needed: "It was on the tip of everyone's tongue; Tyler and I just gave it a name." And the Fight Club segues into "Project Mayhem," a guerrilla or terrorist effort by the anonymous army of Tyler's unquestioning followers to subvert and destroy corporate America, which climaxes in the dynamiting of office buildings. Tyler has a vision of a renaturalized urban landscape, in which men are "pounding corn, laying out strips of venison in the empty carpool lane of an abandoned superhighway." *Fight Club* lodges in a single person, with a split personality, the liberated and the liberating character; where *Titanic* gives us Rose and Jack and *Shakespeare in Love* presents Viola de Lessups and Shakespeare, *Fight Club* offers the narrator and his alter ego, Tyler.

Tyler's methods of self-actualization and self-discovery may seem disturbingly extreme, especially when they are compared to those of the wholesome heroes of sentimental slumming fantasies—Jack teaches Rose to spit in *Titanic* and Lester has fantasies about a teenage cheerleader in *American Beauty*. But there is plenty of precedent for his radical behavior in the American literary, often cult, traditions of naturalist and bohemian writing. As for Tyler, for Beat cult writer Jack Kerouac's alter ego Sal Paradise in *On the Road*, the key question is not "what one should do" but, likewise, "what are we all aching to do? What do we want?" The Neal Cassady character Dean Moriarty advises that "the thing is not to get hung up" and, despite Dean's consistent disloyalty to his friends and wives, Sal argues he is really a true friend because he has brought to others "sexuality and…life."[1] Bohemian writer Henry Miller, likewise, in the initially banned, later best-selling cult novel *Tropic of Cancer* (1934), spreads a gospel of liberation, asking one of his acquaintances, "What is it you'd *really* like to do?" and counsels, "Do anything, but let it yield ecstasy."[2] When he discovers that a friend named Fillmore secretly desires to abandon his pregnant girlfriend and flee the country but feels too responsible to do so, Miller takes charge, ships him out and so frees him, relieving the man of his money in the process. Meanwhile, Miller bluntly admits in *Tropic of Capricorn* that he wanted to see America "razed from top to bottom."[3] Naturalist writer Frank Norris romantically removes his failed dentist in *McTeague* (1899) from the city and the grips of his wife and returns him to the "primeval" female-less American wilderness, where his brute strength is rewarded and an animal "sixth sense" gives him seemingly supernatural powers of perception.[4]

Tyler's therapeutic assault on Raymond, the convenience store clerk, is worth pausing over. While it would be going too far to say that this is a direct reference to the trauma film *Clerks*, it is clear that *Fight Club* has a romantic, "liberating" answer to the paralysis of a Dante Hicks who finds himself in a dead-end convenience-store job he doesn't have the will to shake. (Raymond indeed sounds like Dante when he whines that his goals require "too much school.") All of Veronica's cajoling of Dante to return to college has nothing like the instant effect of Tyler's death threat on Raymond. *Fight Club* clearly rejects the blasted nihilism of the trauma movie and offers a sort of shock-therapy antidote to the defeated. The traumas in trauma films leave characters paralyzed and at best hardened into traumatizers in turn; the traumas that Tyler orchestrates are meant to shake people awake and remind them that they are alive and full of possibility. They are romantic traumas. In short, Tyler has the nerve and the power to change a paralyzed Dante Hicks into a fearless Forrest Gump.

But Tyler's smirking reference to the film *Forrest Gump* and his X-rated tampering with movies such as Cinderella (the classic class-crossing fairy tale), signal *Fight Club*'s hostility to sentimental slumming. For Tyler and *Fight Club*, sentimentalism is an insidious lie that denies the realities of human life and the human body as it promises a fairy-tale experience that doesn't exist. (Indeed, the slumming sentimentalism of such blockbusters as *Titanic* and *Forrest Gump* may be a salute to Hollywood's power to co-opt and sanitize any story whatsoever: after all, the literary tradition of slumming liberation, from Mark Twain and Frank Norris to Zora Neale Hurston and Henry Miller, to the Beat writers and post-Beats such as Kathy Acker, supposedly involved an all-out assault on sentimentalism. It may also be that antisentimental slumming falls into a sentimentality all its own.)

It is no surprise then that the narrator's downward trajectory takes him into the sort of degraded environment and social interactions that sentimental slumming fantasies studiously avoid and that has something in common with the sordid landscapes and transactions of such class trauma movies as *Kids* and *Gummo*. Tyler may be attractive, free spirited, and independent like Jack in *Titanic*, and, thus, unlike the physically undistinguished and peer-identified Telly in *Kids* (played, not incidentally, by an obscure actor who is not, as Roger Ebert attests, "much to look at"[5]). Tyler's great looks and dramatic freedom, though, involve an antiromantic humiliation of his lover, Marla, that is worthy of the repulsive Telly. Not only is Tyler's sexual style rough rather than tender (routinely eliciting screams) but Marla also complains that "you fuck me then snub me." Likewise, Tyler's tenement squat "shithole [where] nothing worked" is a far cry from the clean if crowded lodging in steerage aboard the Titanic; it is much closer to the littered communal tenement apartment in *Kids* or the various rundown abodes of *Gummo*.

But still there is a difference. If sentimental slumming films avoid the sordid while trauma movies depend on the sordid to repulse, slumming trauma cinema mystifies or romanticizes the sordid.

There is that awkward moment in *Titanic* when Jack reveals to Rose that the model for his nude drawings was a Parisian prostitute. Naturally, Rose wants to know if Jack had "a love affair" with the woman, and Jack replies that he was in love with "her hands." He reveals that he didn't have sex with the woman—because she was a one-legged prostitute. But, he quickly assures Rose, she had a good sense of humor.

The dialogue is particularly strained in this scene because the movie is performing a delicate operation, an operation that is central to the sentimental slumming genre and its corresponding PG-13 rating here. Jack's credentials as a bohemian artist are established in this scene: we all know that early twentieth-century American bohemian artists, such as Hemingway and Henry Miller, passed through Paris and had truck with prostitutes. But the wholesomeness of the *sentimental* genre and the innocence of its PG-13 heroes necessitates that Jack not have sex with prostitutes; *Titanic*'s principal audience is girls. The movie must therefore finesse Jack's relationship with the prostitute. On the one hand, he cannot refuse sex with prostitutes on moral principle because then he would hardly be bohemian and free spirited. The prostitute's missing a leg provides a reason for Jack to refrain from sex with her; the missing leg also has the virtue of providing a dose of the harsh realities of life at the social bottom. But, on the other hand, Jack might come off as arrogant or callous for sexually rejecting a woman on the basis of her deformity, so he must go on to affirm her in another way; thus his comment about her pleasant personality. This scene draws attention to an operation that is usually much more smoothly executed in *Titanic*: the movie has essentially excised the *physically* degraded and degrading aspects of lower-class and bohemian life in the early years of the twentieth century (the vermin, the dirt, the substandard housing, the disease, the alcoholism and drug addiction, the prostituted sex). While it can represent the insults and discrimination the poor must endure from the upper classes, it has swept clean the lower-class environment and social world of anything sordid.

By contrast, a woman with a missing leg would attract special sexual interest in a trauma film—provoking repulsion in the audience. *Gummo* indeed managed initially to earn an NC-17 rating on the basis of its overall, unredeemed sordidness; as director Harmony Korine complained, the rating did not issue from any particular sex scene, and its sexual content was milder than many R-rated films. ("Take any scene on its own," Korine reported the Motion Picture Association of America telling him, "and it would be an R, but strung together, the message is so antisocial, so nihilistic, that this is an NC-17 film."[6])

One such R-rated film with stronger sexual content than *Gummo* might indeed be *Fight Club*, which also contains plenty of physical degradation—in the forms of bloody fighting, rough sex, self-mutilation, spliced in pornography shots, car crashing, an "excrement catapult," and even the theft, spilling, and processing of human liposuction waste. But the relation to the physically degraded is different here, and its overtly mystical relation to the sordid—which isn't nihilistic but therapeutic—is what insures the movie's R rating.

Indeed, Tyler's engagement with physical degradation is not ultimately supposed to be about humiliation, but about ennobling humility. When Tyler engineers a car accident for the narrator, he concludes that the narrator has "had a life experience." Likewise, when Tyler ritually pours burning chemicals on the narrator's hand, he declares that "this is the greatest moment of your life." The excruciating pain of disintegrating flesh is meant to enlighten the narrator to the human condition of being mortally embodied: "First you have to know—not fear—know that someday you're gonna die," he lectures, before applying the vinegar that stops the burning. He tells the narrator: "God doesn't like you or want you; we are God's unwanted children." Tyler concludes, "Congratulations; you're one step closer to hitting bottom."

The purposeful physical degradations of *Fight Club*—most obviously the fighting—are supposed to reveal to the narrator and the audience the bottom line of human existence beneath the consumer capitalist twaddle: "You are not the car you drive, not the money in your wallet, not the fucking khakis" you wear; "we are the all-singing, all-dancing crap of the world." Or as Tyler informs the troops of the Fight Club over the megaphone: "You are the same decayed organic matter as everything else." In the paradox of the *romantic* slumming trauma genre, the identification with decay is meant to be purifying, the identification with the degraded to be transcendent. The unusual realization in rich, privileged, pampered America that "we are not special" and "we don't matter," as Tyler says, is precisely what makes Tyler and his group special. The aestheticism and lyricism of Tyler's description of the waste that is humanity ("the all-singing, all-dancing crap of the world") neatly encapsulates the paradox. This formulation is the sort one might find in the oeuvre of Henry Miller. The lyrical embrace of filth and defilement is also a staple of literary slumming trauma. Miller, for example, sings the praises of head lice in the first pages of *Tropic of Cancer*—among other human joys, it promotes intimacy among the victims who end up shaving each other's heads.

The Doubleness of Slumming Trauma

But the mystical paradox of slumming trauma does not seem sustainable here in *Fight Club*—or in the genre generally. The viewer is given reason to suspect that behind the romanticized humility and physical defilement there is actually humiliation and self-loathing, and even a compensatory fantasy of fame. Marla accuses the narrator/Tyler of having "serious emotional problems," and the accusation is borne out by the narrator's own monologue. "I am Jack's inflamed sense of rejection," he reports, and adds later, "My father dumped me; Tyler dumped me; I am Jack's broken heart." Tyler, meanwhile, explains to his fellow Fight Club members that they are "angry" over the false promises of TV that has raised them to believe "we'll all be millionaires and rock stars and movie gods, but we won't." He declares, "Our Great Depression is our lives."

It is important to note though that the narrator will in fact become a "god" of sorts, the leader of a multitude of anonymous men who view him with awe, serve him, and call him "sir." His treatment at restaurants indeed quite closely approximates that of a celebrity. The film claims that the narrator is discovering he is not special, yet it indulges in the fantasy of becoming an underground cult figure or guru—not so different really from the fantastical accidental renown achieved by the constitutionally humble Forrest in *Forrest Gump*, which *Fight Club* mocks.

What begin to emerge in *Fight Club* are two very different accounts of the paths that the narrator and the film are taking. On the one hand, he is throwing off the corporate and consumer straightjacket to reveal a freedom, vitality, and authenticity that are expressed in the masculine pursuits of fighting and sex. On the other, he is pursuing a route of destruction and self-destruction out of a sense of rejection and abandonment by his father and exploitation by bosses and the selling industry. Either the narrator is discovering his aliveness in the body's vulnerability and power to harm, or he is degrading his body and others' out of traumatic self-loathing and depression. Either he is pursuing healthy masculine autonomy and sexual freedom or he is engaging in "therapeutic" sexual humiliation of women and fleeing from intimacy with them out of the terror of further rejection. Either he is splicing in bracing doses of sordid bodily reality to subvert a sentimentalizing culture or he is traumatizing little girls (we see one sobbing in the theater) out of a jealous envy of their innocence, a theme in such trauma films as *Welcome to the Dollhouse* and *Kids*. Either the film is pushing humility or indulging in a martial, even fascist, fantasy of celebrity. The film shimmers between these two very different possibilities. It is stuck between a sentimental slumming drama and a trauma film. Or, to put it another way, the sentimental slumming drama and sardonic trauma genres are inversions or mirror images of one another, and they imply one another.

Again, this doubleness is by no means distinct to the movie *Fight Club*; it is also a trademark of the literary tradition of the slumming trauma—and even of the literary tradition of the sentimental slumming drama. From Frank Norris to Henry Miller to the Beats and Kathy Acker, and from Mark Twain to Zora Neale Hurston, one encounters this double vision. The reader has to doubt that the Norris protagonist McTeague's sadistic treatment of his wife, which culminates in his murdering her, is merely the result of released masculine instinct; it seems to stem from his sense that she, along with the rising professional world that forbids him to practice his dentistry, is "mak[ing] small" of him.[7] Likewise, Miller's pornographic, liberated sexuality of *Tropic of Cancer* is revealed in *Tropic of Capricorn* to involve a revenge upon the mother whom he felt rejected by, and though in *Tropic of Cancer* he praises obscurity, expresses contempt for the literary world, and declares that he will publish the book anonymously, in reality he publishes *Cancer* under his own name and works tirelessly to promote it to the literary establishment. Acker's choice for her heroine Janie in *Blood and Guts in High School* of the "S&M" that is "glorifi[ed]" as sexual liberation over the sentimentalized "nicey-nicey-clean-ice-cream-TV-society"[8] may be the choice of the lesser of two evils, but the choice nonetheless involves a disturbing masochism.

Huck Finn's predilection for the slave Jim in Twain's ostensibly upbeat sentimental slumming tale can be seen as either heartfelt friendship for the outcast or the desire of a lower-class, abused white child to be with someone socially beneath him so he can feel a rare sense of superiority and dominance. After all, Huck is willing to submit this friend he is supposedly willing to go to hell for to considerable unpleasantness and to risk Jim's freedom and life when Huck's own social superior, Tom Sawyer, returns to the scene. Meanwhile, the free-spirited lover Tea Cake's fantastical demise in Hurston's sentimental slumming drama *Their Eyes*—hurricane, flood, dog bite, rabies, gunshot—seems more than a chance ending to a liberating slumming love relationship; the overblown sequence seems to imply a necessary degradation of the dark-skinned male love object akin to the rituals of the voodoo slaughter of animals that Hurston was taking part in on Haiti as she wrote the novel. (After all, in the similar story of *Titanic*, in which rich girl meets poor boy who liberates her and then dies, Jack dies peacefully and in one piece; it isn't necessary for Rose to violently murder him after he devolves into a rabid animal.) Moreover, Hurston's portrait of Janie as only interested in living, in vitality, seems to be belied by the character's return to a middle-class world she has supposedly hated—but where her slumming adventure can inspire awe and jealousy.

The film *Fight Club* never quite settles into either of these genres, the slumming drama or the class trauma. But, as the film progresses and its "gimmick" is revealed, the trauma film content becomes accented. When the audience learns that the narrator and Tyler are two aspects of the same person, the audience also realizes that the fighting between the narrator and Tyler has not been fighting at all (except in the narrator's mind), but rather one man pummeling himself. In fact, when the film definitively reveals that the narrator and Tyler inhabit the same body, the viewer can only conclude that the other men initially attracted to the burgeoning fight club were drawn not to the masculine spectacle of the fight, but to the very different—and arguably pathological and embarrassing spectacle—of a man doing violence to himself. The revelation of the narrator's split personality involves not only a reassessment of the principal characters but also of the Fight Club itself.

But even before the revelation that the narrator is "Dr. Jekyll and Mr. Jackass," as Marla puts it, the Fight Club seems centered on self-destruction. The first fight between the narrator and Tyler begins with Tyler asking to be hit and ends with each character begging to be hit again. Tyler declares at one point, "self-improvement is masturbation; now self-destruction...," affirming the latter with a glance. In this context, Tyler's defeat of the mobster Lou, the owner of the basement space that the Fight Club has co-opted for its meetings, takes on greater significance. Tyler defeats him not by fighting him—but by allowing himself, gleefully, to be pummeled, and then holding Lou down and bleeding on him, saying, "You don't know where I've been." This is something different from the Paul Newman character's famous victory in *Cool Hand Luke* (Stuart Rosenberg, 1967) against the George Kennedy character. Luke's refusal to give up eventually creates a sense of moral shame in the bully who must keep hitting a completely defenseless man or give up. Tyler provokes not conscience but traumatic repulsion in the bully— Lou folds because he cannot tolerate a stranger's insides dripping on him. It is Tyler's ability to take punishment and to be unfazed by his own physical mutilation and the spilling of his and others' bodily contents— the same ability that he teaches the narrator with the burning chemicals and the bags of liposuction waste—which seems to count most of all.

Tyler's masochistic directive to the Fight Club likewise becomes more interesting in this context—"this week, go out, start a fight with a total stranger, and you're gonna lose." It is worth mentioning here that trauma film writer-director Harmony Korine (*Kids*, *Gummo*) actually attempted to make a documentary film with precisely this premise. Korine's now abandoned *Fight Harm* project was a radical experiment in provocation and debasement. Korine explained: "The premise of the film is that I go up to the biggest men I can find and taunt them until they beat up on me. I kinda overlooked the fact that fights don't last very long and how damaging it is when someone really beats you up....And I'd wanted to make a 90-minute feature of just that, just one assault after the next one, and I'd fight every demographic. I'd fight a lesbian one night and fight a Puerto Rican the next. I'd fight a Jew. I tried to get everyone in there but they always had to be bigger than me." "But after six fights I really got messed up and was in the hospital and my ankles were broken and I'd been arrested."[9] Korine promised his worried mother that he'd see "a shrink" and guessed *Fight Harm* "was maybe a way of punishing myself for something":[10] the narrator in *Fight Club* might reasonably take a cue from Korine here. Korine's experience also underlines the essentially romantic attitude that *Fight Club* assumes in regard to violence and self-destruction. The main characters in the film do get hurt and even end up in the hospital, but they are back on their feet and back in the ring the next day: they experience no broken bones or really serious injuries, even in a high-speed car crash.

Finally, the premium on self-mutilation and self-inflicted harm seems to explain an ending that is initially baffling. The narrator somehow kills Tyler without killing himself by shooting himself in the mouth and blowing a hole in the back of his own neck. The audience may indeed wonder why such a wound would kill Tyler, or kill Tyler in particular without killing himself as well. (One might think of similar tales, such as Poe's "William Wilson" [1839], in which the main character's stabbing of his alter ego results in the death of the doppelganger as well as the self.) The answer may be simply that what the narrator has done here is to reintegrate his personality by embracing Tyler's essential quality, his modus operandi, which is self-mutilation. The narrator has killed Tyler by absorbing him, and he absorbs him by embracing self-inflicted harm.

The Desecrated Body

More needs to be said about physical harm here because the desecrated body is a central image in slumming trauma and it may indeed function as a primal expression of humiliation. Bleeding wounds, cuts, incisions, bites, scars, and bruises, especially infected ones, are veritable fetishes in the genre. Slumming drama treats the audience to young, beautiful faces and bodies, which, not incidentally, don't bruise or at least don't stay bruised from fights. The premium on youthful beauty explains the supposedly scandalous desire of Lester Burnham in *American Beauty* for his daughter's cheerleading friend. In fact, his erotic gaze and extended fantasies might be much more scandalous if they were directed at a woman his own age, with wrinkles, graying hair, and other signs of aging. The sentimental blockbuster needs a pretty, wholesome young woman or man to focus on. And Lester's desire is of course safely sentimentalized in his imagination of the red rose petals that adorn and modestly cover his young object of desire.

Meanwhile, blood, bruises, and scars more or less continuously mar the male characters in *Fight Club*. And the female lead sports an emaciated, disheveled, pale, and unhealthy-looking heroin chic. The choice of Helena Bonham Carter here to play Marla is important: the actress was previously especially known for her roles in Merchant Ivory productions (highly civilized films set in upper-class Victorian England) or film versions of Shakespeare. Marla's degradation is all the more shocking because of Bonham Carter's radical transformation from her screen image in, say, *Room with a View* (James Ivory, 1986). Marla toys with suicide and fears bodily decay. She describes herself to paramedics as "infectious human waste" and has the narrator check her breast for infection because she worries that "my tit's going to rot off." This eroticism of infection and dissolution again might seem quite foreign until one consults the literary tradition. In *McTeague* by Frank Norris, masochistic Trina ends up with swollen, infected fingers due to her husband McTeague's bites. Henry Miller claims that he could no more love the prostitute Germaine than he could love "a spider," and in a famous sequence soliloquizes on the "fucked-out crater" of a whore's "crack." What Miller sees there is an image of his own "ugly gash, the wound that never heals" beneath his "carapace of indifference" and self-canonization (*TC*, 42, 225). In much the same way, *Fight Club* glimpses the "serious emotional problems" beneath Tyler's pose of enlightenment and healthful destruction, and reveals these problems not only in Marla's criticism but also in her at once degraded and eroticized physical presence: in her unnerving self-presentation and self-description and in her screams during sex.

Happy Endings

Still, the degradation of the love object in this genre can be distinguished from that of trauma films. In regard to the love object and also more generally, degradation does not have the last word here. It has been a phase. The misogyny is certainly fantastical in *Fight Club*; after all, Tyler makes his money from soap made from female liposuction waste, or, as he puts it, by "selling rich women's fat asses back to them." But in *Fight Club*, Marla is able to step back from her debasing treatment and comment on the man's "problems" that make him abusive. She is also able to reflect on her degradation at the man's hands, even if she can't stop it or withdraw from it, and seems also to enjoy aspects of it. (It should be mentioned that some of this self-consciousness is comic: "I haven't been fucked like this since grade school," she asserts. Also, it is fairly clear that she gets an erotic charge from masochism: at one point she tries to arouse the narrator by comparing her second-hand dress to a "sex crime victim, underwear inside out, bound with electrical tape.")

But more striking still, the abusive (and self-abusive) man and the degraded (and self-abusive) woman actually get together at the end—something seemingly unthinkable in a trauma film. (It is impossible to imagine, say, Telly and Jenny in *Kids* getting together, or Chad and Christine in *In the Company of Men*, or Dante and Caitlin in *Clerks*. The irreversible, traumatic humiliations of these films—visited in each case upon the females—forbid such a "happy ending.") The narrator and Marla are holding hands as the buildings explode and topple across the street and the narrator bleeds from the self-inflicted gunshot to the mouth that has eliminated Tyler. Gruesome and apocalyptic, but nonetheless hopeful, the narrator's absurdly understated summary comment as the skyscrapers tumble—"you met me at a very strange time in my life"—seems to imply that the traumatic but liberating slumming nightmare he has been living through is now coming to an end and his life and his treatment of her are going to be different. (Again, Bonham Carter as Marla is an important bit of casting because the audience can easily imagine the actress restored to her wholesome look of previous movies—now that this phase is over.) As with Henry Miller the character at the end of *Tropic of Cancer*, or William S. Burroughs the character at the end of *Junky* (1953), a new understanding and peace follows a period of confusion, struggle, and violence.

Thus, as sentimental slumming dramas often end with a moving or sappy tragedy that brings the temporary downward mobility to an end—Jack dies in *Titanic*, as does Lester in *American Beauty*; Viola de Lesseps is forever separated from Shakespeare and banished to Virginia—slumming trauma stories tend also to deliver their protagonists from the bohemian depths, or at least point the way out, frequently with a death or symbolic death near the end. Indeed, the gunshot wound that mystically kills Tyler but not the narrator is a deus ex machina akin to the sinking of the Titanic that kills Jack but not Rose. Of course, the trauma aspect of the genre, with its insistence on a desecrated body, demands that the narrator not emerge physically unscathed: he ends up with a gaping neck wound. (By contrast, Rose doesn't lose any toes to frostbite, say.) But also unlike obviously sentimental slumming dramas, which tend to end in tragic death of the liberating figure, or at least loss of the love object, the hero can survive in the slumming trauma, and, as in *Fight Club*, even get the girl. *Fight Club* tries to insure, though, that no one can accuse its ending of sentimentality, not only with the repulsive neck wound, but also through heavy-handed irony and indie-film technique: as the narrator and Marla hold hands and gaze into one another's eyes, buildings crash, the camera gets shaky, and, like a wink to the audience, a final pornographic shot (of a man) is flashed across the screen.

Henry Miller and the Embrace of Defilement

The Artistic Transposition of Humiliation

Stephen Crane and Zora Neale Hurston represent two different artistic accommodations or transformations of humiliation that translate
into two of the three genres at issue here. Crane, who kept no journal
or diary and wrote no autobiography or memoir and few revealing letters (his most recent biographer thus calls his life "enigmatic"[1]), seems
to have projected his shame directly onto the characters in his class
trauma stories and to have said very little about his own anguish,
except in the obscurity of his famously cryptic poetry. He also created
a few heroic figures in his writing (such as Dr. Trescott) that possess
the stoicism, resolve, and stubbornness to resist the humiliators and
stigmatizers. Hurston, who manufactured heroic alter egos for herself
in her liberating fictions of slumming drama and also wrote about herself heroically in her autobiography, reconfigured her shame in almost
mystical terms as a special inner vitality that involved spiritual and
telepathic proclivities (à la voodoo). What little humiliation is evident
in her work (say in Tea Cake's bizarre death) peeps through in richly
reconfigured form. Crane and Hurston shared this: both disliked personal weakness and chose not to admit it, at least not in any direct
way, and both liked to construe themselves as unusually possessed of
moral integrity. Henry Miller makes a nice comparison to the two of
them for the shame theorist because his literary strategy of dealing
with his humiliation was so different and produced the third genre
under discussion: he crafted openly autobiographical and therapeutic

slumming trauma, in which he baldy proclaimed himself wounded and, rather than attempting to present himself (or his fictional Henry Miller) as possessing integrity, exaggerated his happy monstrosity. It is not that Miller was more honest than Hurston (though it is easy to say that both of them were more forthcoming than Crane); it is rather that Miller's fantasy of himself involved an ecstatic embrace of defilement.

Miller has much in common with Crane and Hurston, not only in the fact of the formation of his identity in conditions of humiliation, but also in his nonliterary strategies of coping with his personal difficulties. The sources of his shame were no doubt somewhat different from that of Crane and Hurston: on the one hand, he had a distant mother and a weak father like Crane; on the other, he experienced a class humiliation that was more akin to Hurston's experience of poverty after the breakup of her family. Miller's father had a drinking problem, and if Miller came to rationalize his father's drinking as an escape from an aggressive wife, he was also pretty clearly humiliated as a child by his father's kowtowing to wealthy customers in his tailor shop (*HM*, 29, 32).[2] As for coping as an adult, like Crane and Hurston, Miller found himself on the lam in voluntary exile, abandoning a (hard-won and fortuitous) middle-class and white-collar status in favor of a bohemian existence, and escaping from a romantic relationship he experienced as toxic and crippling. Miller manifested an anxiety about rejection that is similar to those experienced by Crane and Hurston: like George in Crane's *George's Mother*, Miller's first love, which lasted over a year, was of a neighborhood girl whom he never had the courage to approach.

When Miller finally found the mate he thought he truly desired and entered what he recognized as the relationship of his life, he too felt, like Crane, miserable and trapped, and, like Hurston, jealously mistrustful and afraid. "It is Sunday, the first Sunday of my new life, and I am wearing the dog collar you fastened around my neck," he later wrote of June (*Cap*, 347).[3] Like Crane and Hurston, he found his mate overbearing and possessive. He became submissive: "I learned what to do just as though I were part of her organism; I was better than a ventriloquist's dummy because I could act without being violently jerked by the strings" (*Cap*, 235). And, like Cora to Crane, June felt inaccessible to Miller: "I sought relentlessly for her whose name was not written anywhere, I penetrated to the very altar and found—nothing. I wrapped myself around this hollow shell of nothingness..." (*Cap*, 232). "Thou art a skull with ruby eyes," Crane wrote of Cora; Miller wrote of June: "*I could not read her face. I could see only the eyes shining* through, huge....How had she come to expand thus beyond all grip of consciousness? By what monstrous law had she spread herself thus over the face of the world, revealing everything and yet concealing herself?" (*Cap*, 232). She talked endlessly and "though she speaks of nothing but herself I am unable to form the slightest image of her being" (*Cap*, 343). Even when they were having sex, she could not be reached, and they could not connect: they were for Miller "like two maniacs trying to fuck through an iron grate" (*Cap*, 239). Like Crane, who felt trapped by his love in a relationship that caused him jealousy, held him at a distance, and so damaged him ("And I love thee / Woe is me"), and like Hurston, who was surprised that she could suffer so over her doubts about A.W.P., Miller describes himself as caught in "the straight jacket of doubt, jealousy, fear, loneliness" (*Cap*, 240).

The point is not that Cora was very much like June (though both seem charming and self-involved), but that Miller was something like Crane and Hurston, and all found in their love relationships the sense of rejection they felt as children. Hurston felt threatened by A.W.P. and the other men she became involved with; Crane felt a threat of "doom" from Cora. Miller felt himself already dead. He writes, in a wildly mixed metaphor: "That wound went to the heart. By all man-made logic I should have been dead. I was in fact given up for dead by all who once knew me; I walked about like a ghost in their midst...I was buried alive in a void which was the wound that had been dealt me. *I was the wound itself*" (*Cap*, 230). And here—evident in this passage—Miller's literary trajectory began dramatically to depart from that of Crane on the one hand and Hurston on the other.

At this point, during his flight from steady and white-collar work and from his wife, June, Miller had reached a crisis in his life. (His photographer friend in Paris, Halasz Brassai, stated bluntly, "madness and suicide threatened him."[4]) And this was also the point where Crane's and Miller's nonliterary trajectories stopped mirroring each other. Again, though Crane had abandoned Cora for the Cuban war, he eventually returned to her in England, as well as to his prose writing; there would be no more personal poetry or solitary living. Miller did the exact opposite. First, he left June and did not return (he was fortunate enough to have her initial support in this), moved to Paris, and dramatically changed his relationship with women: very soon, he absolutely forbade himself love from June; he rejected monogamy and sought emotional nourishment and romance from a (married) woman, Anaïs Nin, whose demands were low; and he attempted to put his other relationships with women on a purely sexual basis.

But to return to the literary issue, Miller began writing in a different way than he had previously. Whereas Crane left behind (when he left Cuba) his messy personal poetry and returned to a dignified, artistically accomplished prose in which it is possible to decipher an unconscious symbolism of his shame and fear, Miller began *consciously*, and with a frankness that could be called sloppy and would be deemed "obscene" (and result in American censorship), to craft a myth of his emotional origins and development. And though, like Hurston, he began to "sex all things" in his writing, he did so in an idiom that was degraded as well as lyrical. The very language of "the wound" that Miller was to develop, along with his routine and notorious use of the word "cunt," especially in the *Tropics*, indicates his creation of a romantic, slumming trauma idiom, however convoluted, of reality. As for his previous writing, which included three novels, he writes: "The million or so words which I had written, mind you, well ordered, well connected, were as nothing to me—crude ciphers from the old stone age—because the contact was through the head and the head is a useless appendage unless you're anchored in midchannel deep in the mud....I was only a mouthpiece for the ancestral race which was talking through me; even my dreams were not authentic, not bona fide Henry Miller dreams" (*Cap*, 284).

Tropic of Cancer is one of the most savage books in American literature; after a while, despite Miller's claim on the first page that "I am the happiest man alive" (*TC*, 1), one feels the novel is in fact a desperate chronicle of a life and death struggle. The first time Miller and June were ever separated, Miller "realized that the book I was planning was nothing more than a tomb in which to bury her—and the me which had belonged to her" (*Cap*, 334). *Cancer* is certainly the first attempt at such a book: the autobiographical novel as instinctive weapon and crude surgical tool. Banned in America for nearly thirty years for its obscenity and currently damned for its sexism, this book is less known for its fierce asceticism: in the novel, Miller the character will not allow himself love. He can feel the longing, and he cannot help but yearn for the woman he calls Mona (June), but he will not act on it. Helping him in his desperate asceticism is her distance; most of the time an ocean separates them, but an instant of thinking of her can throw him into despair and even terror:

> I had become so reconciled to this life without her, and yet if I thought about her only for a minute it was enough to pierce the bone and marrow of my contentment and shove me back again into the agonizing

gutter of my wretched past....When I realize that she is gone, perhaps gone forever, a great void opens up and I feel that I am falling, falling into deep, black space. And this is worse than tears, deeper than regret or pain or sorrow; it is the abyss into which Satan was plunged. There is no climbing back, no ray of light, no sound of human voice or human touch of hand. (*TC*, 160–61)

This exile from his love with June was a drastic move for a man like Miller, namely a man who yearned for love because he had been denied it from the start, a man who already by the age of eighteen was so lost in books, alienated, and solitary that he was "definitely unhappy, wretched, miserable, despondent."[5] Perhaps a more clinical way of explaining Miller's romantic need and attraction to June in particular is to say that his lack of recognition as a child had given him a tenuous, shaky sense of self, which he attempted to bolster by "merging" with a dynamic woman, by escaping his anxiety and depression with a woman who was especially exciting and dramatic. June was for Miller the woman "one can wait a whole lifetime" to meet; "the woman you never hoped to meet...and she talks and looks exactly like the person you dreamed about" (*Cap*, 343)—in part, no doubt, because she was an expert player of roles, and she responded to her audiences.[6] June talked of August Strindberg and Fedor Dostoevski; she talked of herself; her endless talk "spurts out of her like a flame and consumes everything within reach"; Miller was mesmerized, and, by his own account, his anxiety was quieted (*Cap*, 343). And having once found her, it was almost impossible to give her up, despite all the misery, and he probably would not have done it had he not come to the realization that she could do without him (*Cap*, 333–34).

A man whose alienation and tendency toward solitude seemed to be a good part of his problem, Miller decided in Paris that he had to increase his solitude and sharpen his alienation. Miller's personal answer was not to ignore "the wound"—which in Miller's understanding too involved shame or damage to one's sense of self—or to attempt a relationship despite it, but to plunge into it, "deeper...into the void." "The man which I now am was born out of a wound," he writes in *Capricorn* (*Cap*, 230). It was not possible for Miller to cure himself of longing (or even of romantic involvement), but he could wean himself of *a* love—and really the type of love—that animated and tortured him, hypnotized him and bound him, without giving him communion and emotional nourishment. (Norman Mailer called Miller's type of love with June "narcissistic" and writes, "It is possible that narcissism is a true disease, a biological displacement of the impulse to develop which could bear the same relation to love that onanism does to copulation, or cancer to natural growth of tissue."[7]) Miller could finally be free of such a seduction when he was able to produce a different, somewhat surer, sense of himself based on a sense of his own creative or expressive powers.

Perhaps Crane was never a ventriloquist dummy on Cora's knee, as Miller describes himself in regard to June, but the operative point here is that both Crane and Miller were attracted to women who seemed to them uninterested in their inner lives—and with whom they thus recapitulated their childhood deprivations. From his very first written works, Crane was directing most of his bitter irony against egotism and self-promotion; *Maggie* was ferocious on the subject. In his letters, even before his fame, Crane singled out his own overgrown egotism—which the shame theorist would consider a result of his childhood sense of neglect—and after the success of *The Red Badge*, he saw his ultimate struggle to be just that: he could be seduced by praise. It seems Crane in fact mistook his greatest enemy in deciding to battle his ego; in effect, he tried to treat a (compensatory) symptom of his humiliation, perhaps in part because the obvious threat that came with fame blinded him to another: the fear and hatred of the female that runs through his writing like a cryptographic trace. Miller saw the danger (no doubt with the help of the Freudian revolution) and came to recognize the humiliation he had been dealt, first of all by his cold, stern mother.

Miller's Pornographic Therapy

Cancer is of course notorious for its crude objectification of women; this obscenity is not accidental, but central to Miller's project. He apparently reduced women to their sexual parts first of all in order to prevent them from getting anything but the least emotional hold upon him. He made himself immune to further love (or at least to monogamy or marriage) by developing a rich, sometimes comic, sometimes cosmic, but always pornographic description of his encounters with women. The equation for his own subjectivity in *Cancer* is simple: "I am only spiritually dead. Physically I am alive." He committed a radical surgery in which all players were, ideally, trimmed down to the life of the body: women are "cunts"; men are free meals and buffoons, and Miller is a "hyena," going forth to "fatten" himself—and to laugh (*TC*, 90). This is a book of sexual predation, and one can sense in it Miller's long-suppressed rage and the violent, if gleeful and comic, revenge for his perceived suffering at the hands of women.

Female prostitution obviously provides an ideal theatre for his program. And if he related to prostitutes other than sexually, it is not as with Crane, who instinctively recognized their pain and wanted to save them. Miller identified with some prostitutes too, even with their "wounds," but he admired their detachment from their pain and from other people: and so he remains detached from them as they are detached from him. He writes of a prostitute he calls Germaine that she had a "good heart, a whore's heart which is not really a good heart but a lazy one, an indifferent, flaccid heart...." And he quickly adds: "I could no more think of loving Germaine that I could think of loving a spider" (*TC*, 41–42). Miller was not looking to save her (or any other prostitute) because he was specifically not looking for romantic salvation himself.

Cancer's savage ideal exaggerates Miller's sexual prowess and underplays his relationship to Anaïs Nin, which was not merely sexual, but also provided emotional (and financial) support. But the romantic asceticism of *Cancer* was not simply a lie, as his relationship with Nin was carefully and importantly contained: the fact of her marriage, which she had no intention of leaving, usually safeguarded him against transcendental notions of love and the accompanying emotional dependence. The relation to Nin functioned, perhaps, like a halfway house or an addiction cure; he spared himself the agony of going cold turkey.

Though Miller's language denies it, the book, and his pornographic strategy of emotional ascesis, has a sort of philosophical or psychological harvest. *Cancer* is a radical reassessment of love—conventionally thought of as a relationship between two people—from the point of view of the voluntarily solitary (and humiliated) man. At times, as in Miller's lonely sojourn in Dijon, the novel reads like an emotional version of Descartes' *Meditations*: "Alone, with tremendous empty longing and dread. The whole room for my thoughts. Nothing but myself and what I think, what I fear. Could think the most fantastic thoughts, could dance, spit, grimace, curse, wail...The thought of such absolute privacy is enough to drive me mad. It's like a clean birth. Everything cut away. Separate, naked, alone. Bliss and agony simultaneously...The me and the not-me...Everything has to be learned, tested, experienced" (*TC*, 258). The result of this experiment was that Miller could discover the psychic origins of love or at least of his particular brand of love colored by shame. From the far side of human connection, Miller perceived that love was not a feeling sparked by another; it was a condition of primal longing that a (humiliated) man always carried with him. "Going back in a flash over the women I've known. It's like a chain which I've forged out of my own misery. Each one bound to the other. A fear of living separate, of staying born. The door of the womb always on the latch. Dread and longing. Deep in the blood the pull of paradise. The beyond. Always the beyond" (TC, 258–59).

By being truly alone (for periods of time), by attempting to shave himself down to his physical self, and at points severing all emotional attachments, he was able to see that the feeling of longing required no love object; he was able to isolate it in his person, to discover that longing was fundamentally a reality of his individual psyche. And so he realized that his relationships with June (and all the others) were at bottom a function of a misery that predated them.

When one comes across Miller's dissection of love, his deconstruction of yearning, Crane's blindness in regard to his own romantic longing becomes stunning. Crane, perhaps the premier antisentimental writer of his age, who savagely mocked the sentimental, Cinderella dreams of his protagonist in his first novel (by having them lead her into a life of prostitution and violent death), never cured himself of his own romantic fantasies and seemed hardly to have struggled with them. His love objects were often dramatically inappropriate, women of solid, upper-middle-class backgrounds whom he wildly romanticized as brave or free spirits. And Cora, his nightclub owner who proved to have similar social pretensions to those of the society ladies he hopelessly courted, he doubted, but could not finally leave, hoping always, it seemed, that she would ultimately prove to be a soul mate.

Miller meanwhile analyzed his damaging sentimental habits and was able to withdraw from them. And what he romanticized instead—in a compensatory fashion—was the world of sex. With his unusual sentimental asceticism and his obscenity, he discovered, or rather fashioned, an entire "world of sex" (to use a phrase of his[8])—a world, not incidentally, that he could share to some degree with others, both his female sexual partners and his male cronies. "The Land of Fuck" (Cap, 197), "pure fuck and pure cunt," as he calls it, purified of sentiment and attachment and good and evil, was a compelling realm, an erotic wonderland, which provided a counterweight to that of love. Miller came to imagine "the reality of a realm which was called Fuck, because that was the only name which might be given to it, and yet it was more than fuck and by fucking one only began to approach it"

(*Cap*, 192). If he was nearly devoid of sympathies, he was filled with passion; if he objectified women out of a sadistic desire for conquest and revenge and so, to quote Crane, "uses the cruel one cruelly," his objectification also plunged him into a lively, imaginative, and artistic world that belonged as much to the body as the mind. Miller entered a realm of experience where he could begin to wean himself from the Freudian "virgin/whore syndrome" that Crane never escaped (namely, the neurotic compulsion either to worship or defile women, to ideal- ize or demonize them). Again, Miller rejected his previous writing "because the contact was through the head and the head is a useless appendage unless you're anchored in midchannel deep in the mud" (*Cap*, 284): sexual passion turned out to be such a possible anchor. Rainer Maria Rilke made a similar observation: "Artistic experience lies so incredibly close to that of sex, to its pain and its ecstasy, that the two manifestations are indeed but different forms of one and the same yearning and delight."[9] If Miller was a pornographer, then he was a special kind, for his subject was often not sex acts, but sex emo- tions, sex intuitions, sex metaphysics, sex epistemology, sex eschatol- ogy, sex comedies, sex rubrics, and sex mythology, and his language is often deliriously inventive in its mix of registers:

> There are cunts which laugh and cunts which talk; there are crazy, hys- terical cunts shaped like ocarinos and there are planturous, seismo- graphic cunts which register the rise and fall of sap...there are also masochistic cunts which close up like the oyster and have hard shells and perhaps a pearl or two inside...there are cruising cunts fitted out like yachts, which are good for solitaries and epileptics...there are cunts made of pure joy which have neither name nor antecedent....And then there is the one cunt which is all, and this we shall call the super-cunt, since it is not of this land at all but of that bright country to which we were long ago invited to fly. Here the dew is ever sparkling and the tall reeds bend with the wind. It is here that the great father of fornication dwells, Father Apis, the mantic bull who gored his way to heaven and dethroned the gelded deities of right and wrong. (*Cap*, 194–95)

Miller's biographer Ferguson rightly characterizes Miller's sexual behavior as an escape from guilt and pain about June, but it was also more than that: to see it as merely an escape is to miss the transforma- tive nature of Miller's venturing into a world of sex, especially in the sense of transforming his humiliation. Miller says at the beginning of *Cancer* that he is "dead" (*TC*, 1) and later amends this to "spiritually dead," but, while he was busy in Paris killing off the love he felt for June and the mental life that made that love possible and so desirable (as well as killing off the guilt for leaving her), something else came alive in him, and it was not just his body, unless we understand that body to be the force of a passion that could reprogram his mind and reformulate his shame in a way so that his profoundly intellectual relationship with June no longer had a hold upon him, but appeared to him like a burlesque, a puppet show. The transformation Miller effected upon himself was not finally to kill his humiliation and his emotions of love and guilt and to vivify his body, but to connect his mind, his feelings, and his sexuality in what one might agree with Miller to call a "resurrection of the emotions" (TC, 220): he came alive emotionally by becoming mentally aware of the desires, fears, and humiliations that had been unconsciously driving his actions as a lover, or rather his inaction, his paralysis. His procedure was to resist the blind sentimental impulses (for the "paradise" of love) that again and again brought him to misery, and to do so in part by using sex both as a substitute world and as a release from misery and an aggressive purge of the anger beneath that misery, which he had long repressed out of a fear of alienating the loved one and ending up alone. So his foray into a world of pure sex was not only a leap toward "ecstasy" (TC, 232) but also, like the experience of solitude, another experiment in which he learned about the emotions—including the shame—that had been secretly compelling him.

If his romantic relationships had been a salve on his primal "wound" (of rejection or humiliation) and an escape from himself into the talk, the needs, and obsessions of another person, then the removal of love exposed the humiliation, and the theatre of sex was a stage on which to discover and also act out the shame and anger thus uncovered. In the process, his perception of reality was changed, and eventually June was no longer a bright, warm sun, which lit up his world and around which he orbited, but "a dead black sun without aspect" (Cap, 239). He came to see her constant talk not as giving life and energy but as a "daily flight" "away from the self," motivated by "terror" (Cap, 245, 242). Miller's tour into enforced solitude and sexual passion/exploitation dragged him out of "the stratosphere of ideas, that is…the grip of delirium," where he could find himself a miserable, but helpless, slave to June. He came to believe that "ideas cannot exist alone in the vacuum of the mind. Ideas are related to living: liver ideas, kidney ideas, interstitial ideas, etc." (TC, 220, 219). In a famous episode in Cancer in which he takes to a brothel a novice who mistakenly uses the bidet as a toilet, Miller imagines with glee "what a miracle it would be" if the transcendental meaning that man "attends eternally should turn out to be nothing more than these two enormous turds which the faithful disciple dropped in the *bidet*" (*TC*, 89). Miller was determined to go "off the gold standard in ideas, dress, morals, etc., [off] *the gold standard of love*!...[and] off the gold standard of literature" (*TC*, 219). His new standard was what he called "the mud": the reality of the emotions that stand behind ideas, creeds, and the notion of sentimental love. In *Cancer*, he wrote, "my idea briefly has been to present a resurrection of the emotions....To paint a pre-Socratic being, a creature part goat, part Titan. In short, to erect a world on the basis of the *omphalos*, not an abstract idea nailed to a cross" (*TC*, 220).

Miller's romantic asceticism stands in stark contrast to Crane's indulgence in this regard. But his expatriation to the social fringes of Paris was also, like Crane's escape from the middle-class to the Bowery slums and Hurston's escape from New York to the South and the Caribbean, a strategy for protecting a psyche attuned to shame. He too sought refuge from potential rejection and a sense of failure:

> I had to travel precisely all around the world to find just such a comfortable, agreeable niche such as this....How could I have foreseen, in America, with all those firecrackers they put up your ass to give you pep and courage, that the ideal position for a man of my temperament was to look for orthographic mistakes? Over there you think of nothing but becoming President of the United States some day. Potentially every man is Presidential timber. Here it's different. Here every man is potentially a zero. If you become something or somebody it is an accident, a miracle. The chances are a thousand to one that you will never leave your native village....But it's just because the chances are all against you, just because there is so little hope, that life is sweet over here. (*TC*, 135)

By escaping New York and the United States, Miller thus escaped the expectation and judgment of his countrymen—who valued success and wealth—which he had experienced as a humiliation. "It was scorn which ultimately Miller could not stand," says Brassai. "It was scorn that he wanted to escape."[10] "Nowhere have I felt so degraded and humiliated as in America," Miller wrote (*Cap*, 12). The sweet slum life in Paris freed him from this implicit scorn, lifted the crushing weight of disapproval, and Miller now had the strength to fire salvos back at his native land, a strength he lacked in America. For Miller, the principle fact of America is "the treadmill" (*TC*, 63), and he writes, "I think of all the streets in America combined as forming a huge cesspool, a cesspool of the spirit in which everything is sucked down to everlasting shit." Miller's one "solace" was that "at least I knew I was unhappy, unwealthy, out of step and out of whack. But it was hardly enough....It would have been better for my peace of mind, for my soul, if I had expressed my rebellion openly, if I had gone to jail for it, if I had rotted there and died....Because in the bottom of my heart there was murder: I wanted to see America destroyed, razed from top to bottom" (*Cap*, 12).

It is evident that he also wanted to see the literary establishment brought down: *Cancer* is introduced as "a gob of spit in the face of Art" (*TC*, 2). Miller in the slums of Paris, like Crane in the Bowery and Hurston in Haiti, had the breathing space of a dark corner, a place to avoid the cold spotlight of literary and bourgeois American scorn. He was now safe to rebel in words, to lacerate America in his writing, and he put no brakes on his ranting, indulging in tirades that Crane and Hurston never allowed themselves. As Miller told a friend, "hatred and vengeance" were the motivation for *Tropic of Cancer* (*HM*, 183). Like his anger at women and at his mother (which he expresses in his casual sex as well as his crude language), Miller's rage with the institutions and the society that might call him a failure was liberated in his voluntary exile—and his genre of slumming trauma.

His Parisian "world of sex," then, functioned as the domain where Miller was neither humiliated nor romantically vulnerable. In the emotional prophylaxis of this predatory, sexual, and nonmonogamous world, Miller's "wounds," his rejections in love and the assaults on his sense of self, could be more safely uncovered and observed, and the cathartic experience that ensued was figured in Miller's perhaps central and certainly most intensely concentrated image of the "cunt" or "crack." In the philosophical climax of *Cancer*, the prostitute's vagina that Miller sees in front of his face, on an occasion of sexual acrobatics, is at once a symbol of this purely sexual realm and of Miller's fundamental humiliation, which his immersion in this "pure cunt" has allowed him to realize. Miller's contemplation here is not only on the generative power of the mother and the spiritual exhaustion of a Western civilization that finds sex obscene; the "crack" is also "the wound that never heals," which is, universally, the longing for paradise (and the door of the womb that is always on the latch), but more particularly to Miller, his shame: the rejection of his love by his distant mother and, similarly, the rejection of his person by a "fucked-out crater" (*TC*, 225) of a world that does not value him unless he becomes rich. This world includes, one might imagine, the upper-class individuals that patronized the shop of his working-class father. Miller writes: "When a man appears the world bears down on him and breaks his back....If at intervals of centuries there does appear a man with a desperate, hungry look in his eyes, a man who would turn the world upside down to create a new race, the love that he brings to the world is turned to bile and becomes a scourge" (*TC*, 224).

Laced into Miller's chaotic and fast-shifting free-association on the "crack" is a coherent depiction of the anatomy of his own humiliation, the method of sexual immersion that he used to transform his relationship to his shame, and the nonintellectual sources of his creativity.

> When a hungry desperate spirit appears and makes the guinea pigs squeal it is because he knows where to put the live wire of sex, because he knows that beneath the hard carapace of indifference there is concealed the ugly gash, the wound that never heals. It is no use putting on rubber gloves; all that can be cooly and intellectually handled belongs to the carapace and a man who is intent on creation always dives beneath, to the open wound, the festering obscene horror. He hitches his dynamo to the tenderest parts; if only blood and pus gush forth, it is something. (*TC*, 225).

Beneath the carapace of Miller's infamous indifference and alienation was the cause of this shell and the very thing it is meant to protect: Miller's shame. The "crack" is here both the symbol of that humiliation ("wound" or "gash") and the symbol of the sexual route he was taking to self-definition and specifically the bringing to consciousness of this "open wound," this "tenderest part," this shame, which allowed him to create artistically. He put "the live wire of sex" to use in breaking his shell. It was not sex that was obscene to Miller but rather the paralysis that came from never "div[ing] beneath" one's hard, protective intellectual shell to the buried humiliation and pain. "More obscene than anything is inertia. More blasphemous than any oath is paralysis. If there is only a gaping wound left then it must gush forth though it produce nothing but toads and bats and homunculi" (*TC*, 225). This is the hyperearthy, supersexual, and defiled language in which Miller often speaks of inner reality in the *Tropics*, no doubt because it was sex that had brought him to his understanding. For Miller—a profoundly antitranscendentalist writer—in *Cancer*, the path to self-revelation and artistic creation was downward, through the genitals, to the site of humiliation. To spoof Emerson, as Miller himself does at one point in *Cancer*,[11] one might say that Miller has hitched his wagon to a scar.

Search for Fame

Miller's refuge in his expatriate world of sex, depicted in *Cancer*, was cathartic and also transformative, and it eventually weaned him from the passive and submissive type of love he knew with June. But it was not, of course, a cure for his humiliation, nor his longing for love—which he secretly fulfilled to some degree with Anaïs Nin—nor his longing for recognition as a writer—which he likewise mostly hid from the pages of *Cancer* and which made the novel in important ways definitely fictional and, one might even argue, deceptive. Miller was not free of his massive ambition, out of the United States, any more than Crane when he found sanctuary among the lower class in the Bowery or Hurston when she found solace in the backwoods of Haiti. *Cancer* is no doubt full of poses and the sexual overman that Miller depicted himself as did not correspond, in reality, to the flesh and blood man who was once too shy to approach a girl for a year. But this sexual superman, "part goat and part Titan," was a sentiment, an aspiration born of bodily desires and psychic damage and so has an emotional truth. His understatement of the romance with Nin (Tania in the novel), likewise, did not entirely invalidate his loneliness or his asceticism when it came to a transcendental love. Meanwhile, Miller's pose as the happy orthographer (or proofreader) who lives without grand hopes was not a question of overstatement but of plain fiction and perhaps deception, even self-deception in a book that claimed frankness and honesty for itself, if not about the facts of the main character's life, then about his emotions. In this regard, Miller was like Hurston (in her autobiography), who claims she is driven merely to create and says nothing about her desire for fame. Miller may have been weaning himself from transcendental hopes of meaning but he was not curing himself of hopes of recognition for his writing. His pose of nonambition was perhaps a ruse to protect himself from the fearful stakes of the gamble he was taking with the book, *Cancer*: having retreated from the field of all other achievement, he had to succeed here—or very likely go crazy with self-loathing.

And like Crane, who published *Maggie* under a mundane pseudonym, Miller imagined publishing his novel without his name on it. In *Cancer*, he writes, "Boris and I discussed the book. *The Last*

Book—which is going to be published anonymously" (*TC*, 20). And later, "We have evolved a new cosmogony of literature, Boris and I. It is to be a new Bible—*The Last Book*. All those who have anything to say will say it here—*anonymously*. We will exhaust the age....The world will be able to feed on it for a thousand years to come. It is colossal in its pretentiousness" (*TC*, 23–24). In a 1932 anthology of writing in which a piece of Miller's appeared, his bibliographical note declared, "Last book, a novel, will be published anonymously."[12] However, the book with which Miller was "pregnant" (*TC*, 23) was not a joint effort, but *Cancer*, and though he spoke of publishing it anonymously, he of course did not, and in fact did his best to get it into the hands of writers from the literary establishment he disparaged. As Erica Jong reported, he was "indefatigable in promoting" it.[13]

Miller's Slumming Trauma and Its Appeal

Again—outside of this one large suppression (of his literary ambition)—Miller's genre of slumming trauma represents a different literary strategy for the transformation of shame than those of Crane (class trauma) and Hurston (slumming drama). While Crane and Hurston pillory complainers in their stories, and Hurston simply states in her autobiography that "bitterness is the under-arm odor of wishful weakness" (*DT*, 205), and so decides personally to avoid it, Miller's writing embraces bitter whining.

It can be argued that Miller and Crane shared an ample anger and hatred for America and Christianity, as well as a marked misogyny. But Crane, proud and supermasculine, held his anger in and so remained detached from it; Miller, clearly, held nothing of his anger back—no matter how pathetic and wild his bursts of fury. To reiterate one example of his murderous expressions about the United States: "I wanted to see America destroyed, razed from top to bottom" (*Cap*, 12). And to take one instance of his misanthropy and misogyny: "Henceforth I would live as an animal, a beast of prey, a plunderer....And if rape were the order of the day, then rape I would, and with a vengeance" (*TC*, 90).

Likewise, while Crane and Hurston created proud characters to be mocked for their pretensions (such as Jimmie Johnson and Mrs. Turner, respectively)—and so could be said to have mocked themselves, as Alfred Kazin claims about Crane—Miller indulged in megalomania, even if he denied his specific desire for literary fame. Crane wrote in one letter, after he became famous: "Dear me, how much am I getting to admire graveyards...ignorant of the accursed golden hopes that flame at night and make a man run his legs off and then in the daylight of experience turn out to be ingenious traps for the imagination....If there is a joy in living I cant find it...."[14]

This was typical Crane; there was an ascesis of pride, the refusal to be inspired by his own golden hopes which, intellectually, he saw as embarrassing traps and perhaps also temptations to act badly. Miller, by contrast, refused nothing and avoided gilded traps only by walking into them over and over again until they finally lost their appeal. And he seemed never to tire of his delusions of grandeur. Even as he hid his interest in fame, he made claims about the book he was working on that were "colossal in...pretentiousness" (TC, 24). Miller was not interested in an intellectual anticipation of where his night thoughts would lead, not embarrassed by vainglory, and willfully oblivious to bad form, including bad writing. Cancer might be described as an ode to passion and whenever it came Miller's way, whether in the form of fury or megalomania—or sexual fever—he grabbed at it.

Sexual frenzy is of course the other passion that animates Cancer, and here it is worth distinguishing this sexual mania from the act itself. In a famous sequence in the novel, in which a character named Van Norden has passionless and mechanical sex with a prostitute simply because he has already paid her fifteen francs, Miller is insistent about the difference between the act of sex—performed out of some sense of obligation—and passion. The event becomes for Miller a metaphor for the stupidity of modern, rationalized society and war, and he feels he has put his finger on the answer. He writes: "No, there's the fifteen francs somewhere, which nobody gives a damn about any more and which nobody is going to get in the end anyhow, but the fifteen francs is like the primal cause of things and rather than *listen to one's own voice*, rather than walk out on the primal cause, one surrenders to the situation, one goes on butchering and butchering..." (TC, 128, my emphasis). The problem for Miller with Van Norden is that the obligation to the fifteen francs has usurped his own desire here to decline sex, so the sexual act, rather than liberating, becomes yet another convention. Van Norden is merely the "mouthpiece" of a society that has decreed the nature of the exchange with a prostitute.

Sex is not in itself liberating or close to artistic experience, but as Rilke says, its ecstasy and pain is. It is important to note that Miller's sex life before Paris, despite its amplification and glorification in *Capricorn* and *The Rosy Crucifixion* (1949, 1960, 1963) and despite his bohemian living arrangements with June, was conventional (*HM*, 185). In Paris, Miller anchored his prose in his immediate passions—food is also a large subject in *Cancer* and toilets are celebrated in *Black Spring* (1936).

Miller's indiscriminate retrieval and elaboration of feeling explains the apparent dichotomy between his low, pornographic comedy and his "serious" writing. It also explains the apparent contradiction between his hard-boiled skepticism in the face of dogma and his interest in mysticism. The latter is the material in Miller's oeuvre that his champions often find the most embarrassing—and puzzling. Lawrence Durrell, his friend and probably greatest booster in the literary world was bemused and disconcerted by the apparent anomaly of an interest in religious philosophies, astrology, and the occult in a man who had made his name as a debunker of hypocrisy and humbug (*HM*, 295). Kenneth Rexroth likewise remarks: "Miller...is likely at times to go off the deep end about the lost continent of Mu or astrology or the 'occult.'..."[15] Both Durrell and Rexroth attempt to justify Miller's mystic interests on other philosophical grounds. Durrell attributed them to a reasonable reaction to the extreme materialism of American life (*HM*, 295), and Rexroth similarly proposed that Miller was acting on the principle of the lesser of two evils: "If the whole shebang is a lie anyway, certainly the amusing lies, the lies of the charlatans who have never been able to get the guillotine in their hands, are better than the official lie, the deadly one."[16]

The answer may be simpler. One can find in Miller's work, as Mailer writes, "all the roar of passion, the flaming poetry, the passing crazy wit, and not an instant of intellectual precision, no products of Mind..."[17] To put this in a way that is perhaps a little kinder to Miller, it might be proposed that Miller's angry, solitary debunking and his comic obscenity neither contradicted, nor complemented his mysticism, but rather led to it. Miller's break with his job, his country, and finally his wife and the subsequent loneliness set the stage for both freethinking and free feeling. Liberated from the need to conform (and so keep a job) and to please (which was a fundamental preoccupation in regard to June), Miller began in fact to wean himself from what he calls the "delirium" of an intellectual approach to living, substituting an apparently more nourishing mania of feeling. This "resurrection of the emotions" (*TC*, 220) eventually led to an eclipse of longstanding intellectual reflexes and even the development of little-used emotional muscles, or perhaps emotional hallucinations—depending on how one views mysticism. *The Colossus of Maroussi* (1941) is a remarkable book if only for the fact that Miller's striking portrait of ancient Greece is stubbornly achieved almost without the help of archeological and historical evidence, and his comic description of Saturn is likewise carried out without a telescope: he relies instead on his "impressions and intuitions" (CM, 85).[18]

George Orwell, in trying to decipher the appeal of Miller's work, decides that "it is a voice from the crowd, from the underling, from the third-class carriage, from the ordinary, non-political, non-moral, passive man." He declares, "Miller is simply a hard-boiled person talking about life, an ordinary American businessman with intellectual courage and a gift for words." And he describes Cancer as "the book of a man who is happy."[19]

But this assessment, though it is close to that of other Miller champions, fails, it seems, to understand Miller's genre as well as the appeal of his books. It is clear that Orwell fails to appreciate the path Miller took to writing Cancer when he notes, "Miller is writing about the man in the street," and when he finds it

> incidentally rather a pity that it should be a street full of brothels. That is the penalty of leaving your native land. It means transferring your roots into shallower soil. Exile is probably more damaging to a novelist than to a painter or even or poet, because its effect is to take him out of contact with working life and narrow down his range to the street, the cafe, the church, the brothel and the studio. On the whole, in Miller's books you are reading about people living the expatriate life, people drinking, talking, meditating, and fornicating, not about people who are marrying, and bringing up children; a pity, because he would have described the one set of activities as well as the other.[20]

No doubt Miller, after his experience of loneliness in Paris, could write about marriage; he wrote in an unprecedented manner about his own with June in Capricorn and The Rosy Crucifixion; as Norman Mailer points out, "Miller...is the first American to make the attempt" to describe "the uncharted negotiations of the psyche when two narcissists take the vow of love."[21] Orwell's misconception, it seems, lies in his implicit notion of the novelistic art as a simple mimesis, the author as careful observer and reporter. What Miller ended up changing, in his move to Paris, was not only his distance from white-collar working life but also his perception of it—as he changed his relationship to himself, his intimates, and the working world. (He would devote a good deal of Capricorn to a brutal parody of his white-collar experience in New York.) A man who had not experienced unemployment, demotion, or ostracism would hardly have perceived that "the superstructure is a lie and the foundation is a huge quaking fear" (*TC*, 224). Miller, in leaving the career and working worlds (a process he began in New York with June and finished in Paris without her), experienced the anxiety involved, and so came to realize that the work world is based not only on the desire for goods, wealth, respect, and recognition but, even more basically, on the terror of not having these things.

Miller's art in *Cancer* was not based on accurate reporting of the world around; it was based on the pain, fear, and, yes, sometimes also happiness of bringing to consciousness the hidden emotions, and certainly the humiliations, that unwittingly motivate and agitate working people in everyday, unexamined life. Miller's proper subject was not the reality of the street but the reality of the emotions. He was not a photographic eye but an emotional seismograph. Nor was he an ordinary American businessman but rather a man who had burned away his complacent self-respect, anxious self-doubt, and general self-ignorance (that usually comes with employment, salary, and marriage) in the fires of unemployment, poverty, and loneliness. It is not true that Miller gave average men voice. He seemingly chucked the whole system of marriage and work and somehow survived—as average men imagine they would like to. He did not speak for the average man, or even the average failed man, but *to* him. Miller was quite clear—and, I think, was right—about his distance from the common man in the stark, proud, defiant, final lines of *Black Spring*: "Tonight I would like to think of one man, a lone individual, a man without name or country, a man whom I respect because he has absolutely nothing in common with you—MYSELF. Tonight I shall meditate upon that which I am."[22]

Notwithstanding Orwell's lament, *Cancer* could not have been written from inside corporate or working-class life. If Miller wrote in an appealing way to the average man (and woman), and the sales of his books worldwide appear to bear this out, it was because he removed himself from ordinary life: the result was not just that he got a better vantage point, but that he tore himself up by the emotional roots and so exposed them to himself and wrote about them.

Slumming Trauma as Written Therapy

And once having done that, Miller had to *write* for his life—at least at first—or be swept under in the terror of isolation and humiliation. Here entered his defensive delusions of grandeur, the sort of private fantasies that Crane again and again mocked in his novels. The imperative, to create a new "culture" for himself out of words—in which one is not a failure and a loveless reject, but an artist and a soul in growth—*also* accounts (along with the exhilaration of "passing wit") for Miller's fevered writing style and his mad prolificness. "He had to write himself out of his own dungeons and did," comments Mailer.[23] Wordsworth said that poetry was "emotion recollected in tranquility," but for Miller there could be no tranquility (before he gained recognition, which is to say in the period when he was writing *Cancer* and much of *Black Spring*, and arguably until much later in his life). For Miller in *Cancer* especially, fiction was potentially self-destructive terror and doubt harnessed and mastered, beaten back, swamped, and smashed to pieces by an angry, giddy, and megalomaniacal prolix. As Mailer puts it, Miller "can never feel calm enough to live in the world of art. In this sense, everything Miller writes is therapy." Mailer attributes Miller's literary intensity to the need "to drain the throttled heats of the ego each day,"[24] and it might even be more accurate to say that the writing itself was often another heat, a fierce battle to achieve a precarious homeostasis. Miller in fact characterizes this situation in *Cancer*: "If now and then we encounter pages that explode, pages that wound and sear, that wring groans and tears and curses, know that they come from a man with his back up, a man whose only defenses left are his words and his words are always stronger than the lying, crushing weight of the world..." (*TC*, 224).

Miller was not only "getting the poison out of [his] system"[25] that had built up over his years of humiliation in America but was also expelling daily toxins. The more intense the psychic shock that a person or an event delivered to Miller, it seems, the more he had to strike back, in an equal and opposite reaction. In *Cancer*, his sexual boasting in regard to Tania was perhaps payback for, and certainly denial of, the emotional dependence—and thus potential sentimental weakness—he was developing in regard to Nin (on whom Tania is based), as well as his jealousy of her husband. Likewise, one has the feeling that the "sex crazed" portrait of Van Norden was an attempt to distinguish himself from his real-life acquaintance Wambly Bald (*HM*, 181–83), whose sexual prowess he probably found intimidating. If Miller's works after *Cancer* became somewhat more tranquil, this homeostatic function of his writing never entirely disappeared. Even in the relative calm of *The Colossus of Maroussi*, Miller the incipient "sage" felt the need to attack his enemies in prose (mostly the returned Greek immigrants to the United States who sing America's praises), and in the case of the tavern owner's French wife who misses "civilization" while living in

Greece, he is virulent and untiring: her remark spurs him to spin a lengthy and surreal myth that combines figures from Ancient Greece and American jazz, Agamemnon and Louis Armstrong, and only then is his good humor restored (*CM*, 138–45).

Miller speculated in an interview late in his life about one of the reasons for his popular appeal: "I was getting the poison out of my system. Curiously enough, this poison had a tonic effect for others. It was if I had given them some kind of immunity."[26] Perhaps it was not immunity but, rather, a momentary if vicarious sense of victory, a fantastical feeling that they too could triumph over the petty and not-so-petty humiliations in their lives. What is perhaps most compelling to Orwell's "ordinary reader" is that Miller was once an ordinary man, a failure, a man with his "back up" to the wall, a loser, a victim, an underdog from the working class, who—extraordinarily enough—fought back! And seemingly won. One feels the fight in the very savagery and inexhaustiveness of his prose; as Miller says, his only weapons are words. He fought back against all the dictates, the manners, the bosses, the institutions, the women that oppress the ordinary—if ordinary is meant to include passive and shamed—man. To all these oppressors and oppressions, he responded with a resounding and sometimes eloquent, "fuck it all."[27]

Tropic of Cancer and parts of *Black Spring*, perhaps, can inspire the same kind of catharsis that the Saturnalia or Carnival was meant to effect: a momentary release from the strict rules of everyday life, a pressure valve for feelings of frustration and powerlessness, a controlled bloodletting and rampage. Certainly, a small number of Miller's readers were actually inspired to make changes in their lives, but for most, one imagines, the rebellion remained imaginary, and Miller the character functioned as a kind of trickster for the technological age, a grown-up Huck Finn with a hard-on: a powerful life-spirit that spits on precious ideas of progress and civilization and cares little for modern notions of good and evil. Hungry, oversexed, wandering, conniving, he robs strangers and friends, the rich and the poor, then gives a load of money away in a rush of sentiment, only to "atone" for this goodness with another crime. Women are reduced to sex parts, friends are mocked and eschewed, jobs are quit at the drop of a hat, toilets are extolled, money is literally thrown to the winds, just to round off the sum. The intellect is degraded, and not only intellectually: the main character in a sense does approach the status of a precivilized, animal-god, "a pre-Socratic being, a creature part goat, part Titan" (*TC*, 220).

So raw are some of the emotions touched on in *Cancer*—shame especially—that Miller does not always speak openly or in the first person there. One imagines that such directness would have simply made him too vulnerable. His humiliated psyche can only speak of itself defensively, protectively, obliquely. "The wound that never heals," he writes in this novel, speaking generally; "the open wound, the festering obscene horror" (*TC*, 225). This material was too explosive for Miller except expressed at a certain distance. It was not, as he wildly—and obliquely—claims, that "the world would go to smash" if a man "ever dared to translate all that is in his heart" and tell his entire truth (*TC*, 224); it is more probable that Miller himself would have gone "to smash" in his telling his whole truth. (And a fear of self-obliteration, or madness, might be precisely one of the things in his heart that he dared not translate, at least not directly.)

His soliloquizing on "the crack" was perhaps the only safe way to approach the issue of his shame: covertly and in the pose of the sexual aggressor. The whore is upside down and naked, her legs scissored around his neck; he stands clothed and impassive, staring into her vagina, which is also a Rorschach blot in which he sees his shame: quite a staged scenario for self-therapy. An analysis of his own humiliation glimmers in the interstices of his rant about the decline of Western Civilization and the miracle of creativity; one could easily read this section and miss it entirely. On the subject of what he calls "the wound," the sure, lustful voice of the body is essentially called in to shore Miller up against what might otherwise be the absolutely *maddening* voice of his shame. In this episode, the reader can indeed begin *to feel* that "madness...threatened him."[28]

Compare *Capricorn*. Here Miller could speak directly and in the first person about his wound: "*I was the wound itself*," he says (*Cap*, 230). The wound to his sense of self was now objectified because it had to some extent healed, or rather it had been salved, by the time he wrote this novel: he had been *recognized* in a way that was profoundly meaningful to him, namely, as a writer. His psyche was still tuned to shame, but no longer as dramatically. *Cancer* is written in the present tense; *Capricorn* is retrospective, and he speaks of the wound in the past tense. "I was the wound," this novel tells us, but I am no longer. The very style of his prose on the subject was proof that he was no longer.

Capricorn is more coherent and less disjointed than *Cancer*; his analyses are (more often) pursued at greater length. But something has also been lost. One feels at times in *Capricorn* almost as though Miller was compensating for the loss of the immediate anger and terror that fired *Cancer*: compensating with prose that is overblown and long-winded—even by the radical standard set in the previous novel—as he reached to attain again the poetic flights taken there, and perhaps even to caricature himself, out of a playful self-consciousness about his attempt. For the fuel that Miller was burning in writing *Capricorn* was not only diluted in its anger and fear content; in addition, it is not the premium-grade exhilaration that comes with initial artistic self-transformation but rather the secondary grade that comes with recognition. *Capricorn* was not a life-and-death battle, a war that might still be lost at any moment; it was a clean-up operation and an account of the war; for the moment, he had the thrill and the confidence, but he also had the *relative* complacency of a clear victor.

There is a power, a centrifugal force, then, in Miller's best prose because this writing has the burden of homeostasis, of fight, of aggression. He too is a "devouring soul" (*TC*, 225), as he apparently calls Shakespeare, not simply out of imaginative and linguistic hunger, as the term implies, but also out of shame, anger, terror. His slumming-trauma writing may not give people immunity to these and other poisons, but it does give them an inoculation against passivity and inertia.

It is revealing to compare Miller's writing to the prose of Crane's humiliation tales. The force of Crane's writing breaks in against itself. Yes, there is anger, even anger directed outward against the world, but there is almost always a turn, a secondary movement to that anger—one that moves back against the initial anger at the world. It is bursting with internal tension. James Guetti writes, in regard to Crane's metaphors, of "the extravagance of their disjunctiveness."[29] Miller simply strikes out against his imagined enemies, no matter how mad and childish he sounds.[30] Miller wrote out his delusions of singularity and grandeur; Crane mocked his character's similar fantasies. Henry Fleming, of the *Red Badge*, at points sounds a lot like Henry Miller. But Crane is always looming to puncture his character's imaginings; no such punitive irony is found in Miller's works. There is an absolute difference between Miller's saying, "I know that I spring from the mythological founders of the race" (*TC*, 230) and Crane's writing of his "hero" in the *Red Badge*, "he had, presently, a feeling that he was the growing prophet of a world-reconstruction....And there were many personal advantages in it."[31] Miller's text does not discuss those sorts of personal advantages: he is silent on the subject of the guilt that he would like to escape (guilt about abandoning his second wife, June, as well as his first family); he is also quiet about the fame that he is pursuing in his glorified obscurity.

The Miller character is not, like a Crane hero, a saintly rebel who can resist the mass impulse to swagger, sexually prey, victimize, and traumatize—and stand up for another person. Nor is he, like a Hurston hero, the innocent, good-hearted, and love-seeking saintly rebel of the sentimental slumming romance. Rather, he combines the impulse of the humiliated to trounce, rob, brag, copulate, defile, and traumatize with the saintly impulses of compassion and resistance to injustice, in the figure of the trickster saint. And it is this silly, sloppy, slumming-trauma character, not incidentally, that he introduces into modern literature. The Miller character is a slumming saint insofar as he has withdrawn from society's institutions, from work, from materialism, at first also from country and marriage, and insofar as he criticizes society, its mores, and beliefs. He is a slumming saint insofar as he spreads his gospel of no hope, but no despair either, and helps free his companions from the social traps and illusions that bind and blind them. But he is a traumatizing trickster when he feeds off of the very society he attacks, flouting and exploiting its mores, enjoying its basest pleasures and defilements, exploiting its outcasts, enjoying even the reek of corruption and stupidity, wreaking havoc as he goes. Miller's slumming-trauma hero is the mystic hyena, combing the ground for carrion, philosophizing from the hip, laughing.

Appendix

Michel Foucault's Shame:
Epistemology in a Closet

Michel Foucault once suggested, in his book on Raymond Roussel, that it was necessary, in order to understand a writer's life, to look at his death (*PMF*, 381).[1] Foucault's death also suggests this necessity. Much rumor and speculation—some of it very disturbing—has pointed to Foucault's death as a final, brutal indication of nihilism or even criminal recklessness: that he was attempting to commit suicide by engaging in anonymous S&M sex in the age of AIDS, or, even more sinister, that he had gone to bathhouses in San Francisco, and deliberately infected others with the AIDS virus.[2] My sense of his death is not so sensational or sordid, but maybe more tragic.

James Miller concluded that the rumor about Foucault's intentional infection of others was "essentially false" (*PMF*, 375), that Foucault "had been uncertain, perhaps to the day he died, whether or not he actually had AIDS," but Miller also decided that Foucault was purposefully risking his life. Miller had learned from Foucault's long-time companion, Daniel Defert, that Foucault "had taken AIDS as a 'limit-experience.'" What this meant to Miller was that Foucault was engaged in "potentially suicidal acts of passion with consenting partners, most of them likely to be infected already; deliberately throwing caution to the wind, Foucault and these men were wagering their lives together" (*PMF*, 381). Miller's conclusion is compelling, but a large question remains: why was this world-famous genius making such a wager?

Miller suggests that Foucault was involved in an "ongoing struggle, through the vital alchemy of 'limit-experience,' to get free of himself"; "his own will to know was unflinching and unrelenting," and this was only the final act for a man who pushed "his mind and body repeat-edly to the breaking point" (*PMF*, 382, 383, 385). Miller concludes that Foucault "set a standard for the philosophical life that would be dangerous, if not impossible to emulate. If nothing else, his life-work...proves the wisdom of Friedrich Nietzsche's adage that the 'love of the truth is terrible and mighty'" (*PMF*, 385).

But perhaps Foucault's "lifework" was not so singularly motivated by the love of truth. There is no question that Foucault had a tremen-dous curiosity and bravery. But my memories[3] also tell me that he was in addition a person with significant vulnerabilities and fairly evident strategies for coping with those vulnerabilities. What if Foucault's behavior at the end of his life was not the culmination of ongoing risk taking, but rather a long-deferred, and thus an explosive rebellion against powerful habits of caution and self-protection that included his longtime residence in academia and extended to his writing? And what if these linguistic habits of self-protection, the dazzle, circumlo-cution, evasion, minute analysis, and obscurity, which blossomed into the strange fruit of his hyperrational and omniskeptical histories of the human sciences, what if these habits clouded his vision respecting AIDS, which, until nearly the end of his life, he wanted to see as a medical myth to control and censure homosexuals?

Foucault's earliest writings and his final, secret adventures with sex (and drugs) dramatically affirm something like passion, or the power of raw, disorienting experience to pry one free from the bonds of one's culture. In *Madness and Civilization* (Folie et déraison, 1961),[4] in his use of LSD, in his S&M, and finally in his death, he seemed to glimpse a liberation from all external forms of identity, all imposed forms, all power.

But what happened between his early risks as a writer and his later risk taking in private life? After the 1961 book on madness, his writ-ing less and less affirms this power of experience, except implicitly and in oblique snatches—he makes only a cryptic nod to "bodies in pleas-ures" at the end of *The History of Sexuality* (La Volonté de savoir, 1976).[5] (It could be argued that Foucault after 1961 denied the possi-bility of any experience prior to or outside of discourse and social practice; certainly many current "social constructionists" thus inter-pret Foucault's virtual declaration of "the death of the author.") Foucault seems to lose an initial faith in writing to enliven people, to communicate what he calls in the feverish conclusion to *Madness and Civilization*, "the wisdom and reason" of "the madness of desire,...the most unreasonable passions" (*MC*, 282).[6]

Foucault was clearly inspired by writers who had faith in the power of writing: the Marquis de Sade, Antonin Artaud, Nietzsche. Why did he turn his back on their way? Why the tactics of evasion—which he himself acknowledged? Was he on a course of self-protection, which could also be seen in his remaining in academia despite ambivalence about being a professor? Were these tactics a way of protecting his privacy while still getting recognition? Was his writing a way of flirting with rebellion while escaping the risk of exposure, disorientation, and even the very madness that overtook Artaud and Nietzsche? Perhaps it is no surprise that writing itself in later years felt like a sort of "prison" to Foucault, as he put it (*MF*, 92): perhaps it was a prison he had built out of circumspection, made nearly irresistible by fame and hero worship.

If Foucault was taking desperate risks in bathhouses at the end of his life, then perhaps these risks reflect not an ongoing tendency to push himself to the limit but rather a desperate need to break out of a gnawing sense of self-betrayal (which involved retreating from his brave project of pursuing "'pre-discursive'" or "primitive...experience" [*AK*, 47],[7] both in writing and in life). In addition to this, finally, was his need for a kind of risk taking that still protected him from vulnerability. Foucault had begun as a daring, poetic writer, believing in the power of writing to take one closer to one's nature, but the risk of exposure was too great, and he retreated to the role of "'cold' systematizer"[8] where he found his fame and safety. Ironically, the very theoretical edifice that he had erected as a protective fortress and that came to imprison him caused him to miscalculate the threat of AIDS.

Part of Foucault's career, then, involved the attempt to access and also to conjure in writing a realm of experience at the limits of our codes of behavior and thinking (what he calls "limit-experience"), ending with S&M and starting with *Madness and Civilization*. People who knew him as a young adult took it for granted that his obsessive interest in psychiatry and madness had issued out of his own history. Foucault had had run-ins with madness: there were suicide attempts, an instance of self-mutilation while he was a student, and he had once been put under psychiatric care by his father.[9] What was behind Foucault's mental distress?

It is tempting to say that Foucault's homosexuality holds the key to his suffering, to his radical historicism, and even to his later risk taking and death. There is evidence that as a youth he was ashamed of his homosexuality. In his writing and his behavior, it might be argued, Foucault was asserting the legitimacy of his impulses, showing society's culpability in the "ruin of the body" and the torture of the mind, and in the end refusing to retreat from sexual practices that gave him corporeal freedom and mental insight. Foucault's writing and S&M involvement can be seen as counterattacks against institutions that defined him as immoral and destined for misery.

But the situation does not resolve itself so simply. First of all, why would Foucault's intense problems with homosexuality suddenly return after a hiatus of some thirty years? Then there is the fact that Daniel Defert, closer to Foucault than anyone in his last fifteen years, asserted that Foucault was not suffering from his homosexuality even in his youthful self-destructive phase, but from some distress that remained a mystery to Defert. Defert did suggest that Foucault felt anxiety about "not being handsome" (PMF, 56).[10] How can these two accounts be squared?

The portrait of Foucault that emerges from his collegiate days is of a socially uncomfortable young man with a fierce desire to succeed and a fragile attitude of superiority. After he left home, Foucault had trouble in communal living and boarding situations (MF, 26).[11] Perhaps Foucault was suffering not from shame over his homosexuality but from a deeper sense of ostracism and mental torture: from a shame that comes from being ostracized for being considered "queer." Consider his symptoms from an early age: anxiety and difficulty dealing with others, claustrophobia in social situations, and solitariness combined with a touchy ego. There was a dramatic shyness and discomfort with women.[12] Foucault apparently felt intensely threatened by others; there is even a story of his having chased a fellow student with a dagger. We know he indulged his megalomania at college by demeaning others (MF, 26). He flunked his exams in 1950, according to a professor on the jury, because he attempted to display his erudition rather than discuss the topic at hand (LMF, 44). Toward the end of his studies, he left the country and so escaped the ordeal of competing and being judged.

How was Foucault shamed or stigmatized as a child? To answer this, one must imagine what it must have been like for Foucault to grow up in a conservative, haute bourgeois French family in the 1930s and 1940s, knowing he was different (if not homosexual) and acting differently from other boys from a young age.[13] Of course, prewar France and especially Vichy (Foucault was fourteen when the military occupation began and eighteen when it ended) were not open and were indeed hostile to homosexuality. As a child, Foucault did not engage in sports; he stayed inside and read books and spent a lot of time alone or with his mother. His father was an important doctor in town and usually out of the house;[14] Michel was expected to follow in his footsteps and become a doctor as well, but from early on, his trajectory deviated from his father's expectations. Some of Foucault's anger in college was directed at his father, whom he often mocked to friends. Specifically, Foucault blamed his father for being a *Vichyiste*, in conversation with a lot of people in his hometown of Poitiers and at the École Normale Supérieure. We don't know the truth about Foucault's father's involvement with German officers, but the point here is that Foucault would come to refuse his father on every ground, including the political one. It is not much of a conjecture to imagine that Foucault grew up feeling insulted and rejected, not only by the larger society, but also by his father—because of his homosexuality. It is important here to add that though Foucault was, throughout his life, relatively close to his mother and possibly her favorite child (of three), she helped set a tone in which he would always remain very closed-mouth with her and with his siblings about his personal life and homosexuality. She, for instance, sensed, but didn't want to know or hear about his dislike of his father; fifteen years after Foucault's death, his brother and sister denied, or were unaware, that there had been tension between them. If Foucault ended up feeling ugly, it was because of the shame and isolation he was made to feel both within his family and outside of it.[15]

Foucault's first major book is centered squarely on madness, ostracism, exclusion—the very subjects that were haunting him. *Madness and Civilization* indicted society—and vindicated the madman. Here, Foucault praises the desperate, lonely, and strange artists who attempt to resuscitate the animal impulses of humans—which have been all but stamped out in our civilized world—and who, in the process, go mad or commit suicide: Sade, Gérard de Nerval, Nietzsche, Roussel, Artaud. He justifies their imaginations of cruelty and hatred as inevitable responses to a hostile society. Foucault's obsession with rules and codes of behavior, then, might have originated in the sense of imprisonment he felt as a result of the social ostracism he experienced as a child and youth, as one who feels detached from others and powerless to exert control over his life. Indeed, then, Foucault's writing is intensely personal in its stakes, intended to affirm not only his homosexuality but also his antisocial inclinations more generally, to free himself from the crushing weight of social judgment, and to shift the blame for his suffering to society.

To get an idea of the emotional risk involved, one must remember that he took the precaution of writing *Madness and Civilization* outside of France and its academic world. We know his "exile" turned out to be a cover story or fallback position in case of failure because when the book succeeded, he dropped the pretense and became a professor. The tactic of exile lessened the terrible stakes of the enterprise: in fact, he desperately sought recognition from the very institutions and groups he attacked and fled.

After he received that recognition, his former classmates found "a changed Foucault, a radiant man, relaxed and cheerful" (*MF*, 138). And he was ready to continue the self-revelatory project, to take further steps toward liberation in the realm of writing, with a project advertised as: "Madmen. From the Bastille to Hopital Sainte-Anne,...Michel Foucault recounts the journey to the end of night" (*MF*, 144). He also signed a contract to write the "History of Hysteria" and another for "The Idea of Decadence." But none of these projects were followed up.

Instead, there was a clear retreat from the personal exposure and emotional boldness of *Madness and Civilization*. In that book, he wrote about "the limits rather than the identity of a culture"; he had attempted not "the history of the language [of reason] but rather the archeology of [the] silence" of madness (*MC*, xi). But *The Order of Things* (Les Mots et les choses, 1966) would reverse this formula: he shifted to writing about the identity of a culture—not its transgressions but its codes. He laid aside plans for a series of poetical histories of "limit-experiences" such as madness and instead began a hyperrational analysis of the codes of Western culture. Something clearly happened between the publication of *Madness and Civilization* and the appearance of *The Order of Things*. Somehow, Foucault lost his trust in words as a means of transporting one to the cultural limits.

What happened, most importantly, was that Foucault was publicly— and forcefully—attacked for *Madness and Civilization*. In March 1963, at the Sorbonne, his one-time pupil Jacques Derrida read his paper, entitled "Cogito and the History of Madness," with Foucault in the audience. Derrida branded Foucault's book "metaphysical"[16] or essentialist, and, as Miller writes, "to accuse an avant-garde French philosopher of 'metaphysics' in these years was a...humiliatingly rote gesture of disdain" (*PMF*, 119). Derrida's criticism became brutally invasive, and perhaps chillingly accurate: he said he was "tempted to consider Foucault's book a powerful gesture of protection,...written in the *confessed* terror of going mad" (*PMF*, 120).

It would be hard to overestimate the impact of this event on Foucault. We can guess that Foucault was highly susceptible and sensitive to affront; he had had brushes with madness; he was indeed taking a risk with this book, striking a precarious balance between self-protection and self-exposure. Derrida made direct, callous reference to his most profound fears about his alienation and potential for madness, which he bravely struggled to master in *Madness and Civilization*: this was probably devastating as well as frightening.

Let us consider his response. Eribon writes that Foucault's "legendary touchiness" seemed to have been dormant on the occasion of Derrida's critique. "Foucault does not seem to have taken umbrage either on this occasion or when Derrida reprinted the text in 1967....Foucault even sent him a very friendly letter to acknowledge receipt of the volume. The incident did, however, produce a delayed explosion." In 1971 Foucault wrote "an extremely violent response to Derrida's 1963 lecture," ignoring Derrida's personal attacks and concentrating on their philosophical disagreements. In 1972, Foucault sent Derrida a new edition of his book, with his response in an appendix, and an arch inscription: "Sorry to have answered you so late." "Nine years later!" remarks Eribon (*MF*, 120–21). And after this, he did not speak to Derrida for another nine years.

Nine years later a vicious counterattack: there can hardly be a doubt that Foucault *had* taken tremendous umbrage at Derrida's remarks. Why else hold a grudge for nine years, or perhaps eighteen? In this context, Foucault's initially pleasant letter to Derrida appears as a ruse or an exertion of self-control.

Is it hard to guess why Foucault's explosion was delayed and calculated? To have exploded quickly or recklessly would reveal that Derrida's personal attacks had hit home. If it was humiliating and psychically dangerous for Foucault that the world see him as someone who lived in fear of going mad, his best defense was not to expose himself further. The habits of withdrawal and distrust, which had in part characterized his behavior at college and in exile, were reactivated: he would not confront his adversary but instead hide himself.

He set out to remove what was personal, mysterious, or visionary from his writing, to erase any emotional trace of himself. He publicly criticized *Madness and Civilization*: it "accorded far too great a place, and a very enigmatic one too, to what is called an 'experience.'" He now claimed to recognize that he could not "reconstitute what madness itself might be, in the form in which it presented itself in some primitive, fundamental, deaf, scarcely articulated experience" (*PMF*, 120). (His only source for such reconstitution was personal experience, and that material, which made him vulnerable to shame, would now disappear.)

This is the reason for his movement from experience at the limits to the limiting culture, from the silence of madness to the language of reason. "In the decade after *Madness and Civilization*," as Miller notices, "Michel Foucault set out deliberately to efface himself—to erase the signs of his own singular existence from the texts he composed...." (*PMF*, 123). *The Birth of the Clinic* (Naissance de la clinique, 1963), *The Order of Things*, *The Archeology of Knowledge* (L'Archéologie de savior, 1969): these were very different from his book on madness. His writing became drained of almost all emotional content, stripped of revelatory pain. Foucault now took refuge in the purely intellectual realm where nobody could tarnish him. He retreated to the safe house, as he put it, of "relentless erudition" that was "gray, meticulous, and patiently documentary." His writing now had a "cool objectivity," a "hermetic abstractness" (*PMF*, 123–24); it was peppered with a scholastically precise jargon of his own devising. Any hints of the themes of madness, evil, and revolt were almost hidden.

Because of Derrida's attack, Foucault backed off of a *literary* project that would have boldly revealed himself (and suggested experience with madness). The dramatic success of *The Order of Things* iced Foucault's retreat. Foucault had found a hyperintellectual and arcane style that served at once his desire for fame and his determination to hide himself. He had crafted a literary form in which he could disappear. He says as much in the even more obscure *Archeology of Knowledge*, with a defiant and almost paranoid flourish remarkable for its blunt admission of using writing as a "labyrinth" in which to hide: "'What, do you imagine that I would take so much trouble and so much pleasure in writing...if I were not preparing...a labyrinth...in which I can lose myself and appear at last to eyes that I will never have to meet again. I am no doubt not the only one who writes in order to have no face. Do not ask me who I am....'" (*AK*, 17)

Foucault reveals himself in this stunningly bizarre manifesto as a man who feels dogged at every turn by hostile critics who would brand and so shame him. It had happened to him once with Derrida, and it would never happen again. Just as the "madman" had been created by society and twisted by its constraints, Foucault has begun to be pushed into an extreme intellectualism by academia's callous response to the vulnerability and poetic iconoclasm of *Madness and Civilization*. With *The Order of Things*, Foucault began to wear a mask; it became impossible to penetrate to a human face beneath; nothing remained but layers of intellectual husk. No wonder that, after the euphoria of his celebrity faded, Foucault came to think of

The Order of Things as his worst book, even asking his publisher to stop printing it (*MF*, 185). To suggest that no author has his own face but only an anonymous pen that belongs to discourse, and to be famous for this is the perversion and paradox that Foucault's writing became. There is an almost angry undertone in Foucault's conclusion to *The Archeology of Knowledge* in which he denies readers the possibility of self-expression and dooms them to the anonymity of discourse: his revenge for having been deprived of a written intimacy is to say, "Since I cannot enjoy it, then none of you shall."

The irony runs deep. In *Madness and Civilization*, he attempted to approach the experience of madness and decry the social exclusion and ostracism of the mad; he even demanded works of writing that made society aware of its crimes. In the works that followed, he performed the same operation of excommunication, upon his own text, of "mystical or aesthetic experience"—though he did not denigrate it as madness. Foucault's literary act of exclusion was not justified by an appeal to reason or psychiatry but rather on the solid philosophical ground of systematicity or comprehensibility: yes, Foucault explained, one could approach "some primitive,...scarcely articulated experience," but one would end up with an "enigmatic" text such as *Madness and Civilization* (*AK*, 47, 16), lacking a desired level of certainty. If instead he turned his attention to discourses about madness, then he could describe a "system of formation that...remains stable" (*AK*, 47). Foucault presented the switch as a preference for intellectual rigor.

In much the same way that Descartes, in his description of the physical world, banished "subjective" properties and held onto only those that were measurable, Foucault "wish[ed]...to dispense with 'things'" messily "'prediscursive.'" Foucault declares no wish to "exclude any effort" to approach "what madness itself might be," but such effort will be excluded henceforth from his own project; from now on he will "suppress the stage of 'things themselves.'" Still, he does his best to demean such effort by the end of *The Archeology of Knowledge*, again perhaps out of anger, and maybe also with the pain he ascribes to his readers. Perhaps Foucault cannot be held responsible for people who threaten intellectual humiliation to those who do not "exclude any effort to uncover and free...'prediscursive' experiences from the tyranny of the text" (*AK*, 47–48). But it is hard to imagine he did not feel responsible for such exclusions from his own writing.

And one can speculate that such responsibility would come to weigh on him. No doubt Foucault's refuge in intellectual precision was abundantly safe, but it is hard to imagine that it was entirely comfortable.

Though he construed his exclusions in coldly intellectual terms, such a shift was not emotionally or ethically neutral. How could it have been, for a man who had passionately decried the confinement of the mad, and who so admired his mad philosophers? How could this not have felt to him an act of self-betrayal? Foucault's labyrinth protected him, but it was also a prison. Foucault told his student hosts in California, after their shared LSD trip, "I am happy with my life...not so much with my self" (*PMF*, 283).

It is not too difficult, in this light, to imagine Foucault's ripeness for the LSD and S&M experiences he consented to in 1975. It had been a dozen years since his experience with Derrida; there had been several years of unsuccessful attempts to break out of this self-created prison—or is the better metaphor a closet?—that he had created for himself. He had experimented with relocation to Tunisia in 1968, with political involvements and militancies, with subject matters that had some affinity with his original project (he turned to the prison with *Discipline and Punish* [Surveiller et punir, 1975] and a year later to sexual abnormality with *The History of Sexuality*).

By the beginning of the 1980s, arguably, Foucault had begun, as a friend later wrote, "to dynamite the tunnels of his own labyrinth"[17] in his writing about the self in late antiquity, and in interviews. As Miller sees it, Foucault made that long-promised and "long-deferred turn" from an investigation of codes and transgressions to a study of the self, and there was unusual "candor" in his interviews, particularly in those with the gay press (*PMF*, 318–19). It could even be said that in these interviews, starting in 1979, he essentially "came out" as a homosexual (*PMF*, 257). But it must be added that his writing was as intellectual and impersonal as ever, and his comments about his own homosexuality were also evasive. There were even those who accused Foucault of cowardice for failing to "come out of *the* closet" more publicly. One commentator criticized Foucault for keeping silent about his homosexuality even after it was no longer socially dangerous to confess: "He...never decided to bear personal witness."[18] While this is certainly an exaggeration, it is true that Foucault's by-now trademark abstraction extended to his comments about homosexuality as well. Leo Bersani maintains that Foucault's abstract language about his sexuality has the "perverse" effect of turning "our attention away from the body"—and of denying Foucault's own erotic impulses, obscuring "the terrifying appeal of a loss of ego, of a self-debasement." Of course, Foucault was in part worried about becoming identified with the gay subculture and so having his work marginalized (*PMF*, 259, 256). But Foucault's concerns here were also part of a characteristic desire to avoid being exposed, to remain "closeted," hardly limited to the question of homosexuality.

Part of the point here is that Foucault's personal "counterattack" against the codes of culture, his own unriddling of the self, would not take place in his oeuvre, but outside of writing, in the S&M scene in San Francisco. Leo Bersani remembers being surprised by Foucault's excitement over the discovery of the S&M scene; "There was something explosive about his fascination," Bersani said. "I mean, the scene was fun—but it wasn't that much fun" (PMF, 261). But maybe the explosiveness of Foucault's interest makes sense: he was releasing himself from habits of cautiousness that had long restrained him. Also, he was connecting to others. There are echoes of renewed pride in his writings after 1975; he spoke of an "erotics of truth...transmitted by magisterial initiation, with the stamp of secrecy, to those who have shown themselves to be worthy of it" (PMF, 269).

Why the S&M scene? Why was this the space in which he was willing to risk first disorientation and perhaps even madness and later death by AIDS? Perhaps because its anonymity also served to protect him, allowing him not only to check his identity at the door of the bathhouse, but also to avoid the emotional risks and frustrations that attended sexual interaction. The S&M clubs enabled the possibility of "bodies and pleasures" that freed one from the "tyranny" of the genitals; they also made possible for Foucault sexual interaction with men whom courting might be emotionally risky. The bathhouse did away with the threat of rejection and risk of painful emotional attachment or burdensome obligation. For Foucault, all of these aspects of sexual encounter were no doubt intense, difficult, and troubling. In suggesting that heterosexuals would also benefit from an open access to "fugitive" bodies, Foucault complained that "even...satisfying sexual relationships" could leave him with "appetite" and "torment" (PMF, 264). To have sexual adventure outside the institutional setting of the bathhouse would require assertiveness, openness, and the willingness to risk rebuff. The S&M club was a passive and emotionally safe alternative to sexual courtship and intimacy.

It is also hard to imagine that Foucault's eager participation in S&M wasn't related to the sense of ugliness, or shame really, that he carried with him from childhood. Foucault mocked the Freudian account of S&M, in which S&M is seen as liberating a hidden, innate violence. But a post-Freudian psychological account would link Foucault's predilection for masochism—he preferred to be a "bottom"—to the experience of insult and humiliation.

How therapeutic the bathhouse might have proved for Foucault and to what it extent it might have provided him with a confidence to reveal and express himself openly, other than sexually, will remain an unanswered question. But we know that, with the onset of AIDS, bathhouses began to emerge as something other than sexual carnivals, and Foucault discovered there an openness he was also loathe to surrender. Hervé Guibert, one of Foucault's closest friends at the end of his life, wrote a roman à clef in which the philosopher explained that the threat of AIDS had intensified the experience of the bathhouses, creating new trust and intimacy. "The baths have never been so popular, and now they're amazing," reports the philosopher. "Before, no one ever said a word; now everyone talks. Each of us knows exactly why he is there" (PMF, 29).

Why would Foucault risk his life to preserve these experiences? As David Macey reports, Foucault lived a "compartmentalized" life, keeping groups of family and friends separate (LMF, xiv). He also kept aspects of himself secret from even his closest companions. Defert apparently did not know why Foucault was tortured as a young man or whether he knew in the end that he had AIDS. Foucault's political allies and social contacts shifted. He lived in a variety of countries, finally shuttling back and forth between France and the United States. He had a number of relationships with young men, both gay and straight. Foucault, it might be said, experienced the loneliness that comes with a promiscuous gay lifestyle, intensified in his case by his extreme self-protectiveness. If Foucault preferred the company of students and children to academic peers (LMF, 450) and developed relationships with younger men, it was probably because he found the young less threatening (in their openness, confusion, and lack of professional envy). Perhaps his trademark shaven head was, as for youths who sport it, a means of keeping adults at bay. It is true that Foucault had a strong relationship with his mother, spending a month with her every August, and that he had a partnership of more than two decades: nonetheless, it is fair to say that his emotional life was somewhat fugitive. Defert lent him a stability he otherwise lacked, but he was also harvesting emotional connection in the interstices of a public and intellectual life that gave him little personal sustenance, especially after Madness and Civilization. If the bathhouse became an oasis in which openness was possible, then it is possible to imagine him taking a huge risk to retain such a place.

There is a final tragic element in Foucault's death. His presence in the baths as late as 1983 is in part due to his inability or refusal to see AIDS as other than a social construction. Hans Sluga recalls Foucault's skepticism about the existence of a sexually transmitted virus: "I remember…telling him about some strange disease that was appearing, and didn't even have a name at the time; and telling him, 'You'd better be careful.' He didn't believe it. He thought that Americans were basically puritanical and anti-sexual; and that it was coming out in this sudden hysteria over this mysterious disease" (*PMF*, 345). Foucault would only acknowledge the existence of AIDS after his health began to decline and he was put under a doctor's care (*MF*, 326).

In the early eighties, the American press was writing about the "homosexuals' cancer," and Foucault, I remember, could only see AIDS as a product of social forces hostile to sex and to homosexuality in particular. AIDS was for Foucault a rubric under which disparate diseases could be collected, a social sledge that could be used to hammer the gay community for its promiscuity and immorality. And thus, for Foucault, belief in AIDS was a politically dangerous, even treacherous act. The gay community had to resist this pernicious discourse and refuse to surrender its creative sexual lifestyle. Foucault did just that, even as many gay men were abandoning the bathhouses. By early 1984, in his hospital room, he was admitting that AIDS "exists. It isn't a legend" (*MF*, 326). But it was too late.

Foucault, then, was not nihilistic or criminal; rather, he had been swallowed up in his own intellectual construct. The "theory" that Foucault had developed to protect himself turned out to be mortally dangerous.

Rather than become (like the "madman") a victim of the Reason that attacks and disgraces the irrational and the emotional, Foucault turned himself into a radical historicist and consummate positivist, remaking the rules of the academic game so that it is even more hostile to anything subjective or "metaphysical." It is a testimony to the forbidding climate of the intellectual world in the 1980s that when Foucault resumed his experiments in self-revelation it was not in print but in the secrecy and anonymity of the S&M club.

The examination of Foucault's life provides the opportunity to understand the emotional content behind his radical historicization of subjectivity. Foucault's biographers report that they sometimes met with objection: hadn't Foucault declared "the death of the author," and so wasn't biography obsolete?[19] The camouflage that Foucault had created for himself was still working after his death. Not only can that camouflage be set aside but also Foucault's reasons for using it can be understood. Foucault wrote that history is contingent and that the present situation can always be undone if we know how it got put together. We might apply his suggestion to his own theory of the anonymity of discourse.

Notes

Introduction

1. This typical mix of middle-class condemnation and concern for the poor would not be surprising, except for the theme of the show. Some of the show's commentary was aimed—as usual in middle-class reporting on the poor—at morally distinguishing the middle and working classes from the "immoral" poor. Of course, Gates was contending here with another invidious tradition in America, namely the white tendency to stereotype blacks according to their most "immoral" element.
2. "The Two Nations of Black America," PBS *Frontline*, February 10, 1998.
3. The earlier, pre-Progressive, mid-nineteenth-century account of the thug as "vicious"—by nature or because of corruption—considered him more fundamentally Other, certainly, and there was then too no reason to speak with him, but he was still capable of being morally transformed (through a regimen of discipline and work).
4. Walter Michaels, Lecture at the Fulbright American Studies Institute on Contemporary American Literature, Northern Illinois University, July 14, 2003.
5. William Julius Wilson, "The Cost of Racial and Class Exclusion in the Inner City," in *The Ghetto Underclass: Social Science Perspectives*, Special Issue of *The Annals of the American Academy of Political and Social Science*, no. 501 (1989): 9, 25.
6. See Barbara Ehrenreich, *Fear of Falling* (New York: Perennial, 1990).
7. Mary Helen Washington, foreword to *Their Eyes Were Watching God*, by Zora Neale Hurston (New York: Harper, 1990), ix.
8. New Historical study tends to prefer historical discontinuity. As one current critical series puts it, there is a "focus...on cultural and historical differences, rather than on similarity or continuity." J. Paul Hunter and William E. Cain, series eds., "About the Series," *Maggie: A Girl of the Streets*, Bedford Cultural Edition Series, ed. Kevin J. Hayes (Boston: St. Martin's, 1999), vi. This preference is often reasonable, but it can be misleading in the discussion of long-standing problems, such as that of the inner city.
9. Locke and Wright quoted in Washington, foreword, viii.

10. Some trauma movies—what I call status trauma movies—involve a romanti-cization of the poor. For purposes of style, the term "trauma movies" will be used throughout to refer to "class and status trauma movies," an awkward phrase to repeat.

11. On the subject of gangsploitation as latter-day blaxploitation, see, for exam-ple, Jesse Rhines, *Black Films/White Money* (New Brunswick, NJ: Rutgers University Press, 1996).

12. This motif is sometimes a subtheme in action films that are not focused on the poor, such as *The Patriot* (Roland Emmerich, 2000) in which the hero raises a militia from the lower class, and the Revolutionary War takes on the trappings of a class war.

13. Lippard's book might not be considered a classploitation novel since the plot focused on the seduction of a woman from a "good" family and the book was equal parts sensational sexploitation and social protest, and was consumed to some degree by working-class male readers.

14. Other narrative permutations of class crossing, whose predecessors were once the common tales and folktales of the terrain, still appear today, though they are now less popular than the other variants, discussed above:

1. Status trauma: Weak, vulnerable, innocent, or naive poor girl meets humiliated/humiliating rich boy who trashes her. (For examples, see Chapter 3.) This sort of tale is a fairly direct descendent of the seduction novel; the same seduction narrative is there, but now in a sardonic rather than sentimental mode.

   Note that either the class trauma or status trauma story is similar to the basic formula for the slasher, serial killer, or horror movie. For exam-ple, the widely known *Deliverance* (John Boorman, 1972), with its theme of rural poverty versus urban privilege, is similar to a class trauma film. Horror movies with a class-conflict component differ in the fact that the menacing characters—whether rich or poor—are almost always defeated or foiled; the hero or heroine is not destroyed. Thus, they are not trauma movies but revenge films. For class representations in horror films, see Carol Clover, *Men, Women, and Chain Saws* (Princeton, NJ: Princeton University Press, 1992). See Chapter 3 for a comparison of horror and trauma films.

   One older tale that has not disappeared from the popular media is that of:

2. Cinderella liberation: Poor girl meets rich boy who rescues her from poverty or drudgery. Sentimental/sensational seduction tales of a poor girl by a rich boy could always be redeemed from tragedy in this man-ner, as was the case in *The Quaker City*. In its rags-to-riches trajectory, this Cinderella tale is obviously similar to Alger's American Dream sto-ries. (Alger himself made the connection to the fairy tale in *Ragged Dick* [1868].) For an example in the 1990s, there is *Pretty Woman* (Garry Marshall, 1990). What makes *Pretty Woman* a contemporary tale is that it belongs under the slumming as well as Cinderella liberation categories

because, as the "virgin prostitute," played by Julia Roberts, puts it when the millionaire man proposes to rescue her from her "plight" (Cinderella drama), "she rescues him right back" (slumming drama).

15. But see Chapter 1: the self-made man's ascension theme still remains in the slumming drama.
16. By the 1930s, screwball-comedy films were already exploring the story in which rich girl meets common boy who transforms her. But Hurston's formula is distinct: for example, in *It Happened One Night* (Frank Capra, 1934), the Clark Gable character is a working-class *professional* and is *not* removed (he marries the rich girl).
17. Robert E. Hemenway, *Zora Neale Hurston* (Urbana: University of Illinois Press, 1980), 231.
18. Softskull Press, online notice. URL no longer available.
19. Stephen Crane, *Maggie: A Girl of the Streets* (New York: Norton, 1979), 16.
20. Hayes, introduction, in *Maggie* (see note 8), 18.
21. To quickly sample some later examples of the genre: A comic one, Abraham Cahan's *Yekl: A Tale of the New York Ghetto* (1896) chronicles a Jewish immigrant shamed for his "greenhorn" wife. James Weldon Johnson's *The Autobiography of an Ex-Colored Man* (1912) starts out in the direction of a sentimental slumming romance, as a mixed-race character who can pass for white or black decides to explore his black cultural and musical roots. But the narrator is turned away from his class-crossing quest by the crushing force of white racism. What deters the narrator is not fear of white violence but rather the "shame" of being considered a member of group who can be lynched. Nathanael West is one of the first writers to set a trauma tale outside the lower class proper in his *Day of the Locust* (1939): he chooses the lower middle-class fringe of Hollywood for his setting, the center of the rising celebrity culture. Hubert Selby's class trauma novels, *Last Exit to Brooklyn* (1964) and *Requiem for a Dream* (1978), have recently been retrieved as trauma films with the same titles by Uli Edel (1989) and Darren Aronofsky (2000) respectively.
22. This protagonist can be a vagabond trickster of either sex or he can come as part of a cross-class or biracial pair of buddies (Kerouac gives Sal Paradise working-class Dean; Thompson gives his alter ego a Samoan sidekick) or as part of cross-class or biracial pair of lovers (Mailer's Rojack in *An American Dream* [1964] has his street-girl Cherry). This genre, even when in female hands, remains strongly "masculine" or at least marked by misogyny; see Kathy Acker's *Blood and Guts in High School* (1978). See Keith Gandal, *The Virtues of the Vicious* (New York: Oxford University Press, 1997), 134–35.
23. The authoritative textbook was Thomas Upham's *Elements of Mental Philosophy* (1845).
24. On Riis and Crane and self-esteem, see Gandal, *Virtues of the Vicious*, Chapters 5 and 6. Though comic, Cahan's *Yekl* also sees an amoral shame as the prime mover in the ghetto world. Cahan too breaks with all previous slum literature because his depiction does not center on the moral degradations and physical hardships of poverty, but the social stigmas that attach to immigrant

life. Yekl is so intent on proving himself a regular "Yankee" in the face of mockery that he drops his religious practice and eventually his wife and child.

25. Joel Pfister, "Glamorizing the Psychological," Pfister and Nancy Schnog, ed., *Inventing the Psychological* (New Haven, CT: Yale University Press, 1997), 174.

26. Ann Douglas, *The Feminization of American Culture* (New York: Knopf, 1977) and T. J. Jackson Lears, *No Place of Grace* (New York: Pantheon, 1981).

27. Luc Sante, *Low Life* (New York: Vintage, 1992), 74–75.

28. Ibid., 332. The novel was called *Flowers of Asphalt*.

29. See Eve Kosofsky Sedgwick and Adam Frank, eds., *Shame and Its Sisters: A Silvan Tomkins Reader* (Durham, NC: Duke University Press, 1995).

30. Christopher Lasch, *The Culture of Narcissism* (New York: Norton, 1978), 31–50.

31. For example, Frederick Douglass's *Narrative of the Life* (1845) broaches "self-esteem" theory in the depiction of his fight with the slave-breaker Covey; there he talks about the rekindling of his self-respect as he fends off the violence and degradation of slavery. But his rendition of self-respect is even here shot through with moral and humanitarian notions of justice, equality, and freedom. Douglass's own violence and triumph do not go too far; he does not glory in hurting or defeating Covey. Likewise, the end of Douglass's narrative makes clear that he will transcend the humiliation of slavery; his experience has not left him traumatized. At his first abolitionist meeting, he feels again the slave's sense of inferiority when he contemplates speaking before whites, but when he begins to talk feels his equality and freedom.

    By contrast, Melville's "Benito Cereno" (1856), about a revolt on a Spanish slave-ship, might be considered one of America's earliest approaches to the "trauma" genre. This story is haunted by just the sort of violent retaliatory overkill and mockery that Douglass's tale avoids. Captain Cereno has been fatally traumatized by the extreme social demotion and terror involved in the slaves' turning of the tables of power. Melville's insistence on the outcome of irreversible humiliation is underlined by the fact that, in the true story upon which he based his narrative, the Spanish captain not only recovers, but goes on to sue his rescuers.

32. See Appendix on Foucault.

33. Sedgwick, "Shame in the Cybernetic Fold," in *Shame and Its Sisters* (see note 29), 5.

34. In zeroing in on the motivations and compulsions of these developers of seminal literary tales, I hope merely to suggest something of the imaginative investment we may have in our middle-class fictions of poverty. I hope also to claim for this dusty noncinematic and pre-postmodern literature and its dead practitioners a surprising relevance.

35. Crane, *Maggie*, 40.

36. Eve Kosofsky Sedgwick, who suggests using the word "queer" in a similar way, explains: "*Queer*, I'd suggest, might usefully be thought of as referring in the first place to...an overlapping group of infants and children, those whose sense of identity is for some reason tuned most durably to shame....Race, gender, class, sexuality, appearance and abledness are only a few of the defining social constructions that will crystallize there, developing from this originary affect their particular structures of expression, creativity, pleasure, and struggle." In

Sedgwick's terms, this study, then, is concerned with certain "queer" authors (none of whom are gay except Foucault) and the "particular structures of expression, creativity, pleasure, and struggle," that come out of these shames. The chapters devoted to these authors are about "habitual shame and its transformations," for, as Sedgwick notices, shame cannot simply be gotten rid of. "The forms taken by shame are not distinct 'toxic' parts of a group or individual identity that can be excised; they are instead integral to and residual in the processes by which identity is itself formed. They are available for the work of metamorphosis, reframing, refiguration, *trans*figuration, affective and symbolic loading and deformation." Sedgwick, "Queer Performativity: Henry James's *The Art of the Novel*," *GLQ* 1 (1993): 12–13. These chapters concern this sort of self-transformative "work"—in the lives as well as the works of these writers whose identities are formed through shame.

37. I am limiting myself to films of the 1990s somewhat arbitrarily: for the purposes of focus and relative brevity.

38. One could look to the development of postwar shame theory and self-esteem psychology in: Freudian ego psychology (the Americanized version of the continental radical psychology of Freud), Heinz Kohut's self psychology (beginning in the 1970s) and the related theory of narcissism, and the popularization of these clinical approaches in the self-help and recovery movements played out, with lachrymose intensity, in magazines and on TV talk shows; Silvan Tomkins's non-Freudian affect theory, with its emphasis on shame; the sharp rise since the 1960s of the self-esteem movement in urban sociological and anthropological study, journalistic reporting, social work, and community social policy; the popularization of bohemian writing in the 1950s with the Beats; horror, slasher, and serial killer films of the 1960s through the 1980s; the underground film tradition, including the 1960s cult films of Andy Warhol and the 1970s cult films of John Waters; and comic books, another significant source of the aesthetics of humiliation and shame, especially since several of the biographies of the writers and directors of trauma films indicate an interest in comics. (For the suggestions regarding Waters and comic books, especially, I'm indebted to the anonymous reader for *Texas Studies in Language and Literature*.) Meanwhile, one might investigate contemporary TV shows, such as *The Howard Stern Show*, *Jerry Springer*, *Survivor*, *The Weakest Link*, and *The Apprentice*: whether ostensibly talk shows, game shows, or reality TV, these programs all depend on producing or reproducing situations, and even rituals, of humiliation and social exclusion.

Most importantly, one would want to gage the effects of the crisis of the Vietnam War, which generated national narratives of traumatic humiliation—as well as national narratives of slumming (hippie) liberation from the social constraints of a culture of affluence perceived as failed. Some Vietnam War movies, for example *Full Metal Jacket* (Stanley Kubrick, 1987), produced tales of generalized degradation, conspicuously void of heroes.

A look at post–World War II developments could only answer the question as to why these stories have become popular, have finally moved into the mainstream—not what might have prompted their appearance in initially marginal literature in the first place.

39. Walter Benjamin, "Theses on the Philosophy of History," in *Illuminations*, trans. Harry Zohn (New York: Shocken, 1969), 261.
40. Thus, my somewhat arbitrary focus on the 1990s does not detract from the ultimate aims here.

Chapter 1

1. Zora Neale Hurston, *Their Eyes Were Watching God* (New York: Harper, 1990), 158. Throughout the chapter, quotations will be cited with the page number in parentheses.
2. The kids' scheme to run away in *American Beauty* just begins when the film ends; here the film ending is the deus ex machina.
3. Maitland McDonagh, "Lives of Quiet Desperation," review of *American Beauty*, directed by Sam Mendes, *TV Guide*, http://online.tvguide.com/movies/database/showmovie.asp?MI=41432#review (accessed June 5, 2006).
4. *Forrest Gump*'s theory is apparently that the American experience with the Vietnam War has led to a cultural degradation.
5. On the centrality of luck in Horatio Alger's stories, see John G. Cawelti, *Apostles of the Self-Made Man* (Chicago: University of Chicago Press, 1965), 115–16.

Chapter 2

1. *ZNH* followed by page numbers refers to Robert E. Hemenway, *Zora Neale Hurston* (Urbana: University of Illinois Press, 1980). *ZNH* followed by roman numerals refers to Walker's foreword in the same book.
2. See Houston A. Baker Jr., "Workings of the Spirit: Conjure and the Space of Black Women's Creativity," in *Zora Neale Hurston: Critical Perspectives Past and Present*, ed. Henry Louis Gates Jr. and K. A. Appiah (New York: Amistad, 1993), 289, 299, 303–4.
3. Ibid., 304. More recently, and very similarly, Hortense Spillers has described Hurston as "an enabler" of future black women writers. Hortense J. Spillers, "A Tale of Three Zoras: Barbara Johnson and Black Women Writers," *Diacritics* 34, no. 1 (2004): 94.
4. Alice Walker called *Their Eyes* one of the "most 'healthily' rendered heterosexual love stories in our literature," and June Jordan called it "the most successful, convincing, and exemplary novel of Blacklove that we have. Period." Quoted in Carla Kaplan, ed., *Zora Neale Hurston: A Life in Letters* (New York: Doubleday, 2002), 183.
5. *SO* followed by page numbers refers to Claudia Roth Pierpont, "A Society of One: Zora Neale Hurston, American Contrarian," *The New Yorker*, February 17, 1997.
6. *TE* followed by page numbers refers to Zora Neale Hurston, *Their Eyes Were Watching God* (New York: Harper, 1990). *TE* followed by roman numerals

refers to Mary Helen Washington, foreword to *Their Eyes Were Watching God*, by Hurston (New York: Harper, 1990).

7. Maya Angelou, foreword in *Dust Tracks on a Road*, by Hurston (New York: Harper, 1991), xii.

8. Deborah E. McDowell, foreword in *Moses, Man of the Mountain*, by Hurston (New York: Harper, 1991), xi. Hurston, *Seraph on the Sewanee* (New York: Harper, 1991). *SS* followed by page numbers refers to this text. Hurston, *Tell My Horse* (New York: Harper, 1990). *TMH* followed by page numbers refers to this text.

9. More recently, the preferred strategy of recuperating Hurston has begun to switch: and now her whole oeuvre is seen as subtly, ingeniously progressive. Valerie Boyd's 2003 biography of Hurston, a celebratory and not a critical work, idealizes the younger and older Hurston alike. It takes the deifying, apologist stance to an extreme. *Their Eyes* is seen as subtly criticizing Tea Cake's violence toward Janie and so is considered unproblematic "feminist" "protest literature"; it is also seen as subtly "protest[ing] white oppression," through "not confrontation, but affirmation." Boyd even finds Hurston's later opposition to *Brown v. Board of Education* "prescient" because "some contemporary black intellectuals go so far as to say that integration was one of the biggest tactical mistakes in African-American history." Boyd, *Wrapped in Rainbows: The Life of Zora Neale Hurston* (New York: Scribner, 2003), 303–4, 305–6, 425. Some critical work, such as Susan Meisenhelder's *Hitting a Straight Lick with a Crooked Stick: Race and Gender in the Work of Zora Neale Hurston* (Tuscaloosa: U of Alabama P, 1999), adopts a similar recuperative tactic. According to Meisenhelder, as Keith Leonard puts it in review, "Hurston never pandered to white audiences nor did she grow more conservative in her later years, as various critics have suggested. Instead, Hurston consistently 'hit a straight lick with a crooked stick,' manipulating patrons and publishers through her ingratiating demeanor in order to get published and then 'camouflaging' her racial affirmation and feminist resistance in conventional literary narratives and folk humor." Keith Leonard, Review, *Legacy* 18, no. 1 (2001): 118–19.

10. See also Washington, "'I Love the Way Janie Crawford Left Her Husbands,'" in *Zora Neale Hurston* (see note 2), 106.

11. Back cover of Harper Perennial edition.

12. One of her brothers thinks she might have been married a fourth time, sometime during the fifteen years of her life after her mother's death (in 1904) that she would later seek to erase from the record of her life. This isn't impossible, since her autobiography fails to mention her second marriage (to Albert Price), which is a fact available in public documents.

13. Carla Kaplan lists several unresolved questions in her recent book (2002), including: "Why did she constantly alter her age...?" Kaplan, introduction to *Zora Neale Hurston: A Life in Letters* (see note 4), 20.

14. Court documents of *People v. Zora Neale Hurston*, (General Sessions Court 1948). New York City Municipal Library Archive.

15. Arnold Rampersad, foreword to *Mules and Men*, by Hurston (New York: Harper, 1990), xix.

16. See Kaplan, *Zora Neale Hurston*, 440n47. A.W.P. was actually P. M. P.: Percival McGuire Punter. Boyd, *Wrapped in Rainbows*, 303.

17. According to Boyd, they met in 1935, so Hurston was forty-four and A.W.P. was twenty-three. Boyd, *Wrapped in Rainbows*, 272.

18. This is true if we take her date of birth as 1891: a date that is now widely agreed upon.

19. Boyd makes a similar observation. Boyd, *Wrapped in Rainbows*, 338.

20. This is true of not only Alice Walker in our time but also Richard Wright in her time (*TE*, viii).

21. Hazel V. Carby, foreword to *Seraph on the Sewanee*, ix.

22. Hurston quoted in Carby, foreword, viii–ix.

23. See Baker, "Workings of the Spirit," 289–304.

24. Hurston, *Jonah's Gourd Vine* (New York: Harper, 1990). *JGV* followed by page numbers refers to this text.

25. Rampersad, foreword, xxi–xxii.

26. Kerouac's novel, along with Norman Mailer's essay, "The White Negro," *Advertisements for Myself* (1959), with their romanticization of "the Negro," have inspired extensive criticism; one of the earlier attacks came from James Baldwin, "The Black Boy Looks at the White Boy," in *Nobody Knows My Name: More Notes of a Native Son* (New York: Dell, 1961), 220–21, 228–31.

27. Harold Bloom, introduction to *Modern Critical Interpretations: Zora Neale Hurston's* Their Eyes Were Watching God, ed. Harold Bloom (New York: Chelsea House, 1987), 3, 4.

28. John Berryman, *Stephen Crane* (Cleveland: Meridian, 1950), 268.

29. Henry Louis Gates and Sieglinde Lemke, introduction to *The Complete Stories*, by Hurston (New York: Harper, 1991), xx.

30. I have come across very few interpretations of the dog on the back of the cow; Houston Baker reads it as social commentary. Baker, "Ideology and Narrative Form," in *Modern Critical Interpretations* (see note 27), 38.

31. The doctor tells Janie that his kidney failure has been a couple of years in the making, but it is clear that, at the very least, his demise has been accelerated by an emotional shock.

32. "She battled constantly with W. E. B. Du Bois...and called him Dr. 'Dubious': 'a propagandist' [sic] and 'utterly detestable...[a] goateed, egoistic, wishy-washy...haughty aristocrat.'" Kaplan, Introduction, 17.

33. Angelou, foreword, x.

34. *Dust Tracks* is so thorough in its denial that when Hurston is faced with the word "nigger" at one point, she actually claims in a footnote that there is no racial slur here: "The word Nigger used in this sense does not mean race. It means a weak, contemptible person of any race" (*DT*, xi).

35. Julia Kristeva, *Powers of Horror*, Leon S. Roudiez, trans. (New York: Columbia University Press, 1982), 8. Emphasis original.

36. Ibid., 17, 4.

37. See Hurston, *Moses*, 255. "Aaron is...full of conceit like all little men suddenly elevated to places of power."

38. Washington's reference is to Janie alone.

39. Hurston, *Seraph*, 176.

40. Hurston's novels are consistently, to borrow Kristeva's phrase, "sublimation[s] of abjection." Kristeva, *Powers of Horror*, 26.

Chapter 3

1. The movies under discussion here are distinct from what James Wolcott dubbed "scuzz" films. Those films, which grew out of Quentin Tarantino's movies, *Pulp Fiction* (1994) especially, essentially reverse the "scandal" of these films. Scuzz films accord to low-life characters—who are traditionally one-dimensional in crime and detective movies—three-dimensional consciousnesses permeated by pop culture concerns and New Age psychologies, which were formerly reserved for characters in comedy and drama genres. Thus, the gangsters in *Pulp Fiction* discuss cheeseburgers abroad, and one of them enters a "transitional moment" after a near-death experience. James Wolcott, "Live Fast, Die Young, and Leave a Big Stain," *Vanity Fair*, no. 452, April 1998, 148–58.
2. See Keith Gandal *Virtues of the Vicious*, Chapter 5.
3. *Freeway* stages a contest between slasher film and class trauma movie, and the latter wins out. The upper-class serial killer poses as a Freudian therapist, but lower-class Vanessa, with her shame-theory psychology, is resistant to his brand of (depth) psychological manipulation.
4. *Being John Malkovich* seems finally uncomfortable with the monstrous world it has depicted: at the end, it awkwardly reaches for unlikely compassion and depth of personality (in cruel, cool Maxine) as a way out. Maxine's impregnation (by Lottie through Malkovich) ends up softening and humanizing her. *Boys Don't Cry* likewise pits a female in pursuit of her deep, inner, male self against a community of the demeaned—the trailer-park world of rural Texas. If the hip lesbian romantic comedy overtakes the trauma genre in *Being John Malkovich*, here the trauma movie and the community of the demeaned eventually overwhelm the psychological romance drama and the psychologically transgendered protagonist.
5. M followed by page numbers refers to Crane, *Maggie: A Girl of the Streets* (New York: Norton, 1979). Crane's *Monster* (1899) focuses on deformity; see Chapter 4.

Chapter 4

1. A version of the first part of this chapter originally published as Keith Gandal, "A Spiritual Autopsy of Stephen Crane," *Nineteenth-Century Literature* 51, no. 4 (1997): 500–530, © 1997 by the Regents of the University of California. A version of the second part of this chapter originally published as Gandal, "Stephen Crane's 'Mystic Places,'" *Arizona Quarterly* 55, no. 1 (1999): 97–126, © 1999 by The Arizona Board of Regents.
2. SCAB followed by page numbers refers to Robert Wooster Stallman, *Stephen Crane: A Biography* (New York: George Braziller, 1968).

3. Christopher Benfey, *The Double Life of Stephen Crane* (New York: Knopf, 1992), 12.

4. Richard Chase, introduction to *The Red Badge of Courage and Other Writings*, by Stephen Crane (Boston: Houghton Mifflin, 1960), viii.

5. Chase, introduction, vii.

6. Benfey, *The Double Life of Stephen Crane*, 17.

7. See Gandal "A Spiritual Autopsy of Stephen Crane," 500–530.

8. Ibid.

9. Poem 3 in *The Black Riders*, in Crane, *Prose and Poetry* (New York: Viking, 1984), 1299. Further references to numbered poems and page numbers are from *The Black Riders* in this edition.

10. R. W. Stallman and Lillian Gilkes, eds., *Stephen Crane: Letters* (New York: New York University Press, 1960), 111.

11. In terms of the Cuban adventure, Crane was first ill in England before he left for the war—that is, when something stood in the way of his leaving. He got sick when he was in the midst of his mad desire to rush off to war but felt he could not leave because another writer friend and neighbor, Harold Frederic, was dying. When Crane made up his mind to go anyway, he apparently got better. See Thomas Beer, *Stephen Crane: A Study in American Letters* (New York: Knopf, 1923), 177.

12. "Crane...got out of bed to go to a dinner party in Athens" and got dysentery. Cora quoted (*SCAB*, 303).

13. Later, at Brede, Cora invited "people in such shoals that even the huge manor house could not accommodate them"; she "did not protect Crane's privacy." "Cora to the very end counted on Stephen to solve their money problems by writing" (*SCAB*, 468, 467, 336).

14. Crane, "The Squire's Madness," in *The Complete Short Stories and Sketches of Stephen Crane*, ed. Thomas A. Gullason (Garden City, NY: Doubleday, 1963), 772–79.

15. *SC* followed by page numbers refers to John Berryman, *Stephen Crane* (Cleveland: Meridian, 1950).

16. Chase, introduction, vii.

17. Michael Fried, *Reading, Writing, Disfiguration* (Chicago: Chicago University Press, 1987), 127.

18. Nina Baym, "Melodramas of Beset Manhood: How Theories of American Fiction Exclude Women Authors," *American Quarterly* 33, no. 2 (1981): 123–39.

19. See Gandal *Virtues of the Vicious*, 105–14.

20. Crane, *Maggie: A Girl of the Streets* (New York: Norton, 1979). M followed by page numbers refers to this text. Crane, *The Monster*, in *The Red Badge of Courage and Other Writings* (Boston: Houghton Mifflin, 1960). TM followed by page numbers refers to this text.

21. R. W. Stallman, ed., *The Red Badge of Courage and Selected Stories*, by Crane (New York: Signet, 1960), 217. This is from Crane's original manuscript, which Stallman referred to as the Long Version in this 1960 edition.

22. I am not attempting to reconstruct here a "primal scene" in childhood that traumatized Crane, but rather a primary and ongoing condition of his early years.

23. Crane, *War Is Kind, Prose and Poetry* (see note 9), 1339–40.

24. Crane, *George's Mother*, in *The Red Badge of Courage and Other Writings* (Boston: Houghton Mifflin, 1960), 65.

25. Jayne Anne Phillips, introduction, to *Maggie: A Girl of the Streets and Other Short Fiction*, by Crane (New York: Bantam, 1986), vii.

26. Stanley Wertheim and Paul Sorrentino, *The Crane Log* (New York: G. K. Hall, 1994), 22.

27. Ibid., 31–32.

28. Crane quoted in Beer, *Stephen Crane*, 49.

29. Crane, *War Is Kind*, in *Prose and Poetry* (see note 9), 1340.

30. Crane, "His New Mittens," *Prose and Poetry* (see note 9), 1164–65.

31. Ibid., 1167.

32. Crane, "The Angel-Child," *Prose and Poetry* (see note 9), 1174, 1175.

33. Ibid., 1174, 1175, 1182.

34. Ibid., 1174, 1175, my emphasis.

35. Alfred Kazin, *On Native Grounds* (New York: Reynal and Hitchcock, 1942), 72.

36. Phillips, introduction to *Maggie*, viii.

37. Ibid., viii.

38. Wertheim and Sorrentino, *The Crane Log*, 15–16.

39. Crane, *The Red Badge of Courage and Selected Stories* (the Long Version), 215, 216.

40. Quoted in Joseph Katz, introduction, to *Maggie: A Girl of the Streets: A Facsimile Reproduction of the First Edition of 1893*, by Crane (Gainesville, FL: Scholars' Facsimiles and Reprints, 1966), xiv–xv.

41. To begin with, it must be noted that, though Crane died of consumption, it is doubtful at this point in his life that he knew he had tuberculosis, if in fact he did already have it.

42. Quoted in Edwin H. Cady and Lester G. Wells, eds., *Stephen Crane's Love Letters to Nellie Crouse* (Syracuse, NY: Syracuse University Press), 33.

43. Chase, introduction, xx.

44. Crane, *War Is Kind, Prose and Poetry* (see note 9), 1342.

45. Fried, *Realism, Writing, Disfiguration*, 121; Fried, "Realism, Writing, and Disfiguration in Thomas Eakins's Gross Clinic," *Representations* 9 (Winter 1985), 95.

46. Ibid., 95.

47. Crane, uncollected poems, *Prose and Poetry* (see note 9), 1346.

Chapter 5

1. Jack Kerouac, *On the Road* (New York: Penguin, 1976), 242–43, 194.

2. Henry Miller, *Tropic of Cancer* (New York: Grove, 1961), 241, 220, 278, 227. Subsequently, *TC* followed by page numbers refers to this text.

3. Miller, *Tropic of Capricorn* (New York: Grove, 1961), 12. Subsequently, *Cap* followed by page numbers refers to this text.

4. Frank Norris, *McTeague* (New York: Signet, 1981), 292, 300.

5. Roger Ebert, Review of *Kids*, July 28, 1995, http://rogerebert.suntimes.com/apps/pbcs.dll/article?AID=/19950728/REVIEWS/507280301/1023 (accessed October 25, 2006).

6. Harmony Korine, "Icon Thoughtstyle," 1997, http://www.harmony-korine.com/paper/main/filmography.html (accessed June 5, 2006).

7. Norris, *McTeague*, 282, 287.

8. Acker, *Blood and Guts in High School* (London: Pan, 1984), 99, 94.

9. Korine, quoted in Paul Zimmerman, "Chaos Controlled," *Independent Film Magazine*, August 22, 1999, http://www.harmony-korine.com/paper/int/korine/chaos.html (accessed June 5, 2006).

10. Korine, quoted in Graham Fuller, "Directing on the Edge of Madness," *New York Times*, September 12, 1999, 51.

Chapter 6

1. Christopher Benfey, *The Double Life of Stephen Crane* (New York: Knopf, 1992), 11–12.

2. *HM* followed by page numbers refers to Robert Ferguson, *Henry Miller: A Life* (New York: Norton, 1991).

3. Henry Miller, *Tropic of Capricorn* (New York: Grove, 1961), 12. Subsequently, *Cap* followed by page numbers refers to this text.

4. Quoted in Erica Jong, *The Devil at Large* (New York: Grove, 1993), 45.

5. Miller, *Time of the Assassins: A Study of Rimbaud* (New York: New Directions, 1962), 13.

6. Norman Mailer labels June a narcissist and writes: "Other people exist for their ability to excite one presence or another in oneself. And are valued for that. Of course, they are loved as an actor loves an audience." Mailer, *Genius and Lust: A Journey Through the Major Writings of Henry Miller* (New York: Grove, 1976), 188.

7. Ibid., 189.

8. Title of a book, *The World of Sex* (1940).

9. Rainer Maria Rilke, *Letters to a Young Poet*, trans. Stephen Mitchell (New York: Vintage, 1987), 30.

10. Quoted in Jong, *The Devil at Large*, 45.

11. "'Life,' said Emerson, 'consists in what a man is thinking all day.' If that be so, then my life is nothing but a big intestine" (*TC*, 63).

12. Harry T. Moore, preface to *Henry Miller and the Critics*, ed. George Wickes (Carbondale: Southern Illinois University Press, 1967), v.

13. Jong, *The Devil at Large*, 94, 116.

14. On Kazin's sense of Crane, see Chapter 4. Kazin, *On Native Grounds*, 72. Edwin H. Cady and Lester G. Wells, eds., *Stephen Crane's Love Letters to Nellie Crouse* (Syracuse, NY: Syracuse University Press), 54.

15. Kenneth Rexroth, "The Reality of Henry Miller," *Henry Miller and the Critics*, 124.

16. Ibid., 124.
17. Mailer, *Genius and Lust*, 92; see also, 372: "Anaïs Nin saw that Miller was without philosophy—he had only sentiments, at their best likely to be some of the most eloquent sentiments voiced in English."
18. *CM* followed by page numbers refers to Miller, *The Colossus of Maroussi* (New York: New Directions, 1958).
19. George Orwell, "Inside the Whale," *Henry Miller and the Critics*, 43, 38, 39.
20. Ibid., 35.
21. Mailer, *Genius and Lust*, 186.
22. Henry Miller, *Black Spring* (New York: Grove, 1961), 242–43.
23. Mailer, *Genius and Lust*, 17.
24. Ibid., 84.
25. Miller quoted, ibid., 17.
26. Ibid., 17.
27. He called *Cancer* his "fuck everything" book (*HM*, 211).
28. Halasz Brassai quoted in Jong, *The Devil at Large*, 45.
29. James Guetti, *Wittgenstein and the Grammar of Literary Experience* (Athens: University of Georgia Press, 1993), 139.
30. It is easy to take Miller to task for his eternal immaturity, as some of his biographers and critics do, but this is to underestimate the severity of his childhood alienation and to miss the means of his healing (limited as it was). One need only think of Crane or Hurston's adult loneliness to be reminded of the stakes here: the terrible, destructive power of such deep alienation. Ferguson calls Miller's hatred of his mother "wildly disproportionate" (*HM*, 268), but one asks, disproportionate to what? Ferguson's idea is that his hatred is out of proportion to her coldness to him, but one of Miller's premier messages is that the only reality that counts, in such matters, is subjective or emotional; some objective or reasoned standard here would only underestimate emotional impact. It is a tautology to say that Miller's hatred of his mother is proportionate to his *experience* of her coldness, but that would be precisely Miller's point: his method throughout is to affirm and express these feelings, no matter how antisocial, angry, or embarrassing. Miller pursues William Blake's road of excess, where, from an outsider's point of view, all expression and action seem disproportionate.
31. Crane, *The Red Badge of Courage and Selected Stories*, 216.

Appendix

1. *PMF* followed by page numbers refer to James Miller, *The Passion of Michel Foucault* (New York: Simon and Schuster, 1993). See also Didier Eribon, *Michel Foucault*, trans. Betsy Wing (Cambridge, MA: Harvard University Press, 1991), 147, 325. Subsequently, *MF* followed by page numbers refers to this biography.
2. This last piece of gossip inspired James Miller to write his monumental *The Passion of Michel Foucault*.

3. As a graduate student at Berkeley in the early 1980s, I took part in a seminar with Foucault and worked closely with him on a writing project.

4. Dates for Foucault's texts refer to the initial French language publications whose titles are given in parentheses.

5. Subsequently, *HS* followed by page numbers refers to Michel Foucault, *The History of Sexuality: Volume I: An Introduction*, trans. Robert Hurley (New York: Vintage, 1980), 157.

6. *MC* followed by page numbers refers to Foucault, *Madness and Civilization*, trans. Richard Howard (New York: Random House, 1965).

7. *AK* followed by page numbers refers to Foucault, *The Archeology of Knowledge*, trans. A. M. Sheridan Smith (New York: Pantheon, 1972).

8. Foucault quoted, *PMF*, 151.

9. "All his life he verged on madness," wrote someone who knew him well in this period (*MF*, 26–28).

10. Defert quoted.

11. See also David Macey, *The Lives of Michel Foucault: A Biography* (New York: Pantheon, 1993), 46. Subsequently, *LMF* followed by page numbers refers to this biography.

12. Foucault is often called profoundly misogynist as well, though some women who knew him well deny the charge. See *LMF*, xiv.

13. "I'm sure he was gay from a young age....[He had] always known he was different, if not gay." Didier Eribon, interview with author, October 1998.

14. Eribon said Foucault's mother told him: "Father was always out." Ibid.

15. Ibid.

16. Jacques Derrida, "Cogito and the History of Madness," *Writing and Difference*, trans. Alan Bass (Chicago: University of Chicago Press, 1978).

17. Hervé Guibert quoted, *PMF*, 453n1.

18. Dominique Fernandez quoted, *MF*, 29.

19. Author interview with Eribon.

Index

Please note that page numbers appearing in *italics* indicate an endnote.